Franciscan Books and their Readers

I0585597

Franciscan Books and their Readers

Friars and Manuscripts in Late Medieval Italy

René Hernández Vera

Routledge
Taylor & Francis Group

LONDON AND NEW YORK

First published in 2022 by Amsterdam University Press Ltd.

Published 2025 by Routledge
4 Park Square, Milton Park, Abingdon, Oxon OX14 4RN
605 Third Avenue, New York, NY 10158

Routledge is an imprint of the Taylor & Francis Group, an informa business

© R. Hernández Vera / Taylor & Francis Group 2022

All rights reserved. No part of this book may be reprinted or reproduced or utilised in any form or by any electronic, mechanical, or other means, now known or hereafter invented, including photocopying and recording, or in any information storage or retrieval system, without permission in writing from the publishers.

Trademark notice: Product or corporate names may be trademarks or registered trademarks, and are used only for identification and explanation without intent to infringe.

ISBN: 9789463729512 (hbk)
ISBN: 9781041179702 (pbk)
ISBN: 9781003695974 (ebk)
NUR 684

Cover illustration: Padua, Biblioteca Antoniana, MS 573, fol. 30r.

Cover design by: Coördesign, Leiden

DOI: 10.5117/9789463729512

Every effort has been made to obtain permission to use all copyrighted illustrations reproduced in this book. Nonetheless, whosoever believes to have rights to this material is advised to contact the publisher.

For Product Safety Concerns and Information please contact our EU representative:
GPSR@taylorandfrancis.com
Taylor & Francis Verlag GmbH, Kaufingerstraße 24, 80331 München, Germany

Table of Contents

Acknowledgements

I hope to be able to express my gratitude and convey my appreciation to the many people who have supported me in the process of writing this book. I would like first to thank Dr. Melanie Brunner and Professor Brian Richardson, who offered me advice and encouragement during my research, which was possible thanks to the Fully Funded International Research Scholarship scheme of the University of Leeds. The precious suggestions of Professor Jill Kraye of the Warburg Institute and Dr. Matthew Treherne of the University of Leeds contributed decisively to improving the text.

A poster exhibition at the International Medieval Congress in Leeds led to the publication of this work. Simon Forde managed to see the seed of a book in the poster on Franciscan manuscripts I presented. I must thank his vision and kind encouragement. Dr. Erin Dailey has been the best editor I could imagine, and I wish to thank him, and the publishing team of Amsterdam University Press for their patience and support.

I enjoyed the privilege of being part of the community of scholars of the Institute for Medieval Studies (IMS) of the University of Leeds, and would like to mention the generous guidance of Alison Martin and the support of the then Institute director, Dr. Mary Swan. The original academic collaboration with Dr. Brunner and Professor Emilia Jamroziak has become a wonderful friendship, and that is one of the most rewarding outcomes of my experience at the IMS. A significant part of this work is the result of discussions with colleagues, many of whom were permanent inhabitants of the Le Patourel room of the IMS. I would like to thank especially Drs. Kathryn Maude, Isabella Bolognese, Kirsty Day, Audrey Thorstad, Ana Baeza, Danny Evans, Liz Stainforth, N. Kivilcim Yavuz, Gustavo Carvajal, Alejandra Ortiz and Eleonora Lombardo for honouring me with their input, support and inspiring friendship.

The original idea for my research comes from my work with Professor Nicoletta Giovè Marchioli and Dr. Donato Gallo of the University of Padua. I am greatly indebted to them for their advice and guidance. Dr. Gallo's generosity in sharing his knowledge has been a source of inspiration. Thanks to professor Giovè, I realized that palaeography and codicology are essentially filled with passion and awe, and I hope this book reflects that form of living relation with manuscripts.

The research underlying this book has taken place in many different places. I would like to thank Alberto Fanton OFM and Fabio Salvato from the Pontificia Biblioteca Antoniana of Padua, as well as Luciano Bertazzo OFM from the Centro Studi Antoniani, for their availability, interest and support. The resourcefulness of Michele Agostini from the Biblioteca dell'Istituto Teologico S. Antonio Dottore was extraordinarily helpful for the completion of the manuscript of this book. The staff of the *sala manoscritti* of the Biblioteca Universitaria di Padova provided me with invaluable guidance in the exploration of manuscripts that once belonged to the Observant convent of San Francesco Grande. The staff of the splendid Biblioteca di Storia of the University of Padua offered me remarkable support along all the stages of my research. Dr. Elena Boaga and Dr. Margherita Valenti from the Biblioteca San Francesco della Vigna in Venice and the staff of the Biblioteca Medicea Laurenziana in Florence were especially helpful for completing the early phases of my study. Dom Giulio Pagnoni and Father Dom Francesco Trolese from the Biblioteca Statale del Monumento di Santa Giustina offered me their precious assistance and knowledge of the Benedictine academic tradition.

My work in Italian repositories would not have been possible without the dear friends who helped me not only to manage but even to enjoy the practicalities of researching abroad. I would like to thank especially Edy Linceto and Maurizio Barbiero for offering me a place in their house and their table with extraordinary generosity during my research trips in Italy. Juan P. Valenzuela and Eduardo Guzmán have provided me with the joys of friendship, technical assistance and have been the most enthusiastic supporters of this project. I would like also to thank my students: their questions and suggestions have enabled me to explore some aspects of medieval culture from innovative perspectives. With time, some of them have become close friends. I would like to express my gratitude to Laura A. Moreno, Alejandra Cantor, Juan S. Lima and especially to Laura L. Suárez, Alejandra Ospina and Paula A. Ruiz for their encouragement, care and kindness. I hope this book finds a place in the wonderful library of César Vásquez, my dear colleague and good old friend with whom I have shared literary dreams and my fascination for the Middle Ages since we were students.

My family – in particular, the courage of my mother, Gloria Isabel Vera, and my brother Miguel's unabating devotion to melancholy as the subject of his artistic work – have always been a source of inspiration, especially in difficult times. Finally, I am afraid I cannot properly express how the love of my wife, Genoveva Castiblanco, is the reason why I have been able to complete this work from a mere intuition I shared with her many years ago. I dedicate this book to her as one of the many ways of saying that she is the embodiment of the deepest truth within her favourite quote: 'we are made of stars' dust'.

Illustrations

Abbreviations

AF   *Analecta Franciscana sive Chronica aliaque varia*
    documenta ad historiam Fratrum Minorum spectantia,
    ed. by the Fathers of the Collegii S. Bonaventura, 17
    vols. (Quaracchi: Typographia Collegii S. Bonaventurae,
    1885-2010)

AFH   *Archivum Franciscanum Historicum*

ALKG *Archiv für Literatur und Kirchengeschichte des Mit-*
    telalters, ed. by Heinrich Denifle and Franz Ehrle, 7
    vols. (Berlin/Freiburg im Breisgau: Weidmannsche
    Buchhandlung, 1885-1900)

CHL   *Chronologia historico-legalis seraphici Ordinis Fratrum*
    Minorum Sancti Francisci, I (Naples: Michaele Angelo, 1650)

CHLB *The Cambridge History of Libraries in Britain and*
    Ireland, ed. by Elisabeth Leedham-Green and Teresa
    Webber, 3 vols. (Cambridge: Cambridge University
    Press, 2006)

PL   *Patrologiae cursus completus: series latina* (Paris: Typis
    L. Migne)

RIS   *Rerum Italicarum scriptores*, 2nd ser., 34 vols (Città di
    Castello: Lapi, 1900-17; Bologna: Zanichelli, 1917-75)

Notes on Transcriptions

The transcriptions follow the original text and do not attempt to correct the source's spelling. The main intervention in the original text is the addition of punctuation.

Modern interventions, comments or paratextual information are provided within square brackets, [ ].

For the transcription of poems and marginal comments, a single slash, / marks the end of a line of script, while a double slash, // indicates the end of a paragraph or a stanza within the same textual unit.

Uncertain transcriptions are placed between angle brackets, < >.

Introduction

The book is simultaneously a thing, a force, an event, a history.[1]

In the western part of Colombia, facing the Pacific Ocean, lies Chocó, a region entirely covered by tropical rainforest. This place has some of the heaviest rainfall levels on the planet and perhaps it is the most humid place in the world. Thanks to these particularly challenging conditions, Chocó became a refuge for enslaved men and women who fled from the wealthy colonial centres of the Caribbean, beginning in the seventeenth century. Today, every year, from mid-September to mid-October, the whole population of Quibdó, its capital city, participates in the most important celebration of the entire region, the festival of San Pacho, a celebration of the African heritage of the community, and commemoration of the figure at the centre of their cultural agency: brother Francis of Assisi.[2] The colourful festival of San Pacho illustrates the extent of the success of Franciscan missionary work, a worldwide campaign inspired by the example, words and figure of a thirteenth-century preacher from a small city on the hills of central Italy.

The impact of Franciscan preaching was possible thanks to a demanding programme of training based on intensive study. Thus, we may assume that books were at the core of Franciscan identity from its origins, but this did not mean that the relation between Franciscans and books was ever smooth. From the very beginning, Francis wanted the order to rely on something more fundamental than intellectual achievement, and feared that affection for books could endanger the original apostolic spirituality of the community. Nevertheless, Franciscans soon became an order of learned individuals, that is, intellectuals who were familiar with the complexities of the cultural practice of medieval universities, and who contributed to all areas of knowledge. Despite the warnings of their founder, Franciscan

---

1   Dane, *What Is a Book?*, p. 7.
2   *Pacho* is the colloquial word used in Colombia to refer to those named 'Francisco', that is, Francis.

Hernández Vera, R., *Franciscan Books and their Readers: Friars and Manuscripts in Late Medieval Italy*. Taylor & Francis Group, 2022
DOI 10.5117/9789463729512_INTRO

friars fell in love with books and tried by all means available to reconcile the spirit of Francis with their devotion to manuscripts and learning.

This book will explore the relation between Franciscans and books in terms of the interaction between friars and manuscripts in the male convents of the city of Padua from the thirteenth to the fifteenth centuries. To do so, four aspects, or dimensions, of the Franciscan manuscripts will be discussed. First, the ideal, as expressed by the regulations on study and the use of books; second, the space, that is, the libraries where these manuscripts were collected, read, studied and written; third, their purpose, as revealed by their physical characteristics; and finally, their readership, that is, their interaction with their writers and readers. This layered consideration of the reality of manuscripts used and produced by Franciscan friars in northern Italy will allow us to gain a better understanding of key transformations in manuscript culture, especially in readership, that paved the way for significant developments in literacy, among which humanism. But before considering these features in detail, it will be helpful to explore briefly the development of our knowledge of the relationship between the Friars Minor and manuscripts during the Middle Ages.

Franciscans and Manuscripts: An Overview

Our insight into the manuscripts used by the Franciscans derives from fields of study such as the history of Franciscan education, the history of Franciscan libraries, the development of Franciscan regulations on study and books, and the discussion of the modalities of the use of books by friars within Franciscan schools or *studia*.

The history of Franciscan education is one of the most developed fields of research and has undergone a remarkable and constant growth. In its early phases, from the end of the nineteenth century, it focused on editing sources, mainly the constitutions regulating the discipline of study.[3] In 1904, Hilarin Felder published the first comprehensive study of the development of education and intellectual training in the Franciscan order, a work that was swiftly translated into French and Italian.[4] Felder explored themes such as the relation of the Franciscans to the establishment and growth of the schools and the organization of studies during the thirteenth century. The effort to make comprehensive and accurate editions of the sources

3   See, for instance, Ehrle, ed., *Die ältesten Redaktionen.*
4   Felder, *Geschichte der wissenschaftlichen Studien im Franziskanerorden.*

continued during the first part of the twentieth century, as shown by the work of Andrew G. Little and the editions carried out by the Collegio di Quaracchi.[5] As a result, the evidence needed to explore certain problems and cases became available. The first studies of the history of education in the order were carried out mainly by its members, who focused on three main topics, namely the biographical profiles of renowned Franciscan masters, the study of canon law, and the role of Franciscan friars as masters at the University of Paris.[6] A more structured view of the process of education and the development of the network of Franciscan schools was achieved thanks to contributions to the congress in Todi in 1976.[7] The papers at the congress explored the role of schools, comparing the processes of training and learning of the Franciscan friars to the model of the Dominican experience. The contributions also explored methodological questions, for example, how the availability of the sources shaped the perspectives of scholars on their fields of research. This explains how the presence of a structured and specific corpus of Dominican sources on learning conditioned the perception of early Franciscan scholarship. Other fields proposed by the congress were the diffusion of the mendicant schools, the constitution of networks of centres for training, and the techniques of teaching and learning, as revealed by the sources. Concerning the relation of the mendicants, and in particular the Franciscans, to manuscripts, the contribution of Gabriella Severino Polica on books, reading and practices of learning in mendicant schools has become a fundamental reference for the study of book culture within the order.[8] As will be discussed further on, the papers at Todi are a significant contribution to scholarship on Franciscan intellectual history and further validate the idea of a Dominican influence on Franciscan book culture.

In 1988, the Sixteenth Congress of the Società Internazionale di Studi Francescani in Assisi investigated the relation between the Franciscan order and the culture of medieval universities. As a result of the new approaches proposed by the contributions, the role of masters such as Anthony of Padua and Bonaventure of Bagnoregio as promoters of scholarly culture was explored within the wider context of the institutional development

---

5   A. Little, *Grey Friars in Oxford*; A. Little, 'Franciscan School at Oxford'; A. Little, 'Definitiones capitulorum generalium'; A. Little, 'Statuta provincialia'; Abate, ed., 'Memoriali, statuti ed atti'. For an overview of the editorial work of the Collegio di Quaracchi, see Iozzelli, 'Le edizioni scientifiche'.

6   Benoffi, 'Degli studi nell'Ordine dei Minori'; Brlek, *De evolutione iuridica studiorum in ordine*; Glorieux, 'D'Alexandre de Halès à Pierre Auriol'; Doucet, 'Maîtres franciscains de Paris'.

7   *Le scuole degli ordini mendicanti.*

8   Severino Polica, 'Libro, lettura, "lezione"'.

of the order.[9] More recently, there have been attempts to explore new fields within the scholastic culture of the mendicants, for example, the vocabulary of the mendicant schools.[10] To achieve a better understanding of the complexities of the Franciscan educational system, scholarship has recently focused on the actual practices of learning, training and reading in the Franciscan schools to relate them to the general development of the order.[11] Nevertheless, the efforts of scholarship focus almost exclusively on the early history of the order and on the rise and affirmation of Franciscan scholastic thought – particularly at the University of Paris – and usually do not venture further than the beginning of the fifteenth century. As a consequence, the role of Franciscan Observance has been neglected. In this context, the work of Bert Roest is particularly relevant for several reasons: first, it has gone beyond the fourteenth century and has explored the educational context of the Franciscan Observance; second, it has proposed bringing Franciscan libraries into analytical focus as parts of a system of training; and third, it has proposed a study of the 'lectors', or instructors at the schools, as agents of Franciscan intellectual achievement.[12] His description of the Franciscan curriculum of studies and the organization of the network of schools within the provinces has been discussed recently by William Courtenay, who warns against the perils of generalizations and suggests focusing on the specific characteristics of the provinces.[13] Luigi Pellegrini, however, returned to the topic of the relation between mendicant orders and medieval universities, proposing that they were medieval innovations or 'inventions' that reflected the dramatic transformations of the social and cultural context, providing new answers and interpretations to the question of why mendicants engaged so quickly and effectively with universities.[14] More recent studies have explored an approach to Franciscan learning in the specific context of the order's provincial organization. An interesting example is Emanuele Fontana's work on the relation between friars, books and modalities of teaching in the province of Sant'Antonio, in northern Italy.[15] His work also discusses the organization of studies, the practices related to production and acquisition of books and study in the province, and

9   *Francescanesimo e cultura universitaria.*
10 Pacheco, ed., *Le vocabulaire des écoles des mendiants.*
11 For example, Maierù, 'Formazione culturale e tecniche'.
12 Roest, *History of Franciscan Education*; Roest, 'Role of Lectors'; Roest, 'Sub humilitatis titulo; and Roest, *Franciscan Learning, Preaching and Mission.*
13 Courtenay, 'Franciscan Learning', p. 59.
14 Luigi Pellegrini, *L'Incontro tra due invenzioni.*
15 Fontana, *Frati, libri e insegnamento.*

the works of some of the lectors in the convent of Sant'Antonio. Fontana's contribution is a suitable continuation of the work previously carried out by Paolo Marangon, who significantly enhanced our understanding of the development of Franciscan scholastic culture, and explored the relation between friars, the university and the study of philosophy and natural sciences in the school of the convent of Sant'Antonio.[16]

The recent work of Neslihan Şenocak discusses a wide range of issues such as the historiographical debate about the 'Franciscan question', or the original intention of Francis regarding his own order, the influence of the members of the order on early Franciscan historiography, and the overstatement of the apparent incompatibility between using books, on the one hand, and the Franciscan rule and vow of poverty, on the other.[17] As will be seen in Chapter 1, even the most rigorous reconstruction of the 'intentio' of Francis does not entail condemning the use of books. Additionally, Şenocak argues that, concerning learning and the use of books, historiography has so far considered the question of humility a secondary topic and has focused instead almost exclusively on poverty. With regard to learning and study, Şenocak also discusses the fact that even though Franciscans argued that preparation for preaching and pastoral care was the reason to pursue a course of study, their level of training, active participation in all fields of scholastic discussion, and achievements as intellectuals clearly go beyond the simple task of fulfilling pastoral duties. Additionally, she explores the questions of why friars engaged so profoundly in the scholastic culture of their time and whether this engagement by the Franciscans and mendicants in general reflected a process of glorification of learning which was characteristic of medieval society.

In the context of scholarship on Franciscan learning, the present volume assesses Franciscan regulations to understand the distance between the ideal proposed by the rule and the actual practice of learning. The application of reception criticism and its categories, such as the interpretive community and the analysis of manuscript evidence, offers insight into the friars as flexible readers who integrated the world of their audiences into their discipline of writing.

As to the second field of research, that is, the history of Franciscan libraries, one could say that it has mainly been about Franciscan institutional developments or Franciscan education.[18] Further research has produced

---

16 Marangon, *Ad cognitionem scientiae festinare*.

17 Şenocak, *Poor and the Perfect*.

18 Clark, *Care of Books*, pp. 199-207; Abate, 'Manoscritti e biblioteche'; Humphreys, *Book Provisions*; Humphreys, *Friars' Libraries*, and Roest, *History of Franciscan Education*.

editions of library inventories, complemented by the identification and description of the volumes registered in those documents.[19] Another set of studies has focused on processes such as the creation of regulations for the libraries and the acquisition and circulation of books within the Franciscan houses.[20] Recent contributions focus on the description and assessment of the book collection with the help of inventories and legal documents, and explore the modes of circulation and use of the library as a resource within the convents.[21] In regard to the regulations of the community on study, books and libraries, research has produced a significant contribution in terms of the edition of the sources and more recently a comparative study of the Franciscan regulations and their relation to the order's internal debate on the ownership and use of books.[22]

The consideration of manuscripts in Franciscan environments as an independent object of study had its origin in the description of sets of manuscripts that could be considered Franciscan in terms of their provenance.[23] Scholars such as Attilio Bartoli Langeli, Nicoletta Giovè Marchioli and Neslihan Şenocak have explored and discussed the circulation of books in the Franciscan order and have contributed significantly to the transformation of the topic of books and mendicant orders into a field of study in its own right.[24] Their work continues to offer interesting results and to introduce prospective fields of inquiry such as the dynamics of the circulation of books within reformed houses, the signatures of the saints of the Franciscan Observance, and the dynamics of writing and reading within female Franciscan communities.[25] Two topics are particularly relevant to the object of this book, and they are, first, the real extent of the Dominican

19   Humphreys, *Library of the Franciscans of the Convent of St. Antony*; Humphreys, *Library of the Franciscans of Siena*; Cenci, ed., *Bibliotheca manuscripta*; Frioli, 'Gli antichi inventari della Biblioteca Antoniana di Padova'; Govi, 'Il fondo manoscritto'; Pantarotto, *La biblioteca manoscritta*; Frioli, ' Gli inventari delle biblioteche degli ordini mendicanti'; and Somigli, *'Hoc est registrum omnium librorum'*.
20   Gavinelli, 'Per una biblioteconomia'; Şenocak, 'Book Acquisition'.
21   Grauso, 'La biblioteca francescana medievale di Assisi'; Cicarello, 'Tra grandi biblioteche e grandi lettori'; Granata, 'Dalle povere origini alle grandi biblioteche'.
22   The main contributions to the field are due to Pietro Maranesi. For instance, Maranesi, *Nescientes litteras*, and Maranesi, 'La normativa'.
23   Lopez, 'Descriptio codicum franciscanorum'; and Tosti, 'Descriptio codicum franciscanorum'.
24   Bartoli Langeli, 'I libri dei frati'; Giovè Marchioli and Zamponi, 'Manoscritti in volgare'; Giovè Marchioli, 'I protagonisti del libro'; Giovè Marchioli, 'Circolazione libraria e cultura francescana'; Giovè Marchioli, 'Scriptus per me'; Giovè Marchioli, 'Il codice francescano'; Giovè Marchioli, 'La cultura scritta al Santo'; and Şenocak, 'Circulation of Books'.
25   Giovè Marchioli, 'Sante scritture'; see also Benvenuti, 'L'Osservanza e la costruzione'; and Giovè Marchioli, 'Scritture (e letture) di donne'.

influence on Franciscan book culture and, second, the nature and typology of the books used by Franciscan friars.

Franciscans or Dominicans? A Question of Influence

The discussion of the role of books in Franciscan life has been determined by a useful but inevitably schematic opposition between Franciscans and Dominicans built up in the historiography of both these orders. Previously, scholarship on the role of books within mendicant orders defined the field, by suggesting a model according to which book culture was adopted by Franciscans under the influence of the Dominican success. One of the clearest examples of this approach is the contribution presented by Gabriella Severino Polica at the congress in Todi in 1976, where she discussed mendicant practices of study, as well as the use of books during the thirteenth and fourteenth centuries.[26] One of her main conclusions was that the Dominicans represented a cultural and intellectual avant-garde that succeeded in making study into an essential part of their identity from the very beginning. Franciscans, however, barely managed to follow the Dominican example, since they were dramatically limited by their internal conflicts.[27] Accordingly, although both orders reproduced the dynamics of the university *lectio* in their own schools, their divergent cultural ideologies determined opposite roles for books within each community.[28] Moreover, although preaching was a distinctive element of the orders' identity, Dominican preaching had the purpose of fighting heresy, while the purpose of Franciscan preaching was the call to penance. Consequently, the preparation for preaching reflected the difference between the orders. For the Dominicans, only intensive study could provide the necessary exegetical tools to guarantee the proper interpretation of scripture. For the Franciscans, preaching was essentially an apostolic exhortation and therefore based rather on living in an exemplary way than on learned reflection. As a consequence, an incomplete Franciscan theological interpretation developed later.[29] This approach suggested that

26 Severino Polica, 'Libro, lettura, "lezione"'.
27 Severino Polica, 'Libro, lettura, "lezione"', pp. 381-83.
28 Severino Polica's analysis proposed an ideology focused on intellectual achievement for the Dominicans, as opposed to a Franciscan ideology centred in the apostolic exhortation to penance. See Severino Polica, 'Libro, lettura, "lezione"', pp. 378-81.
29 'Risulta chiaro a questo punto che l'ideologia del libro elaborata dai Domenicani esprime un rapporto di consapevole e approfondita continuità fra cultura scritta e predicazione [...] I Francescani, al contrario, stenteranno sempre ad inquadrare la riflessione del libro in un'ottica

only Dominicans considered intensive study and use of books to be essential to pastoral care, which reinforced the perception of the Dominican order as an intellectual community centred on study. This assessment is emphatically conditioned by the assumption that mendicants should have a suitable model of intellectual development, a model that Franciscans could not provide, at least not in the early phases of their history.

Any set of observations on the very early phases of the Franciscan cultural experience is unquestionably useful but still insufficient to understand phenomena such as the role of books in, say, fifteenth-century Observant preaching. Since the kind of analysis Severino Polica undertook was based on a scheme that opposed 'active Dominicans' to 'passive Franciscans', it was natural to arrive at the conclusion that the Dominican book was essentially a 'scholastic' tool adapted to the intellectual vocation of an order focused on study, while the Franciscan book, as expected, was a continuous source of conflict.[30] This kind of perception has its roots in the overstatement of the conflict between the presence of books and the poverty of the order, and a lack of understanding of the role of humility in the whole picture. As shown in the first chapter, even the most rigorous interpretations of the rule did not condemn books in themselves. Nevertheless, the conflictual approach to the question of study and books has been very influential. One of the reasons for its success is that it is inherently schematic and therefore useful in simplifying complex phenomena. Another reason is the fact that it followed a comparative approach that focused on the differences between the orders, providing a simple characterization of the communities during their complex early phases: 'intellectual, disciplined Dominicans' were the opposite of and complementary to 'apostolic, passionate Franciscans'. Only very recently has this approach been questioned, particularly by Bert Roest, Neslihan Şenocak and Nicoletta Giovè Marchioli.[31] In fact, there are two important problems with the traditional approach: first, it implies a value-judgement in terms of the perception of the early phase of Franciscan history as some kind of failure in terms of scholarly achievement; and second, it fails to establish clearly the extent of the influence of the Dominican example.

culturale-professionale, proprio perché il nesso fra acquisizione della scienza e sua professionaliz-zazione, fra cultura scritta e predicazione, fra esegesi e comunicazione, si afferma presso di loro in modi incerti, sfocati, segnati da un non risolto rapporto con una vocazione "evangelica".' See Severino Polica, 'Libro, lettura, "lezione"', p. 408.
30   Severino Polica, 'Libro, lettura, "lezione"', pp. 387-93 and 402-3.
31   Roest, *History of Franciscan Education*; Şenocak, *Poor and the Perfect*, pp. 16-20; and Giovè Marchioli, 'I protagonisti del libro', pp. 51-53.

The Franciscan Book: Ideal Models and Perspectives

In 2004, during the Thirty-Second Congress of the Società Internazionale di Studi Francescani in Assisi, Nicoletta Giovè Marchioli offered the results of her research on the books used and produced by Franciscans in her search for a specific type of book to be considered especially Franciscan.[32] Indeed, to identify a model for the Franciscan book, Giovè Marchioli discussed what she labelled as the 'physiognomy' of the Franciscan manuscript, that is, the set of physical characteristics of the manuscripts used and produced by Franciscan friars. One might think that the books used by the early community of friars would provide such a model, but Giovè Marchioli points out that a question then arises regarding which kind of manuscripts produced by the early Franciscans constituted this model: the humble miscellany of devotional texts gathered and copied by the first friars or the liturgical books for the divine office?[33] Liturgical books such as breviaries and missals were perhaps the first manuscripts available in Franciscan houses, even before the foundation of any library. However, they arrived through donations or bequests; and even when they were later produced by the convents themselves, they followed established patterns that left no room for the affirmation of any original Franciscan style. As a consequence, the liturgical books used by Franciscans had only two possible variations: a big manuscript for collective use with a high level of ornamentation or breviaries of a smaller dimension intended to be portable books to be carried by the friars. The manuscripts produced by the friars in the early stages of the history of the order were mainly devotional texts, not tools for study or for the friars' preparation for preaching. The appearance of manuals and compilations of sermons within the Franciscan convents reflected the further engagement of the community in forms of preaching beyond the exhortation to penance. These manuscripts, which usually contained sermons, had a low level of sophistication, were smaller than books for study and contained a great variety of hands and decorative elements. For these reasons, the Franciscan compilations of sermons did not fit the model of any archetypical Franciscan book.[34]

To find a suitable archetype, Giovè Marchioli proposed to start by formulating an independent ideal of the Franciscan book, that is, a manuscript

---

32 Giovè Marchioli, 'Il codice Francescano'.

33 Bigaroni, 'Catalogo dei manoscritti', pp. 10-11; see also Giovè Marchioli, 'Il codice Francescano', p. 382.

34 Giovè Marchioli, 'Il codice Francescano', pp. 394-95 and 406-9.

written by a Franciscan friar, containing the work of a Franciscan author and belonging to a Franciscan house.[35] In these respects, the volume Assisi, Biblioteca del Sacro Convento, MS 338, a compilation of early writings on Francis of Assisi, is the realization of such an ideal.[36] However, a manuscript that satisfied the requirements of the ideal was rather exceptional, and therefore it becomes practically irrelevant to the nature and readership of the Franciscan book. Some Bibles used by friars in Franciscan convents were unequivocally made to be part of a Franciscan library, as shown by the decoration depicting Francis and Franciscan saints. Nevertheless, they were magnificent manuscripts of large dimensions, far from reflecting any humility or poverty.[37] At the same time, the production within a Franciscan centre is not a necessary condition for a manuscript to be Franciscan. There are some examples of Franciscan manuscripts whose scribe was a layman living outside the convent, as happens with the volume Florence, Biblioteca Riccardiana, MS 1287, a miscellany with excerpts from Bonaventure and other Franciscan masters, written by Dino Brunaccini, a wool merchant who transcribed the book for himself and for his heirs.[38]

As already mentioned, Franciscan manuscripts containing sermons were usually far from the proposed ideal. At the beginning, Franciscan sermons were gathered into compilations that reproduced the format of the manuscripts used as tools of study in the university, that is, they were parchment manuscripts of regular size, usually between 300 × 200 and 330 × 220 millimetres, written in gothic script, normally by a single hand, and with a *mise en page* organized in two columns. The more modest paper volumes of sermons, written in cursive script, with a smaller size, were incorporated later, usually as miscellanies, and were characteristic of the Observant reformed convents.

Evidence shows that books used and produced by Franciscans had a remarkable variety: they were written in many different scripts, from the formal gothic to the most informal cursives, and had an enormous

---

35 Giovè Marchioli and Zamponi, 'Manoscritti in volgare', p. 312.

36 A complete description of the manuscript can be found in Cenci, ed., *Bibliotheca manuscripta*, I, pp. 236-37.

37 Examples of this kind of manuscripts are the volumes Cesena, Biblioteca Malatestiana, MS D.XXI.1, 2, 3, 4, and Trento, Castello del Buonconsiglio, Monumenti e collezioni provinciali, MS 1597, or the Bible in various volumes: Padua, Biblioteca Antoniana, MS 267, 274, 276, 277, 280, 283, 284, 285, 289, 309, 310, 313, 316 and 342, and Assisi, Biblioteca del Sacro Convento, MS 1, 2, 3, 4, 5, 6 ,7, 9, 10, 11, 12, 13 and 15. See Giovè Marchioli, 'Il codice Francescano', p. 385.

38   'Per se e per le sue erede del libro dello armario dello studio del chonvento di frati minori di Firenze.' See Giovè Marchioli, 'Il codice Francescano', pp. 401-2; see also Giovè Marchioli and Zamponi, 'Manoscritti in volgare', pp. 314-16.

variation in size, style of decoration, and *mise en page*. These volumes contained single works, compilations of works by one author, miscellanies of excerpts or even composite volumes, being the result of the process of assembling several manuscript unities. A similar variety can be found in the types of books and their size. At least three different kinds of manuscript were employed by friars: the big liturgical book, the medium-size book of study that followed the model of the books used in the universities and the small, portable book. With respect to the general dynamics of production, it seems that the same types of manuscript were continuously reproduced, with one significant variation. The unreformed friars of the Community, or Conventuals, continued using books, but there are indications that by the late fifteenth century they no longer produced many new manuscripts: the number of colophons indicating the convent as the place of production decreased dramatically. It seems that those who undertook the task of producing new books were the Observant friars.[39] Until the end of the fifteenth century, the three main forms of the Franciscan book continued to be the book of study, characterized by the influence of the university book; the compilation of sermons; and the book with a high level of realization, destined for devotional purposes but certainly not a book of study. Taken altogether, these considerations led Giovè Marchioli to question the existence of a single model that could summarize the different types of book produced and used by Franciscan friars during the Middle Ages.[40] The proposal of the ideal Franciscan book, or rather, its failure, is helpful in understanding that the complex reality of the manuscripts written and read by Franciscan friars escapes any attempt at methodological simplification in terms of a unitary model, and this understanding constitutes one of the findings of this book.

The discussion proposed by Giovè Marchioli was a significant contribution to the discovery of new paths for Franciscan codicology as a field of research, and constituted a sound alternative to the approach of a sector of Franciscan historiography that separated preaching from an intensive discipline of study. Actually, evidence shows that preaching had an important role in university studies and that it was at the centre of book circulation

---

39 Giovè Marchioli, 'La cultura scritta al Santo', p. 375.

40 'Non esiste un codice francescano con un'identità certa e assoluta, o comunque non esiste un modello dominante, quanto piuttosto esiste una costellazione di modelli simili ma tutti devianti o deviati, quasi fossero una rifrazione, una scomposizione all'infinito di un'immagine e dunque di una realtà solo inizialmente o astrattamente nitide e poi sempre più complesse.' Giovè Marchioli, 'Il codice Francescano', p. 381.

in Franciscan houses.[41] Thus, a broad conception of study – one closer to actual practices in the use of books in Franciscan culture – is necessary to gain a better understanding of the role of books in the order.[42] As a result, Giovè Marchioli further explored the question of whether her model might be useful in the description of the manuscripts in use during the fifteenth century. The most relevant preliminary result of her research is perhaps the presence, from a codicological standpoint, of a 'deconstructed' Franciscan book by the end of the Middle Ages.[43]

Franciscans Manuscripts: Elements of the Late Medieval Book

Manuscripts written, collected and read by Franciscans have been the object of study of different disciplines, for example, codicology, which has offered a complete description of the physical characteristics of some of the manuscripts collected in Franciscan convents. Histories of libraries have focused on the development of collections of books, including the edition and description of valuable sources such as medieval library catalogues. Religious historians have explored the manuscripts written, collected and used by Franciscans as a significant element in the general debate on the 'Franciscan question', that is, the historiographical discussion of the original intention of Francis for the development of the order. Cultural historians have outlined the significant role of books in the development of the scholastic culture of the Franciscans. Despite their great significance, these lines of enquiry have only further underlined the fact that the manuscripts written, collected and used by Franciscan friars have been an important piece of evidence in the historiographical debate. However, apart from Giovè Marchioli's assessment, Franciscan manuscripts have rarely been studied for their own sake, by engaging directly with their 'Franciscan' distinctiveness. A clear example of this is the historiographical approach to Franciscan manuscripts as an element of potential conflict between the rule and the vow of poverty. As shown recently by Neslihan Şenocak, historiography has overstated the conflict between the vow of poverty and use of books within the order

---

41   Roest, *History of Franciscan Education*, pp. 281-84 and 290-97. Neslihan Şenocak argues that preaching played a fundamental role in the life of the order, not as the ultimate purpose of intellectual training, but rather as a means to justify the centrality of learning in the life of the friars. See Şenocak, *Poor and the Perfect*, pp. 145-48.

42   Giovè Marchioli, 'Il codice Francescano', pp. 404-6.

43   Giovè Marchioli, 'Note sulle caratteristiche dei codici francescani'.

and has downplayed the role of humility.[44] By doing so, scholarship has inadvertently also participated in the reconstruction of Francis's 'intentio'.

Apart from these areas of scholarly debate, other important fields of study concerning Franciscan manuscripts have remained unexplored. The most recent discussion of the topic does not go beyond the fourteenth century, and even in the few cases where consideration is given of manuscripts or libraries in the fifteenth century, it refers almost exclusively to the friars and libraries of the unreformed Community, excluding the centres of production and study of the Franciscan Observance.[45] A second area in need of research is related to the fact that current analysis of the book within the Franciscan order focuses on the scholastic model of reading used in the universities.[46] The reception of Franciscan manuscripts employed for devotional purposes, for pastoral care and as tools for preaching, especially during the second half of the fifteenth century, remains unexplored. A discussion of practices of reading is necessary in order to improve our models of analysis, particularly in the case of the Observant manuscripts, and would constitute a solid base from which to propose a more accurate typology of the Franciscan manuscript. A third field left unexplored concerns the use of a comparative approach to study cases of Franciscan libraries and their organization to verify whether it is possible to establish a particular type of manuscript in relation to reformed or unreformed communities of the order. Another area of extraordinary importance is the consideration of female Franciscan communities and their relation with writing and reading manuscripts, which has been so far painfully neglected by scholarship.[47]

This book fills some of these gaps by studying the manuscripts written, collected and read in the male Franciscan convents of Padua from the thirteenth to the fifteenth century. As mentioned, Padua was one of the most important Franciscan centres and could count on the presence of two convents that had a school and a functioning library from two different branches of the order during the second half of the fifteenth century: the unreformed convent of Sant'Antonio and the reformed or Observant convent of San Francesco Grande. The study of these manuscripts is undertaken

---

44   Neslihan Şenocak presented a set of considerations on the matter in the paper 'Making of Franciscan Poverty', presented at the International Medieval Congress in Leeds in 2012.

45   Remarkable exceptions are Giovè Marchioli, 'Note sulle caratteristiche dei codici francescani'; Bartoli, 'La biblioteca e lo *scriptorium* di Giovanni da Capestrano'; and Pellegrini, 'Cultura del libro e pratiche'.

46   Hamesse, 'Scholastic Model of Reading', pp. 108-11.

47   Among the few exceptions are the studies of Gabriella Zarri, especially Zarri, 'Le monache e i libri', and Giovè Marchioli, 'Scritture (e letture) di donne'.

using an interdisciplinary approach, and explores the relation between Franciscan friars and their books, as well as whether this relationship reflects a particular conception of the book. It will also discuss the question of the 'Franciscan book' by establishing a difference between the 'Franciscan book' as an abstraction and the 'Franciscan manuscript' understood as a category encompassing the concrete volumes analysed and studied. In what follows, a more detailed description of this work will be presented, but it is necessary first to dedicate some words to the terminology adopted and the fields and questions that this book does not cover.

'Conception' is understood in a wide sense as the inner representation or a set of ideas related to an external physical object. Accordingly, the conception of the book is the way in which Franciscans, through interaction with manuscripts, perceived the book in multiple forms: as an object that was a recipient of information, as a source of information, as a tool for the preparation for preaching, as a recipient of their own thoughts, as a portable library and as a defining element of their identity. It is clear, then, that the Franciscan conception of the book was not a unitary one.

'Book' and 'manuscript' as individual words and as nouns both in the singular and the plural – book/books, manuscript/manuscripts – are practically interchangeable in this work and refer to a material object in a specific time and place which is a written recipient of information in the form of a codex.[48] Nevertheless, as explained earlier, this study will discuss the theoretical notion of the 'Franciscan book' as opposed to the reality of 'Franciscan manuscripts'. The 'Franciscan book' is used for the conceptualization of an ideal unitary model for the books written, collected and used by Franciscan friars. 'Franciscan manuscripts' refers to the concrete handwritten volumes or books that were used by friars as the source of information for the practices of reading and study. I have tried to avoid confusion by reducing to a minimum the instances where the 'Franciscan book' is employed.

The term 'library' refers not only to a space where the books were collected and kept but also to a system of collection, circulation and retrieval of written volumes characterized by specific patterns of organization. It also acquires the sense of a collection of works, and that is why, as will be seen in Chapters 3 and 4, it could also refer to a single manuscript that contains a melange of different works.[49] The term 'study' is understood in its medieval scholastic

---

48   Teeuwen, *Vocabulary of Intellectual Life*, pp. 168-69.
49   Teeuwen, *Vocabulary of Intellectual Life*, pp. 159-60.

sense of 'to devote or apply oneself to one's books'.[50] It implies mainly the act of reading, and in the case of the Franciscan interpretive community, also the act of writing. To study therefore was a form of interaction with the text, as examined in Chapter 4. 'Learning' has a broader general sense, and comprises the multiple practices of study but also the teaching methods and all the forms of intellectual training of the friars. In this sense, learning was a long-term process that implied a continuous devotion to study and consequently to book culture. 'Study' and 'learning' usually appear together in this work, but they are not interchangeable, although they were closely related. 'To read' and 'reading' will be understood as the process of interaction between an agent, the reader and a written object, the text, within the specific context of an interpretive community, that is, the community of shared values and practices of writing to which the reader belongs. A detailed description of the sense of 'reading' and 'interpretive community' is offered in Chapter 4.

It is also necessary to mention the fields this work does not discuss for reasons extending from the methodological to the practical. For example, concerning the community of readers, this book will not explore the female branch of the Franciscan order. Also, in regard to the book collections, the manuscripts kept in the sacristy of the convents usually employed for the divine office are not included in this analysis, mainly because, from the point of view of the interpretive community, they were not part of the book collection but rather of the valued goods of the sacristy. Another type of book that is not the object of analysis in this work is the printed book. Franciscans enthusiastically welcomed printed books into their collections, but these volumes were no longer the result of the physical action of a scribe. As such, the texts reached their readers in the form of unitary, complete and finished objects; and even though they could be personalized in different ways, they were not the kind of intellectual tools that, for example, were intended to satisfy the specific needs of an individual scribe. They were books, certainly, but no longer manuscripts.

Now, concerning the main topics of this book, Chapter 1 may be said to explore the first aspect of the Franciscan manuscript, namely the ideal, by discussing the relation between the regulations of the order and the use of books in the Franciscan convents. Using books became a problematic issue for Franciscans as a result of the warnings of their founder against the glorification of study and learning. This chapter proposes that the Franciscan rule, as established by Francis, aimed to preserve a balance in the

50   Teeuwen, *Vocabulary of Intellectual Life*, pp. 139-40.

presence of unlearned and learned members of the community. The order's intellectual achievement was possible thanks to a tradition of interpretation of the rule that reconciled the parts of it that seemed to prohibit learning as a goal in its own right with a dedication to the study and use of books. This chapter traces the interpretation of the rule proposed by the friars of the Community, to which the convent of Sant'Antonio belonged, and the reformed friars of the Franciscan Observance, to which the friars of the convent of San Francesco Grande belonged. The chapter focuses on assessing the ideal Franciscan relationship to books, as revealed by the regulations – both implicitly and explicitly. According to this ideal, the 'intention' of the founder could be reconciled with the intellectual agency of the friars because the latter was justified by the need for preparation for preaching and pastoral care. Again, the remarkable achievement of Franciscans in all areas of intellectual endeavour surpassed the stated aim of helping to fulfil pastoral duties. This chapter also shows how the ideal book, as described in the first versions of the regulations, was perhaps never used, mainly because it could not satisfy the expectations and needs of the friars. Accordingly, the regulations had to evolve and reflect the needs of a community that came to share certain intellectual expectations. The main sources used to carry out the analysis in this chapter are the two versions of the Franciscan rule and the different interpretations of the masters of the order under the form of answers to particular questions, treatises on the proper observance of the rule, admonitions, letters and commentaries on the rule.

Through a study of the Franciscan libraries in Padua, Chapter 2 explores the second dimension of the Franciscan manuscript, that is, the space. The starting point is the discussion of the development of the medieval library with the help of two models of book collection: the first is the library as it was conceived and used by Boethius, that is, as a scholar's personal library that reflects the expectations and needs of its owner; the second is represented by Cassiodorus, who assembled the book collection of Vivarium, his monastery in southern Italy. The library of Vivarium was intended to satisfy the needs of a community whose members shared reading and writing skills, and it became the predominant type of library during the Middle Ages. With the development of scholastic culture, significant transformations occurred in the setting of this type of communal library. One of the most important was to split the book collection into two: one part made up of books chained to the tables, and the other of copies available for loan. The mendicant orders, and particularly the Franciscans, both adopted and improved on this model of the library. This chapter offers new insights into the field of study by comparing the libraries of the two Paduan convents. After describing the history, size and main characteristics of each book collection, this chapter analyses the distribution of volumes and the composition of the library. Although both libraries were intended to be the repositories of a collection focused on the education and training of Franciscan preachers, the comparison reveals interesting differences in the topics and physical characteristics of the manuscripts collected. The older library of Sant'Antonio seems to have been devoted to the study of the 'classic' masters of Franciscan culture, while in the library of the Observant convent there is a significant presence of treatises on cases and procedures related to pastoral care and devotion. Most of the manuscripts collected in the Observant library are modest in format and materials and appear to be miscellanies written as personal copies, that is, books to be used by their own scribes. The presence of this kind of manuscript challenges the assumption that a functional, personal collection of books returned only with the rise of humanism. The study of these Franciscan libraries also shows that friars were highly skilled readers, capable of reading more than one manuscript at a time; they were also readers who employed manuscripts as a source for producing new manuscripts, and in this respect their libraries show that Franciscans were agents of writing. The main sources for this chapter are the medieval inventories of the Paduan libraries, contained in surviving manuscripts in Padua and in the Vatican Library.

Chapter 3 studies the physical characteristics of a representative set of volumes collected in the Paduan libraries, as well as traces of use that can be found in them, in order to explore a further dimension of the Franciscan manuscript that could be called, in the Aristotelian sense, as its form. To do so, it establishes two sets of manuscripts, one from the library of Sant'Antonio and the other from the library of San Francesco Grande. The set from Sant'Antonio is constituted by the copies of a theological treatise and a collection of sermons, while the set from San Francesco Grande is constituted by manuscripts used as tools for the composition of sermons and collections of sermons. These two sets are representative selections from the two libraries that exemplify some of the larger issues treated in this work. The study of the manuscripts begins with a codicological examination, before comparing the volumes from the same set and finally comparing the two sets. This codicological comparative approach reveals unknown features of the organization of the library of Sant'Antonio; for example, it has made it possible to establish the order of arrival of the copies of the Bonaventure of Bagnoregio's commentary on the first book of the *Sentences*. At the same time, interesting information is also discovered on the way in which the library guaranteed the availability of manuscripts. The overall comparison allows one to establish common features in the manuscripts, depending on their library of provenance. The library of the convent of Sant'Antonio held mainly parchment manuscripts of study and theological treatises of medium size, the library of the convent of San Francesco Grande was a repository of mainly paper manuscripts of smaller dimensions that were usually compilations for devotional purposes or tools for pastoral care and preparation of sermons. These manuscripts contained works of different genres in both Latin and the vernacular.

Chapter 4 explores the fourth dimension, namely, the readership, through the assessment of the practices of reading within the Paduan convents. Using methodological tools from the history of reading and reception theory, as well as codicological and palaeographical tools, this chapter establishes a relation between the manuscript evidence and the notion of an interpretive community, and applies it to the convents to identify not only particular forms of reading within the convents but also a characterization of Franciscan friars as readers. This chapter also discusses models of analysis of medieval readers as proposed by historical criticism, and shows that in relation to their interpretive community, Franciscans were professional agents of culture characterized by an outstanding flexibility as readers and writers. As readers familiar with different levels of writing and, in the case of Observant friars, as users of personalized collections of works, Franciscans challenge the definition of the lay humanist reader as the pioneering figure of a readership characterized by its flexibility, multilinguistic competence and cultural agency through personal libraries. The main sources for the discussion of the practices of reading in the convents are the manuscripts read by the friars, specifically the traces of use that can be identified in the form of marginal comments, notes, cross references and ownership inscriptions.

In summary, the present work explores four dimensions of the Franciscan manuscripts: the ideal of these manuscripts, as expressed in the regulations on study and use of books; the space of the Franciscan manuscripts, that is, the libraries where they were collected; the purpose of the manuscripts, as reflected by their physical characteristics; and the readership of these manuscripts, as revealed by textual evidence. At this point one might justifiably ask why this book focuses on Franciscan manuscripts instead of broadening the field to the Franciscan book. As will be shown, the notion of the Franciscan book is unhelpful as a category of analysis, which is an additional reason why it is proposed instead to focus on the Franciscan manuscript as a concrete, functional and verifiable reality that reveals the interaction between Franciscans and the written page, showing that medieval Franciscan friars are worthy of further study as writers, readers and agents of literacy.

1. The Ideal

Regulations and Franciscan Manuscripts in Padua

Introduction

By the middle of the fifteenth century, Franciscans were facing an internal conflict that menaced the unity of the order. Two groups of friars – the unreformed friars of the Community, or Conventuals, on the one side, and the reformed or Observant friars on the other – embraced almost opposite views concerning the nature and purpose of Franciscan spirituality. When, in 1443, a general chapter was summoned at Padua to elect the new minister general of the order, Pope Eugenius IV decided to intervene to solve the problem of increasing division within the order. The pope's project should have been confirmed by the election of the virtuous Observant friar Alberto of Sarteano. However, as Duncan Nimmo describes, during the first session of the chapter,

> Alberto of Sarteano as president mounted the rostrum and began to read out a message from the pope, which may very well have expressed the wish that he be elected General. He never reached the end of it. With cries of 'Liberty!, Liberty!', a crowd of Conventuals surged forward, tore the missive from his hands, and dragged him bodily from the chamber, and on the floor of the hall the delegates of the two factions came to blows.[1]

Two bands of friars fiercely, and perhaps enthusiastically, exchanging blows to settle a question of spiritual leadership was certainly not the most encouraging display of Christian charity. Nevertheless, the fight at the Paduan chapter was dramatic evidence of a dispute about the proper way of following Francis. In other words, the fight was in essence the physical expression of a debate on the proper way of reading and, if necessary, interpreting the Franciscan rule.

---

1   Nimmo, *Reform and Division*, p. 630.

Hernández Vera, R., *Franciscan Books and their Readers: Friars and Manuscripts in Late Medieval Italy*. Taylor & Francis Group, 2022
DOI 10.5117/9789463729512_CH01

Francis explicitly forbade any glossing of his writings; nevertheless, Franciscan friars found themselves torn between those who wanted a strict and even literal observance of his dispositions and those who considered that interpretations and adaptations of the rule were necessary. In this debate, one of the most important questions was the role of study and books. In effect, learning and the use of books were intrinsically connected to two fundamental aspects of the Franciscan life: the principle of humility and the apostolic mission of preaching. An early biography of Francis of Assisi described his concern for the fact that, apparently, knowledge had become more attractive to friars than virtue. He feared that his companions could find themselves empty-handed on the 'day of reckoning', when all of their precious books would be absolutely useless and would be thrown out the window.[2] According to this passage, Francis attributed a low level of useful-ness to books because their value depended on circumstances. Therefore, they were superfluous and unnecessary for achieving the goal of living according to apostolic principles. This excerpt reflects how, from the early stages of its history, the Franciscan community perceived an incompatibility between Francis's intentions and the presence of books as tools for learning. Actually, very soon Franciscans became an active part of the international community of learned scholars. Thus, it became difficult to both respect the original intention of the founder in terms of humility and poverty and to develop a discipline of study and learning.[3] Naturally, at the root of Francis's apprehensiveness was the anxiety that books could easily become objects of ownership and intellectual achievement, which would contradict the principle of humility established by the rule.[4] The order made a continuous effort to solve this problem by developing different interpretations of the

2   In chapter 147 of the *Vita secunda*, a biography of Francis written by Thomas of Celano in 1246-47: '[Franciscus] Dolebat si, virtute neglecta, scientia quareretur, praesertim si non in ea vocatione quisque persisteret in qua vocatus a principio fuerit. "Fratres", ait, "mei, qui scientia curiositate ducuntur, in die retributionis manus invenient vacua. Vellem eos magis roborari virtutibus, ut cum tempora tribulationis venirent, secum haberent in angustia Dominum. Nam et ventura est", inquit, "tribulatio, qua libri ad nihilum utiles in fenestris proiciantur et latebris". Non hoc dicebat quod Scripturae studia displicerent, sed quo a superflua cura discendi universos retraheret, et quosque magis charitate bonos, quam curiositate sciolos esse vellet.' Thomas of Celano, *Vita secunda*, pp. 190-91; see also Prinzivalli, 'Un santo da leggere', pp. 97-99, and Merlo, *Nel nome di san Francesco*, pp. 159-60.
3   Şenocak, *Poor and the Perfect*, pp. 107-8; Robson, *Franciscans in the Middle Ages*, pp. 58-59.
4   The first version of the Franciscan rule established: 'Regula et vita istorum fratrum haec est, scilicet vivere in obedientia, in castitate et sine proprio, et Domini nostri Jesu Christi doctrinam et vestigia sequi qui dicit: "Si vis perfectus esse, vade et vende omnia quae habes, et da pauperibus et habebis thesaurum in caelo; et veni, sequere me."' Esser, ed., *Die Opuscula*, pp. 377-78.

regulations to guarantee the constant presence of books without violating, at least not formally, the spirit of the founder's dispositions.

This chapter will explore one aspect of the Franciscan manuscript, that is, the ideal of the manuscript as proposed by the regulations. To do so, it will follow the attempts to solve the problem of the apparent incompatibility of the original Franciscan regulations with the presence of books within the convents. It will consider the development of the main source of regulations, that is, the rule of the order, and its application in the two male Franciscan convents in Padua: the unreformed convent of Sant'Antonio, which followed the interpretation of the regulations proposed by masters such as Bonaventure of Bagnoregio, Hugh of Digne and other representatives of the hierarchy of the order; and the reformed or Observant convent of San Francesco Grande, which followed the model proposed by John of Capistrano and Bernardino of Siena, two of the four 'pillars' of the Observant reform. The discussion of the different approaches to the regulations will be useful in understanding the ways in which the Paduan convents conceived of their respective relation to books and how they perceived the role of books within the life of the community as an element of Franciscan identity. The assessment of the regulations on books as interpreted by the Community and the reformed friars will also provide elements for a comparison between the ideal Franciscan manuscript, as derived from the rule, and manuscripts as they were conceived in later interpretations of the rule. This discussion will help us in subsequent chapters to understand the actual practices of collection, production and use of books, and will also provide evidence valuable to an appreciation of how the ideal of the Franciscan manuscript developed and adapted to the necessities and expectations of the friars.

Learning and the Use of Books: Two Problematic Practices for Franciscans

When Francis of Assisi died in Porziuncola on the night of 3 October 1226, he left a 'troublesome inheritance' to his community of friars.[5] Although Francis in his *Testamentum* described himself as ignorant and unlearned – 'ignorans et idiota' – his writings covered various genres such as letters, regulations, canticles, admonitions and exemplary tales written in

---

5   Lambertini and Tabarroni, *Dopo Francesco*; Robson, *Franciscans in the Middle Ages*, p. 44; and Moorman, *History of the Franciscan Order*, pp. 83-85.

Latin and in the vernacular.[6] All of them were shared, read, studied and interpreted thoroughly by the friars, not only for their spiritual significance, but especially because most of them were either their founder's answer to a question addressed by a single friar or group of friars or Francis's solution to a specific problem experienced by the early community. Within this context, the most complex of those documents, the Franciscan rule, went beyond the specific purpose of fixing the principles for the order's identity and government to also serve as an authoritative source to solve issues in the proper application of Franciscan principles to everyday life. Consequently, the rule was not only read and studied but – despite the founder's exhortation – interpreted by the community's masters and chapters in an attempt to harmonize the swift growth of the order with his original intention.[7] Preaching is one of the activities that best illustrates these changes. Franciscan friars embraced preaching as one of the essential traits of their identity, as reflected in the ninth chapter of their rule. Early Franciscan preaching consisted in a simple and universal call to penance and remission of sins; but with the affirmation of learning within the order, and with the diffusion of the Franciscan presence in every layer of society, preaching became an activity entrusted to those who had received suitable preparation in the *studia* of the convents or in the university, and very soon learning and preaching became inseparable in the Franciscan world. In this trajectory, the different interpretations of the Franciscan rule on study, books and libraries reflected the evolution of the order's spirituality, as well as its internal conflicts on the role of learning within the community. In what follows, there will be a brief description of the general development of the Franciscan rule, as well as of the rule's treatment of the study and use of books.

The Franciscan Rule

Once the charismatic preaching of Francis of Assisi began to attract his first followers, the question of how to organize the group of companions according to an apostolic model became apparent. Most probably, Francis did not have in mind any specific form of organization for the brotherhood, but simply intended to reproduce the way of life of the first Christian

---

6   Da Campagnola, 'Introduzione'; see also Esser, ed., *Die Opuscula*, p. 262.
7   Şenocak, *Poor and the Perfect*, pp. 59-60; Pásztor, *Intentio Beati Francisci*, pp. 181-96.

community, as it was described by the Gospels.[8] However, very soon he realized that it was necessary to reach a certain degree of formalization and to obtain institutional approval. Accordingly, by 1210 he wrote a collection of evangelical principles and asked and obtained papal approval for them.[9] Unfortunately, no copies of this rule, known as the *Regula primitiva* or *Protoregola*, have survived, but most probably it reflected the fact that Francis regarded his companions as members of a *fraternitas*, and consequently, establishing a new religious order was not his main purpose.[10] Nevertheless, the swift growth of the community and the arrival of clerics, masters of theology and priests dramatically changed the nature of the first group of his followers. By the autumn of 1220, Francis gave up the government of the community, and by 1221 he completed, with the aid of friar Caesarius of Speyer, a different text intended as a normative document.[11] This 'first rule', also known as the *Regula non bullata*, lacked papal approval. Hence, the question of a canonically valid normative document to regulate the life of the friars was still open.

On 23 November 1223, Pope Honorius III officially confirmed a rule for the Franciscan community with the letter *Solet annuere*. This new rule, known as the *Regula bullata*, was an attempt to combine, or rather, to translate the Franciscan spirit into precise, normative language. This time, in addition to Francis, the heads of the order and even perhaps members of the Roman curia participated in its composition. The result was a Franciscan text in inspiration, but with a sharp normative twist.[12] By the autumn of 1226, Francis dictated his famous testament. Intended as a synthesis of his spirituality, the testament, according to his words, should be considered to complement the rule and, like the rule, should be preserved carefully in its original integrity.[13] Nevertheless, very soon the rule and the testament

---

8   'Et postquam Dominus dedit mihi de fratibus, nemo ostendebat mihi, quid deberem facere, sed ipse Altissimus revelavit mihi, quod deberem vivere secundum formam sancti evangelii.' Esser, ed., *Die Opuscula*, p. 439; see also Merlo, *Nel nome di san Francesco*, p. 20.

9   'Et ego paucis verbis et simpliciter feci scribi et dominus Papa confirmavit mihi.' Esser, ed., *Die Opuscula*, p. 439.

10   Some scholars have proposed a reconstruction of the *Regula primitiva* based upon surviving sources. See Moorman, *Sources for the Life of S. Francis of Assisi*, pp. 38-54; see also Manselli, *San Francesco*, pp. 259-61.

11   See Merlo, 'Storia di Frate Francesco', pp. 10-11.

12   See Armstrong et al., eds., *Francis of Assisi: Early Documents*, I, p. 99; see also Esser, ed., *Die Opuscula*, pp. 363-72.

13   'Et non dicant fratres: "Haec est alia regula, quia haec est recordatio, admonitio, exhortatio et meum testamentum quod ego frater Franciscus parvulus facio vobis fratribus meis benedictis propter hoc, ut regulam, quam Domino promisimus, melius catholice observemus [...] Et generalis

became the subject of study, critical reading and controversial interpretation in order to adapt the normative dispositions to challenging situations such as the arrival of learned members in the community, their engagement in scholastic culture or the appointment of friars as prelates.

The Rule and the Question of Study and Books

Even before the composition of the *Regula non bullata* the question of the use and ownership of books was a problem for the first Franciscan community, as shown by the dispositions of an early general chapter of the order – gathered in 1220 – which established that friars should not have books and that novices should not keep the psalter with them.[14] The use and access to books was also considered by the *Regula non bullata* in its third chapter, which prescribed that clerics should have only those books useful to the performance of their duties, that the laypeople capable of reading the psalter could have a copy but that books should not be available to those who could not read:

> 'Clerics [*clerici*] [...] may have only the books necessary to fulfil their office. The lay brothers [*laici*] who know how to read the psalter may have one. Those who do not know how to read [*nescientibus litteras*], however, may not be permitted to have any books.'[15]

This reveals three important features: first, that by the time of the compilation of the first version of the rule a distinction was drawn between *clerici*, *laici* and the *nescientes litteras* within the community; second, that one of the key criteria to establish the distinction was the ability to read books; and third, that this ability was perceived as a skill with a specific and practical purpose. This passage also leads to the question of a restriction in

minister et omnes alii ministri et custodes per obedientiam teneantur, in istis verbis non addere vel minuere. [...] Et omnibus fratribus meis clericis et laicis praecipio firmiter per obedientiam, ut non mittant glossas in regula neque in istis verbis dicendo: "Ita volunt intelligi." Esser, ed., *Die Opuscula*, pp. 443-44.

14   Only three decrees from this chapter are known. All of these dispositions were related to the question of possession. Two explicitly forbade possession of books in general and possession of a psalter for novices. See Şenocak, *Poor and the Perfect*, pp. 31-32.

15   'Clerici [...] libros tantum necessarios ad implendum eorum officium possint habere. Et laicis etiam scientibus legere psalterium, liceat eis habere illud. Aliis vero nescientibus litteras, librum habere non liceat.' Flood, ed., *Die Regula non Bullata der Minderbrüder*, p. 57.

the access to literacy for those *nescientes litteras*. Some scholars see in this disposition a 'damage-control strategy'; that is, since Francis knew that the increasing influence of literate friars was unavoidable, he tried to guarantee the presence of illiterate active members in the community to prevent the 'intellectualization' of the order.[16] Although it is very difficult to establish the original intention of Francis, this interpretation seems in accordance with his declared purpose of living according to the spirit of the Gospel.

The distinction between *clerici, laici* and *nescientibus litteras* remained in the second rule or *Regula bullata*; thus, it was established in the third chapter that clerics should perform the divine office in accordance with the prescriptions of the holy Roman Church, that they should use breviaries instead of the psalter and that lay brothers should pray twenty-four paternosters at established times of the day:

> The clerical brothers should recite the Divine Office according to the rite of the holy Roman Church excepting the psalter, for which they may have breviaries [...] The Lay brothers may say twenty-four Our Fathers for Matins, five for Lauds; for Prime, Terce, Sext, and None, seven for each, but twelve for Vespers and seven for Compline.[17]

This is confirmed further in the tenth chapter, where Francis reminds and exhorts in the name of the Lord that friars should beware of any sense of pride, personal glory, envy, avarice, anxiety for the things of the world or spirit of division and that they should not try to teach literacy to those unable to read:

> I admonish and exhort the brothers in Lord Jesus Christ to beware of all pride, vainglory, envy and greed, of care and preoccupation for the things of this world, of detraction and murmuring, and those who are illiterate [*nescientes litteras*] should not trouble about learning, but should pay attention to what they must desire above all else: to have the Spirit of the Lord [...][18]

16 See Menestò, 'Francesco, i Minori e i libri', pp. 9-10; see also Paolazzi, 'I Frati Minori e i libri', pp. 22-27, and Maranesi, *Nescientes litteras*, pp. 56-63.

17 Clerici faciant divinum officium secundum ordinem sanctae Romanae Ecclesiae excepto psalterio, ex quo habere poterunt breviaria [...] Laici vero dicant viginti quatuor *Pater noster* pro matutino, pro laude quinque, pro prima, tertia, sexta, nona pro qualibet istarum septem, pro vesperis autem duodecim, pro completorio septem [...]. Esser, ed., *Die Opuscula*, p. 367.

18 Moneo vero et exhortor in Domino Jesu Christo, ut caveant fratres ab omni superbia, vana gloria, invidia, avaritia, cura et sollicitudine huius saeculi, detractione et murmuratione et non

An interesting question relevant to the use of books is whether some sort of development takes place between the two rules – namely, the rule moves from a restriction on possession of books to one on learning to read – or whether the *Regula bullata* is just a concise and refined reformulation of the first version of the rule. Carlo Paolazzi proposes that the rules are complementary: the restriction concerning the psalter in the first rule implies a restriction on reading, while the curb on learning how to read implies a restriction on the use of books.[19] Therefore, although the Franciscan rule did not encourage, and even restricted, learning, it is possible to say that it did not condemn it.

As noted earlier, it seems that the rule aimed to keep a balance between, on the one hand, learning and intellectual achievement and, on the other, Francis's conception of the pure spirituality of an apostolic way of life. A strict observance of the Franciscan rule would not have stimulated learning, schools or any kind of deep engagement with book culture. The image derived from the rule of the manuscript to be used by Franciscans is, then, that of a devotional volume, produced outside the community and available only to a restricted number of friars. Nevertheless, Franciscans very swiftly became agents of knowledge and culture, a transformation that raises the question of how this was possible, given the importance of adhering to the rule. The key to the answer is to be found in the development of interpretations of the rule which allowed for the accommodation of university masters and intellectuals within the setting of the order while keeping a direct link with the figure of the founder.[20] In what follows a more detailed description of the various interpretations of the rule's regulations on learning and the use of books will be considered, as well as their relation to the Franciscan convents in the city of Padua.

The Convent of Sant'Antonio in Padua and the Interpretations of the Rule of the Friars of the Community

There is no precise record of the arrival of the first Franciscans in Padua; nevertheless, it is very likely that an active campaign of Franciscan preaching

---

curent nescientes litteras litteras discere; sed attendant, quod super omnia desiderare debent habere Spiritum Domini [...]. Esser, ed., *Die Opuscula*, p. 370.

19   Paolazzi, 'I Frati Minori e i libri', p. 55.
20   Şenocak, *Poor and the Perfect*, pp. 35-37.

began shortly before 1229, as recorded by a chronicle of the time.[21] Most probably the nearby convent of Arcella offered support for the Paduan preaching, and as a result friars from that convent were called by Bishop Jacopo Corrado to settle in the city, in the small church of Santa Maria Mater Domini located on the site of the current Chapel of the Virgin in the Basilica of Sant'Antonio.[22] There are grounds to suppose that Anthony of Padua himself established the convent's *studium*, which should have responded to the increasing need of preparation for preaching. In a very short time, the convent established a strong relationship with the university, following the model of the University of Paris.[23] The relation between the University of Padua and Franciscan culture is illustrated by the fact that, according to St. Anthony's legend, professors and students of the university were among the first who asked for his canonization, even though he did not study or teach there.[24] In actual fact, the transformation of the convent's school from *studium provincialis* into *studium generale* in 1310, and from 1363 into a section of the theological faculty, was only possible thanks to the interaction with the university.[25] Further evidence of the reciprocal influence between the Franciscan convent and the academic centre may be found in the composition of the book collection held by the friars in

21 'Hic speravit Padua pacem amodo permansuram in ea. – Nunc circa unius anni spacium civitates de Marchia tarvisina adeo quieverunt in pace, quod quasi circa finem anni domini MCCXXVIIII, et circa principium subsequentis nulla fuit terrarum predacio, nulla hostium incursio vel insultus, preter supra dictum exercitum, set bonorum omnium copia; tantum gaudium et leticia intergentes, ut a pluribus crederetur quod amodo nulle sediciones esse debeant in Marchia nulle werre. Imo et religiose persone totum quasi populum in laudabili contemplacione manentem divinis predicacionibus recreabant. Nam et in illo tempore inter ceteros viros religiosos et iustos advenit beatus Antonius, sicut dicetur inferius, et in diversis locis per Marchiam verba Dei voce melliflua predicavit.' Rolandinus Patavinus, *Cronica in factis et circa facta Marchie Trivixane*, p. 40; see also Lombardo, 'Ecclesia huius temporis', p. 98.

22 Sartori, *Archivio Sartori*, I, p. 1309; see also Bernardino Bordin, 'Profilo storico-spirituale', pp. 74-75.

23 Marangon, *Ad cognitionem scientiae festinare*, pp. 65-69 and 115-25; Fontana, *Frati, libri e insegnamento*, pp. 52-56.

24 'Clamat nimirum sacer cleri conventus; vociferatur devotus populus; omnes una voce et unanimi voluntate concordant; ut probeati Antonii canonizatione [sic] ad curiam mittatur modis omnibus instant [...] Scribit proinde favore digna magistrorum atque scholarium universitas tota et litteras, visus et auditus testimonium prehibentes, mittit litteratorum concio, non leviter repulsam passura.' Kerval, ed., *Sancti antonii de Padua vitae*, pp. 75 and 77; see also Marangon, *Ad cognitionem scientiae festinare*, pp. 65 and 81; Bortolami, 'Studenti e città', pp. 6-18; and Rigon, 'San Antonio e la cultura universitaria'.

25 Marangon, *Ad cognitionem scientiae festinare*, p. 120; Poppi, 'La teologia nell'Università e nelle scuole', pp. 6-12; Roest, *History of Franciscan Education*, pp. 28, 36 and 39-41; Fontana, *Frati, libri e insegnamento*, pp. 65-66 and 84-88.

their library. According to Cesare Cenci, during the first two centuries of the convent's history there was a predominance of Franciscan authors with emphasis on pastoral content; however, the influence of professors and students at the university became more evident as the composition of the collection changed and reflected their needs.[26] The activity of the friars, the strategic location of the city and the continuous interaction with the university made of Padua the most important Franciscan centre in Italy after Assisi. The arrival of the Observant friars and the foundation of the convent and hospital of San Francesco Grande during the fifteenth century enriched the scholarly exchange, since the Observants, apart from becoming active students, offered accommodation and support to fellow scholars.[27] As a result, by the second half of the fifteenth century, Padua hosted two Franciscan convents from two different branches of the order, each of them with a group of active students and masters and with a remarkable book collection in its library.

Concerning the question of learning, study and more importantly the use of books and their compatibility with the Franciscan rule, the friars of Sant'Antonio followed the interpretation developed by the masters of the Community such as Bonaventure of Bagnoregio and Hugh of Digne during the thirteenth and fourteenth centuries. A brief summary of the main aspects of that interpretation will be offered in the following.

As shown in the description of the development of the Franciscan rule, the attitude of Francis to learning and the use of books was very difficult to grasp.[28] By the mid-thirteenth century, a significant part of the Franciscan

---

26 Cenci, 'Manoscritti e frati studiosi nella Biblioteca Antoniana di Padova', p. 498; see also Sartori, 'Gli studi al Santo di Padova', where there is a comprehensive documentary overview of the activities of friars as agents of culture in society and the practices of study in the convent.

27 Collodo, *Una società in trasformazione*, pp. 510-11.

28 To establish the 'intention' of Francis has proven to be a very elusive goal, especially with regard to study and the use of books, as Malcolm Lambert has confirmed: 'It is a dangerous thing to make unrestricted use of scholastic methods in analysing the nature of Francis's intentions. Many of the historians who have given us outlines of the ideal of Francis have been Franciscans themselves, trained in systematic theology and naturally enough employing the categories of scholasticism [...] Yet Francis was never able to think or write in such terms.' Lambert, *Franciscan Poverty*, pp. 34-35. Other interesting considerations on the topic may be found in Felder, *Histoire des études*, pp. 65-104; Landini, *Causes of the Clericalization of the Order*, pp. 51-55; Barone, 'La legislazione sugli "studia" dei Predicatori e dei Minori', pp. 208-9; M. Ferrari, 'Gli scritti di san Francesco d'Assisi'; Desbonnets, *Dalla intuizione alla istituzione*; Bartoli Langeli, 'I libri dei frati'; Maranesi, *Nescientes litteras*, pp. 63-66; Merlo, *Nel nome di san Francesco*, pp. 113-15; Menestò, 'Francesco, i Minori e i libri', pp. 11-15; Pásztor, *Intentio Beati Francisci*, pp. 195-96; Courtenay, 'Franciscan Learning', pp. 55-56. See also Godet-Calogeras, 'De la "Forma vitae"'; and Şenocak, *Poor and the Perfect*, pp. 25-54.

community wanted to completely reconcile the activities and spirituality of the order with study. Nevertheless, a feeling of suspicion regarding
intellectual achievement was growing, in part due to the dissemination
of Joachite ideas within the order. In fact, the special interpretation of the
spiritual prophecy of Joachim of Fiore cast a deep shadow over the real
meaning and importance of study. In 1254 Gerardo of Borgo San Donnino
wrote the *Liber introductorius in evangelium aeternum*, a work that proposed
a radical interpretation of the eschatological work of Joachim of Fiore.[29]
According to Gerardo, the Franciscans were Joachim's 'prophets of the
Spirit', the preachers of the *evangelium aeternum* and the agents of salvation
that would lead to a new age, the age of the Spirit. In this new age, learning
would not be required because Francis's words and precepts would have
comprised all knowledge and science. Gerardo believed that the *evangelium
aeternum* was confirmed by three works written by Joachim: the *Concordia
Novi et Veteris Testamenti*, the *Expositio in Apocalipsim* and the *Psalterium
decem chordarum*. Gerardo's propositions were condemned as heretical by
Pope Alexander IV in 1255.[30] This is the context in which masters such as
Hugh of Digne and Bonaventure of Bagnoregio wrote their commentaries
on the question of books and study.[31] The latter offered a good synthesis of
the position of the friars of the Community on study, books and libraries
during the thirteenth century.[32]

Bonaventure presented his point of view on the relation of Franciscan
spirituality to books and study in two works. The first of these is the *Epistola de tribus questionibus*, a letter dated 1254 and sent as an answer to an
unknown master who had asked specific questions on three contradictions
between the Franciscan life and rule. The first question regarded material

---

29   On the life, profile and influence of Joachim of Fiore, see McGinn, *Calabrian Abbot*.

30   See Luigi Pellegrini, *L'Incontro tra due invenzioni medievali*, pp. 147-48; Reeves, *Influence
of Prophecy*, pp. 175-90; Merlo, *Nel nome di San Francesco*, pp. 163-65; and Maranesi, *Nescientes
litteras*, p. 93.

31   Maranesi, *Nescientes litteras*, pp. 97-109.

32   Bonaventure was born Giovanni di Fidanza, most probably in 1221 in the small town of
Bagnoregio, central Italy. According to testimonies for his canonization, he was educated
by Franciscans in his home town. In 1234-35 he set off for studies in Paris, where he studied
under master Alexander of Hales, who became the first Franciscan to hold a chair in theology
at the University of Paris. He entered the Franciscan order in 1238 and received the name of
'Bonaventure'. In 1254, he obtained the licence to teach theology but was admitted into the
guild of masters only in 1257, due to the dispute between secular and mendicant masters. That
same year he was elected minister general, and in 1273 he was appointed cardinal. Bonaventure
died unexpectedly in 1274. Further references to Bonaventure's life and work can be found in
Gilson, *La philosophie de saint Bonaventure*, pp. 9-88; Brooke, *Early Franciscan Government*;
Noone, 'Franciscans and Epistemology'; and Cullen, *Bonaventure*.

goods, especially the use of money by proxy, or 'interposita persona' and the possession of books. The second question put forward the problem of the absence of manual work in the life of the friars. Finally, the third question concerned the incompatibility between teaching in the universities or the dedication to study and the regulation that prohibited teaching illiterate friars how to read: 'non curent nescientes litteras, litteras discere'.[33]

To answer the question on the circulation of money, Bonaventure argued that the rule prohibited the ownership of goods, among which were books, but it did not forbid their use. Bonaventure clearly distinguished 'to use' and/or 'to have' from 'to own'. According to his interpretation, only the latter would be against the rule, which implied that the use of books was a perfectly valid option for the followers of Francis.[34] Moreover, books had an extraordinary value for the order, because they were absolutely necessary to the mission of preaching, the very *raison d'être* of the Franciscans.[35] Consequently, not the presence, but the absence of books was the true menace to the existence of the order. In this sense, due to their fundamental role, books should not be seen as part of the question concerning the poverty of the order, because they were a fundamental part of the apostolic commitment at the heart of Franciscan identity. The perfection of the rule, depended on them, that is, its true fulfilment is to have books and to preach.[36] Interestingly, though, Bonaventure chose *habere* instead of *studiare*, *legere* or *utor* to be linked to the perfection of the rule. Since Bonaventure had established a distinction between having and ownership, his reflection suggested that the possession of books, understood as a continuous use in time, was a legitimate option for the Franciscan order and that such an option was not only in accordance with the spirit of the rule but also essential to Franciscan identity. This last reflection is of great importance in the understanding of further developments in practices related to manuscript culture such as loan of books for long-term periods in Franciscan libraries.[37] Regarding

---

33 Bonaventure of Bagnoregio, *Opera Omnia*, VIII, p. 331.

34 'Dico, ergo, quod Fratribus horum concessus est usus, sed vetatur appropriatio. Nam non dicit Regula, quod fratres nihil habeant nec aliqua re utantur, quod esset insanum; sed, quod "nihil sibi approprient."' Bonaventure of Bagnoregio, *Opera Omnia*, VIII, p. 333.

35 'De libris autem et utensilibus quid sentiam, audi. Clamat Regula expresse imponens fratibus auctoritatem et officium praedicandi, quod non credo in aliqua regula alia reperiri. Si igitur praedicare non debent fabulas, sed verba divina; et haec scire non possunt, nisi legant; nec legere, nisi habeant scripta: planissimum est, quod de perfectione Regulae est libros habere sicut et predicare.' See Bonaventure of Bagnoregio, *Opera Omnia*, VIII, pp. 332-33.

36 'De perfectione Regulae est libros habere sicut et predicare.'Bonaventure of Bagnoregio, *Opera Omnia*, VIII, p. 333.

37 A more detailed discussion of these practices will be offered in the next chapter.

dedication to study and teaching, Bonaventure made clear that study was not forbidden, nor even questioned by Francis. When he said in the rule 'non curent nescientes litteras litteras discere', Francis's principle did not hinder study to learned friars, but forbade teaching illiterate members of the community how to read. In other words, each one should remain in their original vocation: 'The rule does not forbid the study of letters, but only to those illiterate and laymen. As the apostle rightly says, each one should remain in that vocation to which has been called.'[38]

A second document in which Bonaventure referred to books and the role of study is the *Determinationes quaestionum circa regulam Fratrum Minorum*.[39] In this work, Bonaventure, already minister general of the order, answered some problematic questions concerning the rule. The third question regarded the proper place of study in the life of the community: was it necessary to study to accomplish the friars' spiritual duties?[40] Bonaventure answered the question with two arguments. The first dealt with the importance of preaching and the pastoral role of the order, a very delicate task that required proper preparation.[41] The second argument was related to the danger of being guilty of heresy due to an inaccurate reading of scripture. To avoid this danger, it was necessary to be able to read properly, and that was possible only through study and the use of books.[42]

Another interpretation that illustrates the attitude of the friars of the Community towards the question of the use of books is Hugh of Digne's commentary on the rule.[43] There is general agreement on the year 1252 as the

---

38 'Dico ego, quod Regula non vetat studium litteratis, sed illiteratis et laicis. Vult enim iuxta Apostolum, quod unusquisque in ea vocatione, qua vocatus est, permaneat.' Bonaventure of Bagnoregio, *Opera Omnia*, VIII, p. 334.

39 Bonaventure of Bagnoregio, *Opera Omnia*, VIII, pp. 337-90.

40 'Cum Religiosi debeant simpliciter ambulare et orationibus et virtutibus abundare et ad hoc operam dare, cur usum impendunt studio literarum, quae olim sancti Patres postposuisse laudantur, ut Benedictus et alii, in secreta conversatione studentes?' See Bonaventure of Bagnoregio, *Opera Omnia*, VIII, p. 339.

41 'Predicationis officium ex regulari professione Ordini anexum sit et confessionis, quae notitiam requi sacrae Scripturae, quae subtili indiget in plerisque locis expositione, ne ex imperitia errores pro veritate doceamus; necesse est nos sacrae Scripturae habere studium et magistros.' Bonaventure of Bagnoregio, *Opera Omnia*, VIII, p. 339.

42 'Hereticorum etiam versutiis, qui in scripturis sanctis occasionem erroris per falsas interpretationes assumunt, oportet per ipsarum diligentem investigationem diligentius obviare et fideles contra illorum fraudes et latentes decipulas praemunire.' Bonaventure of Bagnoregio, *Opera Omnia*, VIII, p. 339.

43 As a master of the Franciscan order, Hugh of Digne could be considered an outsider. In fact, he was not among the learned friars who shared with Francis the first development of the community, nor was he part of the ruling entourage of the order, nor was he among the great

date of composition of Hugh's commentary. The date is important because it places the commentary under John of Parma as minister general of the order, and shortly after Pope Innocent IV issued the bull *Ordine vestrum*.[44] This bull was a significant institutional shift against a sector that asked for reform within the Franciscan order; and it is possible that John of Parma himself, who also believed in the need to rediscover the original principles of Franciscan spirituality, conceived of the commentary as instrumental to an articulated rejection of *Ordine vestrum*.[45]

The commentary was addressed mainly to those who claimed to be living according to the rule while ignoring it.[46] At the same time, by establishing that the rule was not against learning, Hugh was responding to those who had attacked the order, particularly the secular masters who had questioned Franciscan masters and students' fidelity to the rule in the context of the dispute over the role of mendicants as masters at the university, especially William of Saint-Amour.[47] The commentary followed the structure of the rule, glossing each chapter. For example, when discussing the second chapter, and particularly the conditions for entering the order, Hugh followed the established distinction between *clerici* and *laici*, and explained that the substantial difference between these two groups within the order was their intellectual background. The commentary on the sixth chapter discussed poverty, property and the use of goods. Commenting on the passage where the rule specifies that friars should not possess anything, Hugh discussed the difference between ownership and use, especially in relation to books. Proper use did not imply any disobedience to the rule, and therefore the real question to be discussed should be the purpose of using the goods.[48]

philosophers of the University of Paris. Nevertheless, although the contours of his life are not very clear, he is one of the most influential Franciscan figures of the thirteenth century. A profile of this Franciscan master may be found in Poulenc, 'Hughes de Digne', and Brooke, 'Hugh of Digne'. A complete study of Hugh of Digne may be found in Ruiz, *La vie et l'ouvre de Hugues de Digne*.

44   Flood, ed., *Hugh of Digne's Rule Commentary*, pp. 11 and 54; see also Paul, 'Le commentaire de Hughes de Digne', pp. 231 and 240-41, and Maranesi, *Nescientes litteras*, p. 98.

45   Flood, ed., *Hugh of Digne's Rule Commentary*, p. 54; see also Brooke, *Early Franciscan Government*, pp. 255-74.

46   'Quosdam vero ex nostris periculose quod scire necesse est ignorantes, non enim excusat ignorantia regulae professorem.' Flood, ed., *Hugh of Digne's Rule Commentary*, p. 91.

47   Maranesi, *Nescientes litteras*, p. 100; see also Flood, ed., *Hugh of Digne's Rule Commentary*, pp. 53-54. Brief descriptions of the conflict between mendicant and secular masters at the University of Paris can be found in Merlo, *Nel nome di san Francesco*, pp. 161-67; Gratien, *Histoire*, pp. 205-15; Felder, *Histoire des études*, pp. 186-242; and Luigi Pellegrini, *L'Incontro tra due 'invenzioni' medievali*, pp. 139-61.

48   'Attende tamen quod in praecentibus tetigi, quod proprietas tam locorum librorum quam aliarum rerum Ordini licitarum quae ad usum fratrum simpliciter et absolute nulla sibi retenta

This implied that the question whether the order should or should not have an intellectual vocation was already solved, as two examples showed. First, the example of Francis himself, who made extensive use of the written word; second, the example of Alexander of Hales, who became a friar after establishing himself as a renowned scholar in Paris, thus illustrating how study and the use of books could lead to the highest levels of virtue. Nevertheless, an important question remained to be solved, namely the question of how the rule's admonition to avoid teaching illiterate friars to read – 'non curent nescientes litteras litteras discere' – should be interpreted. Like Bonaventure, Hugh's answer explored Francis's *intentio*. According to Hugh, Francis did not mean that study and the use of books should be prohibited, but intended to allow it only to those who already had an intellectual background, because each one should remain in and cultivate his proper vocation in complete agreement with the apostolic principles.[49] Thus, the original vocation of those learned friars could only be reinforced by studying the words of God.[50]

This brief consideration has shown some uniformity in the reflections of two Franciscan masters on the role of learning and books. Both Bonaventure and Hugh of Digne tried to provide a definitive answer to the question of whether Franciscans should or should not have an intellectual profile. By offering a reconstruction of the *intentio* of Francis, Bonaventure concluded that the founder not only did not condemn

proprietate sive dominio conferuntur cum fratrum esse non possint regula obsistente, ad diocesanos ut dicitur de iure pertinebit. [...] Ita quod fratres nec locum nec librum nec aliquam rem extra Ordine alienare quomodolibet possunt [...]. Quod pater qui dat filio suo librum non contra ordinem et animam filii dare intendit, sed dat librum ut Ordo et filius iuxta Ordinis formam utatur.' Flood, ed., *Hugh of Digne's Rule Commentary*, p. 146.

49 'Sanctus hoc loco primas in Ordine litteras et senes elementarios non commendat. Multis studium litterarum studii orationis devotionis et caritatis ad fratres negligentiam parit. Religio ad virtutes potius quam ad apices vocat. Si bonus studens vis esse bonitatem et disciplinam scientia anteponere stude. [...] Sed cum regula dicat quod non curent nescientes litteras litteras discere, et Dominus in Evangelio: Nolite vocari rabbi [Matt. 23:8]; numquid fratres studium litterarum et maxime cathedram magisterii possunt assumere? Possunt utique. Non sanctus regulae conditor litteratis sed laicis et illiteratis studium vetat, ut unusquisque secundum apostolum in qua vocatione vocatus est in ea permaneat [1 Cor. 7:24]. Nescientes litteras litteras discere noluit. Sed scientes litteras in litteris proficere non vetuit.' Flood, ed., *Hugh of Digne's Rule Commentary*, pp. 186-87.

50 'Alioquin suae contrarius regulae ipse fuisset, qui existens in Ordine cum paucas litteras sciret, postmodum non solum orando sed etiam legendo profecit. Et alios fratres in divinis studere litteris voluit. Et ut sacrae scripturae doctores in magna reverentia haberent mandavit, tamquam illos a quibus perciperent verba vitae'. Flood, ed., *Hugh of Digne's Rule Commentary*, p. 187.

studies but conceived of them as an important feature of the order's work. By linking the use of books to the very essence of the order, that is, apostolic preaching, Bonaventure made books an essential part of Franciscan identity.[51] A similar solution to the problem is proposed by Hugh of Digne. He also tried to reconstruct the *intentio* of Francis and found evidence that decidedly supported the intellectual vocation of the order in the rule.[52] These interpretations remained practically without variation over time, since they effectively reflected the needs and expectations of the friars of the community, such as those of the Paduan convent of Sant'Antonio. As a matter of fact, Anthony of Padua had been a remarkable example of how a learned friar could follow Francis's example through devotion to preaching. Nevertheless, a part of the community felt the need for renewal and reform in a return to a strict application of the rule and the original principles of the Franciscan brotherhood. Perhaps the most important of the initiatives of reform were the Spirituals and Observant movements. The latter is of special interest because one Observant community had an important settlement in the city of Padua, with a convent that became one of the most influential centres of the Franciscan Observance in Italy.

The Observant Convent of Padua and the Interpretations of the Rule of the Movements of Franciscan Reform

The convent of San Francesco Grande followed the Franciscan Observant approach to learning, books and study. As a movement of reform that strove for a return to the original simplicity of the first Franciscan brotherhood, the Observance had to reconcile the presence of study and books with Franciscan spirituality, and once again, it found the answer through an interpretation of the original intention of Francis. Nevertheless, the Observant conception was in part the result of the development of previous attempts to find an answer, particularly, from the movement known as the Spirituals. Accordingly, it is necessary to describe the main features of the Spirituals' interpretation of the rule in order to explain the Observant solution to the incompatibility between the strict application of the rule and the development of learning and study at the highest levels.

51   Şenocak, *Poor and the Perfect*, pp. 146-48.
52   Maranesi, *Nescientes litteras*, pp. 104-5.

Franciscan Movements of Reform and their Views on Study, Books and Libraries

At the General Council of Lyon in 1274, the question of the status of the mendicant orders was raised. As a result, while the small mendicant communities were suppressed, the major orders were preserved and reinforced, since the Holy See saw in them an evident benefit to the universal church.[53] However, in the same year, according to the chronicle of Angelo Clareno, alarming news began to spread. There were rumours that Pope Gregory X had forced the Franciscans to accept common property in the style of monastic orders and canonical communities.[54] A group of Franciscan friars reacted to the rumours by vehemently opposing those at the top of the order's hierarchy. Among the rebels were friars especially loyal to the rule such as Angelo Clareno and Pietro of Macerata, who, once summoned and asked to recant, refused and therefore were punished by the ecclesiastical authorities with imprisonment.[55] This group of rebel friars willing to fight for the privilege of poverty were known as the 'Spirituals'. They saw themselves as the heirs of a tradition in strict accordance with the first Franciscan group and fought for the observance of the rule and Francis's *Testamentum* in a literal way. Their sources were oral tradition and the written testimonies produced by the first companions of Francis; and it is likely that Angelo Clareno, one of the main figures of the movement, had had direct personal contact with one or more of the first companions of Francis.[56]

The theoretical basis of the Spirituals was summarized in the writings of Peter John Olivi and Ubertino of Casale.[57] In their works, poverty was placed at the core of Franciscan identity, and thus the question of use and ownership became extremely important.[58] In this context, the conception

---

53   Merlo, *Nel nome di san Francesco*, pp. 181-84; see also Moorman, *History of the Franciscan Order*, pp. 177-78, and Andrews, *Other Friars*, pp. 1-4 and 231-32.

54   Angelo Clareno, *Liber chronicarum*, pp. 528-34. David Burr observes that this chronicle is a reconstruction made by Clareno in his late years, which means that it may be 'artfully constructed'. See Burr, *Spiritual Franciscans*, pp. 44-45.

55   Merlo, *Nel nome di san Francesco*, p. 232; see also Burr, *Spiritual Franciscans*, pp. 43-46, and Moorman, *History of the Franciscan Order*, pp. 188-90.

56   Nimmo, *Reform and Division*, pp. 79 and 90-93.

57   For Peter John Olivi, see Manselli, 'Pietro di Giovanni Olivi spirituale'; for his *Quaestio* on the *usus pauper*, his treatise on the same subject and his commentary on the Franciscan rule, see Petrus Ioannis Olivi, *De usu paupere*, and *Peter Olivi's Rule Commentary*, ed. Flood; and for Ubertino of Casale, especially his treatise *Sanctitas vestra*, a passionate response to some objections that came from the friars of the community, see Ubertino of Casale, *Sanctitas vestra*.

58   See Ubertino of Casale, *Sanctitas vestra*, pp. 72-76.

of the principle of *usus pauper* was developed by Olivi as central to the
Franciscan life: friars were required to be poor, not only by rejecting any
kind of ownership, but also by restrictions in the use of material goods.
Moreover, it was also necessary to make a 'meagre use' of goods to be in
complete accordance with the vow of poverty. Accordingly, a breach in the
principle of *usus pauper* was a substantial breach of the vow of poverty,
which was a mortal sin.[59] As a result, the order found itself torn on the
question of the proper observance of the rule, and a division developed
concerning the interpretations of the rule and the Franciscan principles.[60]
After a phase of controversy, Pope Clement V proposed a solution to the
conflict with his bull *Exivi de Paradiso*, in 1312. The bull aimed to offer a
common ground of observance. There followed a short-term compromise
that lasted until Clement died, but afterwards the conflict started again.[61]
On 7 October 1318, Pope John XXII issued the bull *Quorundam exigit*, which
was basically a commentary on two decisions of the preceding bull *Exivi de
Paradiso*. As a result, a difficult alternative was presented to the Spirituals:
full obedience to the pope's decree or persisting in disobedience, which
meant to be declared heretics. The formula was as simple as it was effective,
and was synthesized by the bull's conclusion: poverty was great, and even
greater was integrity; nevertheless, the greatest good of all was obedience,
and it should be strictly kept.[62]

The Spirituals doctrine concerning books and studies is clearly reflected
in Ubertino's *Sanctitas vestra* and in the works of Angelo Clareno. Ubertino's work is an answer to some questions about the Spirituals' point of
view concerning the right observance of the Franciscan life. According to
Ubertino, study represented one of the main risk factors to the spiritual
health of the order. Actually, the principle of simplicity illustrated by the
life of Francis should lead the friars to the refusal of pagan or scholastic
studies and simultaneously stimulate them to preserve carefully the words
of the Fathers. Nevertheless, for many, study had become an instrument
to achieve power and privilege and to enjoy a life of easy work, exercising

---

59 See Burr, *Olivi and Franciscan Poverty*, pp. 43-81. Ubertino went further and affirmed that
the poverty of Jesus, his mother and the disciples implied the *usus pauper*, and therefore the
refusal of such a sacred principle constituted heresy. See Nimmo, *Reform and Division*, p. 103;
see also Ubertino of Casale, *Sanctitas vestra*, pp. 57-66.

60 See Nimmo, *Reform and Division*, pp. 109-19.

61 See Nimmo, *Reform and Division*, pp. 119-34.

62 'Magna quidem paupertas, sed maior integritas; bonum est obedientia maximum, si
custodiatur illaesa.' See Moorman, *History of the Franciscan Order*, p. 311, and Nimmo, *Reform
and Division*, p. 137.

unfair authority over the other friars.[63] Ubertino condemned what he called the 'evil spirit' of many learned brothers, but did not condemn study or the use of books in themselves. Accordingly, for Ubertino the only way to remain in the rightful Franciscan spirit was to respect faithfully the original *intentio* of the founder, clearly expressed in the rule where he said, 'non curent nescientes litteras litteras discere'.[64] This meant that the main purpose of Franciscan life was not to study but to live in simplicity, by preaching and praying, according to the evangelical model.[65] Any other way of considering the matter of books and study was simply contrary to the *intentio* of Francis, since it was evident that books and study played a secondary role in Franciscan spirituality.[66] Only the spirit of prayer and simplicity could defeat the arrogance and pride that usually characterized scholars, because Franciscan identity, contrary to that of other orders, did not depend on books and study but on prayer.[67]

The second source of the Spirituals' views on study, learning and the use of books was in the *Liber chronicarum sive Tribulationum Ordinis Minorum* and the *Expositio regulae Fratrum Minorum* written by Angelo Clareno.[68]

---

63 'Et omnes dissensiones quasi, que sunt in provinciis multis ordinis, sunt propter ambicionem promocionis ad studia, ut sint lectores et prelatis et aliis dominentur. [...] Quia non multis sunt ingeniosi et apti ad subtilia et tamen, ut honorentur, volunt mitti ad studia et habere nomen lectoris, licet parum sciant, ideo postea fastidi de studio efficiuntur ociosi et vagi et aridi et indevoti nec curant chorum sequi, sed uno socio habito servitore discurrunt, ut volunt, et stant in terris propriis ceteris fratribus dominantes. [...] Et quia a talibus ordo regitur cum quasi semper sint de corporibus capitulorum provincialium et postea generalium; ideo semper Ordor tendit ad ima.' Ubertino of Casale, *Sanctitas vestra*, pp. 73-74.

64 Esser, ed., *Die Opuscula*, p. 370.

65 'Non fuit hec intentio regule nec beati Francisci, quin immo dicit Regula quod "non curent nescientes litteras litteras discere, sed attendant, quod super omnia desiderare debent habere spiritum domini et sanctam eius operacionem, orare semper ad deum puro corde" etc. Et in legenda dicit, quod vult fratres esse discipulos evangelicos et in scientia simplicitatis excrescere et magis orationi quam studio vacare exemplo Christi, qui magis orasse dicitur quam legisse.' Ubertino of Casale, *Sanctitas vestra*, p. 74.

66 'Et multa dicit de hoc, expresse asserens, hoc genus studii esse contra suam intencionem, et horrebat tantam apropriacionem librorum.' Ubertino of Casale, *Sanctitas vestra*, p. 74.

67 'Et dicebat, quod nolebat, quod fratres cupidi essent de scientia et libris, sed volebat quod studeret habere sanctam simplicitatem et oracionem devotam et dominam paupertatem. Et hanc dicebat securiorem viam pro salute anime et vocacionem ordinis sui na domino principalem. [...] Et si aliorum religiones vocantur ad studia ex sui institucione, licet ubique reprehendenda sit abusio studiorum, huius religionis vocacio ex expressione fundatoris, superius est descripta, ad orationem et studium modiis aliis moderatum.' Ubertino of Casale, *Sanctitas vestra*, pp. 74 and 76.

68 Angelo Clareno was born in Fossombrone around 1247. He became a Franciscan friar by 1262. Shortly afterwards he retired to a hermitage with a few companions and formed a group of Franciscan hermits known as the 'Clareni' who searched for a strict observance of the rule. The group was soon united with the main body of the order, but he persisted in following the

The main purpose of the commentary on the rule was to establish the real *intentio* of Francis. Like Ubertino, Clareno paid special attention to the rule's exhortation to abandon any form of arrogance and pride, a principle that also applied to books and their use: the friars should not be eager to possess books or to become learned because such a spirit was contrary to true Franciscan humility and simplicity.[69] According to Clareno, Christ himself, through Francis, made an exhortation concerning the perils of vanity, showing simplicity as the only real and secure path for any true Franciscan. At some point in the order's history, holy simplicity was betrayed by some friars who, like Eve in paradise, fell victims to temptation.[70] Therefore, for Clareno, the pursuit of profane knowledge brought an excessive reliance on secular knowledge and the growth of vanity and pride. These very same feelings encouraged the community to build up great houses in the centres of cities and to search for material goods instead of cultivating poverty in holiness.[71]

The Spirituals' interpretation of the rule concerning the problem of study and the use of books had two main consequences. First, the Spirituals aimed to

original Franciscan way of life under the influence of an interpretation of the Joachite prophecy in a historical sense, which led to a dispute with the government of the order. After a period of wandering and preaching, he was summoned to Avignon to answer the charge of heresy. As a result of the final dispositions of Pope John XXII, he became a member of the Poor Hermits of Celestine V. When the cardinal protector of the Celestines, Giacomo Colonna, died on 1318, Angelo left Rome and went to Subiaco, where he lived among the Benedictines. In 1337 he retired to the small hermitage of Santa Maria d'Aspro in Basilicata, southern Italy, where he died. For further details on his life, spirituality and legacy, see *Angelo Clareno francescano*, and Accrocca, *Un ribelle tranquillo*.

69   'De hoc etiam in prima regula erat scriptum: "Et clerici libros tantum necessarios ad eorum officium possint habere." Voluit beatus Franciscus quod fratres omnes non essent cupidi de scientia et libris et quod literas nescientes non curarent literas discere sed quod clerici et layci actendant ad id, quod super omnia habere et desiderare debebant et tenebantur, quod illud est, quod se habentes Deo placentes facit, et gratia et veritate plenos, ad regnum glorie absque impedimento perducit, habere videlicet spiritum Domini et sanctam eius operationem, orare semper ad Dominum puro corde et habere humilitatem et patientiam in persecutione et in infirmitate et diligere eos, qui nos persequuntur et reprehendunt et arguunt, et cetera.' Angelo Clareno, *Expositio regulae*, pp. 208-9.

70   'Beatus Franciscus previdit quod religionem suam ad similitudinem Eve sub specie mala et bona sciendi, et excellentiam habendi deorum, idest sublimium doctorum ecclesie et sapientium magistrorum, antiquus serpens seducendo corrumperet et a simplicitatis innocentia, ad quam tenendam et amandam tanquam sue plenitudinis et integritatis formam et speciem singulariter creata et condita erat, finaliter elongaret, et miseriis innumeris et erumpnis multiplicibus, proprio decore perdito, obnoxiam faceret.' Angelo Clareno, *Expositio regulae*, p. 209.

71   'Futura enim prospiciens cognoscebat per spiritum ait fr. Leo, et etiam mulotiens fratribus dixit, quod fratres sub specie hedificandi alios dimicent vocationem suam, scilicet puram et sanctam simplicitatem, orationem sanctam et dominam paupertatem nostram'. Angelo Clareno, *Expositio regulae*, p. 209.

establish and use an interpretation of the *intentio* of Francis as an argumentative strategy. Second, based on the interpretation of the *intentio*, the Spirituals did not condemn the use of books and study. Instead, they preserved their close relationship with books by identifying pride and vanity as the real dangers for Franciscan spirituality. This suggests that, for the Spirituals, a humble activity of study could be an acceptable form of the *usus pauper* of books.

The Franciscan Observance and Study, Books and Libraries

The group of the Spirituals was completely dissolved during the first half of the fourteenth century. This did not undermine the ideal, however, of living under the strictest observance of the Franciscan rule, as shown by the several attempts undertaken during the second half of the fourteenth century.[72] One of the most important was the initiative of John of Valle, a former disciple of Angelo Clareno. In 1334, John established a small hermitage at Brugliano, in Umbria, that, despite its rigour, attracted many followers. One of them, Gentile of Spoleto, became the leader of the fraternity, and under his direction, the fraternity grew significantly. Gentile requested in 1350 an authorization to incorporate four existing Franciscan hermitages into his fraternity. Against all odds, the community obtained the approval in the form of a papal privilege, *bonorum operum*.[73] However, the friars of the wider Franciscan community saw this small group of hermits as dissidents.[74] When in 1354 the general chapter approved a new set of statutes for the whole order, the minister general, William Farinier, asked the hermit friars if they intended to accept the new regulations. The hermits considered the statutes to be incompatible with their strict observance of the rule and rejected this new set of norms. The community then proceeded to declare the group of hermits heretical. At this point the Holy See intervened and, after an inquisitorial procedure, it was determined that the hermits' privilege should be revoked.[75]

---

72   Nimmo, 'Franciscan Regular Observance', p. 189.

73   See Moorman, *History of the Franciscan Order*, pp. 369-70; Nimmo, *Reform and Division*, pp. 382-86; and Merlo, *Nel nome di San Francesco*, p. 284.

74   'Eodem anno quidam frater laicus, dictus Gentilis de Spoleto de Provincia sancti Francisci, et quidam alii quadam fatua devotione seducti in tantam audaciam proruperunt, ut se toti Communitati Ordinis opponentes Ordinem magno schismate dividere molirentur. Supplicaverunt namque domino papae Clementi, instantibus pro eis aliquibus viris notabilibus eorum fatua devotione deceptis ut eis aliqua loca Ordinis concederentur, in quibus possent regulam ad litteram observare.' *Chronica XXIV Generalium*, p. 547.

75   Wadding, *Annales Minorum*, VIII, pp. 120-22.

The experience of the Umbrian hermits was significant for the history of the Franciscan order because one of the members of the suppressed community, Paoluccio of Trince, persisted in gathering together a Franciscan community that lived under a strict observance of the rule. In 1367 he met the new minister general, Thomas of Frignano, and obtained permission to go back to Brugliano and revive the experience of rigorous Franciscan life. Consequently, in 1368 Paoluccio assembled a community devoted to the strict observance of the rule. This is commonly accepted as the origin of the reform movement known as the Franciscan Observance.[76] The reputation for holiness of the Observance grew and the movement rapidly spread. The growth of the movement within the order raised the question of the compatibility of a strict form of life within the order and a more relaxed interpretation of the rule. A solution to the problem was possible under one of three forms: first, to make a general reform of the order in a stricter sense; second, to institutionalize the existence of two parties with different interpretations of the rule, both of them under the authority of one minister general; and third, to divide the order into two. The history of the Franciscan order during the fifteenth century could be summarized as the attempt to solve the question of coexistence by exploring each one of these solutions.[77]

The appointment of Observant friars to play a role in the governance of the order reflected the diffusion of the movement within the community and their growing influence. By 1443 John of Capistrano, one of the four 'pillars of the Observance', was elected as vicar for the Italian provinces and, in fulfilment of his duties, he prepared a set of directions for the friars under his care. These directions became the core of the Observant constitutions. In 1447 the Observants held a chapter general that confirmed the dispositions of John of Capistrano. Two years later, the unreformed Franciscan friars, or friars of the Community, held a chapter general in Florence. The impossibility of holding one general chapter for both Franciscan branches showed that there was an effective distinction between two forms of Franciscanism within the same order.[78]

As defenders of a strict interpretation of the rule, Observants may appear to be a group of friars hostile to learning, study and the use of books. Nevertheless, for the Observance, learning was a means to achieve spiritual

---

76   Wadding, *Annales Minorum*, VIII, pp. 246-47; see also Moorman, *History of the Franciscan Order*, pp. 371-73, and Nimmo, *Reform and Division*, pp. 394-405.

77   Moorman, *History of the Franciscan Order*, p. 441.

78   *Chronica fratri Nicolai Glassberger*, pp. 308-9; see also Moorman, *History of the Franciscan Order*, p. 479.

strength. The programme of John of Capistrano of 1443 confirmed the important role of proper guidance in order to avoid the risk that blind pursuit of knowledge might suffocate the humility that should characterize the spirit of the Franciscan mission.[79] The most important sources for the doctrine and regulations on study and books are the writings of Bernardino of Siena and John of Capistrano. Bernardino of Siena established a school of moral theology and pastoral training at Fiesole, where the friars could receive preparation to preach. In 1438 Bernardino went to Assisi and, as vicar of the Cismontane Observants, issued at the convent of S. Damiano an important vicarial decree pertaining to study and the organization of pastoral care. Albeit a short document, it became the source of legislation on study for the Observants.[80]

The decree stated first that the friars who had entered the Observance as unlearned laypersons and had later passed on towards the clerical state should not be allowed to hear the confessions of laypeople.[81] Secondly, the decree prohibited uneducated lay friars from learning and from entering the clerical estate, in accordance with what had been established by the tenth chapter of the rule.[82] The only way to solve the contradiction between these decrees would be to assume that the unlearned laypersons of the first decree were capable of reading and writing at the moment of arrival in the order, which would have enabled them to perform the divine office with the required books. As for the uneducated lay friars of the second decree, it should be assumed they were unable to read, and therefore they should not be taught to. Bernardino offered two clear restrictive clauses concerning the order and study that derived their authority directly from the tradition of interpretation of the rule. This illustrates how the conception of the role of study within the Observance was carefully designed to be presented as the valid realization of the original purpose of the founder.

When John of Capistrano was designated vicar for the Italian provinces in 1443, he prepared a set of regulations for the friars under his care.[83] Capistrano presented his constitutions in the form of a detailed commentary

79   Roest, *History of Franciscan Education*, p. 156; see also Bartoli, 'La biblioteca e lo *scriptorium* di Giovanni da Capestrano'.

80   Fois, 'La questione degli studi nell'Osservanza'.

81   'In primis, quod nullus ad professionem receptus pro laico, postea effectus presbyter, possit audire confessiones saecularium personarum, sed dumtaxat fratrum.' Bernardino of Siena, *Opera Omnia*, VIII, p. 314.

82   'Item, quod nullus laicus permittatur addiscere litteras, aut ad clericatum ascendere.' Bernardino of Siena, *Opera Omnia*, VIII, p. 315.

83   See Maranesi, *Nescientes litteras*, p. 226.

on the rule, and so the Observant regulations were to be understood as directly derived from Francis's *intentio*. Capistrano started by considering the requirements for admission into the order. The dispositions put special emphasis on the precision with which the hard conditions of Franciscan life should be explained to the new members of the community.[84] Another point concerning the admission of novices to the order established that the candidate should be apt to good works and be able to carry the burden of religious life.[85] Capistrano stressed the importance of the willingness to undertake physical activity instead of showing special competence in study. This had a special importance because it was customary to separate the new friars according to their previous ways of life so as to be considered potential lay friars (*pro laico*) or clerics (*pro clerico*), and one of the fundamental criteria used to establish the difference was their level of education. Since Capistrano's constitutions apparently did not assign particular importance to the knowledge of grammar, but instead stressed the role of physical capability, it would seem that Observants were not interested in establishing a distinction between *pro laico* and *pro clerico*. However, the Observant constitutions established the exclusion of laymen from clerical life, in accordance with the traditional understanding of the rule's passage that prohibited teaching illiterate friars to read: 'And do not care for teaching to those illiterate how to read, but instead pay attention to wish for the spirit of the Lord and his holy work'.[86] Moreover, according to Capistrano's constitutions, the only way to avoid the restriction was to obtain a special authorization from the general vicar for the Observant friars.[87] In this sense, one could say that the Observant constitutions followed the traditional interpretation of the Franciscan rule, that is, identifying the *nescientes litteras* with the lay friars.

Naturally, in the spirit of reform the friars' spiritual duties were considered of vital importance, and it was in order to satisfy this need that the dispositions on study, learning and the use of books became of great

---

84 'Et nullus fratrum iuvenem quempiam vel aetate provectum, adulationibus, suasionibus, vel blanditiis, praesumat attrahere ad nostram Religionem: Quinimmo vitam nostram accipere volentibus, diligenter et seriose exponatur rigor potius nostri status quo ad obedientiam, paupertatem et castitatem et cetera quae in nostra Regula continetur.' *CHL*, p. 103a; see also Maranesi, *Nescientes litteras*, p. 227.

85 'Sit idoneus ad honestos labores, et Religionis onera supportanda.' *CHL*, p. 103b.

86 'Et non curent nescientes litteras, litteras discere, sed attendant quod super omnia desiderare debent habere Spiritum Domini et sanctam eius operationem.' Esser, ed., *Die Opuscula*, p. 262.

87 'Nullus etiam Laicus nostri Ordinis ad Clericatum praesumat accedere nisi a me prius licentiam obtinuerit: et nescientes literas, non curent literas discere, nisi suscepta obedientia, vel obtenta licentia sui Vicarii, vel mea.' *CHL*, p. 108a.

significance. To guarantee that confessors and preachers were able to exercise their duties properly, the constitutions established that one or more Observant houses in each province should be designated for the teaching of friars *in primitivis scientiis* and in *sacra pagina*, that is, theology. The study of those subjects was considered to be on the same level as preaching, hearing confessions or providing spiritual advice.[88] Consequently, the establishment of centres of study with specific programmes of training and study acquired an extraordinary value for the Observance.[89] Observant *studia* were founded in Bologna, Ferrara, Mantua, Fabriano, Florence, Pavia, Milan, Verona Padua and Venice – all of them furnished with libraries.[90]

In February 1444, Capistrano wrote a letter directed to all provincial vicars of the Observance in Italy with the purpose of ensuring the fulfilment of directions he had established in 1443. The letter is an interesting source that confirms the great importance of study for the Observance as a resource to guarantee the proper undertaking of the duty of preaching.[91] For Capistrano, the possession of correct knowledge was not only necessary for the clerical friar in charge of pastoral care but also had spiritual significance, because it was directly linked to the deepest nature of humanity as a creation of God. Those who despised knowledge therefore inevitably sinned against human nature and the gifts of the Holy Spirit.[92] At this point one might wonder how the Franciscan Observance would respond to the restriction on teaching illiterate friars (the *nescientes litteras*) to read. Capistrano established that the rule's admonition was not intended to be interpreted in an absolute,

88 'Quod etiam sane intelligendum est circa spiritualia exercitia cum corporalibus intermixta; ut neque in praedicationibus, neque in confessionibus, neque in studiis, sive lectionibus; vel etiam spiritualibus consiliis, personis regularibus, vel saecularibus exhibendis, adeo se occupent, quod divinas laudes et ordinarium officium praetermittant.' *CHL*, p. 105a.

89 'Iuvenes idonei ad studia literarum non occupentur in aliis exercitiis a suis prelatis.' *CHL*, pp. 111-12.

90 'Omnibus Vicariis suae curae commissis quatenus quilibet Vicarius in sua Provincia determinaret unum vel plura loca, iuxta possibilitatem et aptitudinem Fratrum Provinciae, in quo vel quibus locarentur Fratres idonei ad docendum pariter et discendum, qui proficere valerent, nedum in principiis scientiae sed etiam in Sacra Pagina, Deo Duce.' *CHL*, pp. 106-8; see also Roest, *History of Franciscan Education*, pp. 164-65.

91 'Quomodo poterit quisquam benefacere se nescit? Quomodo sciet, si non didicerit? Quomodo discet, sine docente?' See Chiappini, ed., 'De studio promovendo', p. 129.

92 'Turpissima est iactura quae fit per ignorantiam et negligentiam. Inimicus nature est, qui scire contemnit; quia naturaliter est homini scientiam concupiscere. Contra naturam ergo peccat, qui scientiam despicit; Spiritum Sanctum blasphemare convincitur qui Spiritus Sancti donum negligit et talentum.' See Chiappini, ed., 'De studio promovendo', p. 128; see also Roest, *History of Franciscan Education*, pp. 164-65.

restrictive sense: it was a means to an end.[93] One example of this was given by Francis himself when he authorized Anthony of Padua to teach theology to friars with the admonition that it should not inhibit the spirit of prayer and devotion: for Capistrano, this meant that it was not study but its abuse which was the real danger to spirituality.[94]

A perspective complementary to the general Observant regulations on learning and the use of books is offered by Bernardino of Siena, who not only instituted places of learning in Observant convents, but also developed a doctrine on the character of study as a part of Christian life. Bernardino's thought is summarized in three works: his sermon in Florence on 20 February 1425; another sermon in Siena in the same year; and the sermon *De scientiarum studiis*, at the University of Padua in 1443. These works showed how, in Bernardino's conception, study was necessary to arrive at true wisdom. In this sense, knowledge had a moral value because, if ignorance was the cause of social unrest and civic disaster, knowledge guaranteed civil harmony. Accordingly, there was a universal obligation to become learned, that is, to have knowledge of the principles of faith. This meant that everybody should learn, because that was a moral, honest and a virtuous way of glorifying God.[95]

With regard to the Franciscan Spirituals' and Observants' approach to the issue of learning and books, it may be concluded that both movements were expressions of the wish to return to the origins of Franciscan spirituality, and that both held learning to play a determining role in such reform, despite the fact that learning, study and books were not considered to be part of the original brotherhood's identity. All the emblematic figures of the movements of reform – Peter John Olivi, Ubertino da Casale, Angelo Clareno, Bernardino of Siena and John of Capistrano – were outstanding examples of the discipline of study and book culture of Franciscan schools.

In the specific case of the Franciscan Observance, there are two important remarks to be made. First of all, study in the Observant world was considered

---

93   'Eia ergo agite prudenter, et circumspicite diligenter, ut laici nescientes litteras non curent litteras discere; clerici vero et presbiteri, qui iam litterarum studio sunt professi, vacent litteris et scientiae, sine dispendio regularis observantie et spiritualis discipline.' See Chiappini, ed., 'De studio promovendo', p. 130.

94   Francis's authorization took the form of a short letter: 'Fratri Antonio episcopo meo frater Franciscus salutem. Placet mihi quod sacram theologiam legas fratribus, dummodo inter huius studium orationis et devotionis non exstinguas, sicut in regula continetur.' Esser, ed., *Die Opuscula*, p. 153. Capistrano's admonition aimed to evoke the spirit of Francis's authority: 'Non in scientia, sed in abusu scientie acquisite vel aquirende: scilicet in modo acquierendi vel ministrandi, defectus aut vitium implicatur.' See Chiappini, ed., 'De studio promovendo', p. 130.

95   Roest, *History of Franciscan Education*, pp. 161-62.

a fundamental, complex and rewarding activity with a practical purpose: to support the mission of preaching.[96] Secondly, the Observant constitutions were not only the expression of an awareness of the importance of intellectual activity, but also reflected an increasing interest in creating a link of uninterrupted tradition with the original intention of the first brotherhood. In this regard, they followed the same path as the unreformed friars of the Community.

Conclusion

This overview of the development of the Franciscan regulations on learning and the use of books allows us to understand that the friars of the Community and those of the movements of reform followed the same approach to assessing the role of books within the order, that is, to reconstruct the *intentio* of Francis. Naturally, that was only possible because Francis did not clearly establish his view on the matter. Following the path of the reconstruction of Francis's intentions, one can say that although he aimed to preserve a delicate balance between learned and unlearned members within the order, he did not consider books to be fundamental to their spirituality, especially because he did not provide the community with a set of procedures and rules on study and learning. Yet none of the developments in the interpretation of the rule, even the most rigorous, condemned the use of books or found any illegitimacy in the role of learning within the *intentio* of Francis. Naturally, the interpreters of the founder's ideals were all products of the sophisticated training and intellectual discipline of Franciscan schools, and therefore they were, one might say, unintentionally the most compelling evidence of how the order could offer comfortable room for the coexistence of the highest levels of learning and the apostolic spirit.

A second observation regards the fact that the key argument to justify the role of learning and the presence of books within the order was the preparation for preaching and to a lesser extent for pastoral care. The intellectual achievements of some members of the order swiftly surpassed all expectations, and the declared purpose of limiting the activity of study to the preparation for preaching became more a reminder of an aim than an effective determinant of actual practice.[97] The significant distance

---

96 'Praedicationis officium est substentamentum Fidei Christianae, lumen veritatis, schola virtutum, ruina vitiorum, via salutis, doctrina morum, camera sanctitatis.' *CHL*, p. 106a.
97 Şenocak, *Poor and the Perfect*, pp. 145-46.

between study as a support for preaching, as expressed by the regulations, and the actual development of the order allows us to reflect on the extent to which the first Franciscan regulations also expressed the ideal of a book to be used by the friars.

The first significant feature of the ideal book to be used by Franciscans is that it was not to be written by Franciscans. Early regulations do not refer explicitly to the activity of writing within the convents, and the first specific reference to writing appears in the constitutions of 1239, which describe it as an activity related to the general development of skills rather than to the continuous production of manuscripts.[98] By 1260 an interpretation of the section of the rule on activities of work suitable for friars established that writing was an acceptable option, and for the first time it related writing to study.[99] It was still unclear whether friars were encouraged to produce the manuscripts they needed for study or if they were allowed to work as scribes for external patrons. Nevertheless, as a significant development in terms of the conception of the practices of study and production of manuscripts within the convents, specific regulations, such as those of the provincial chapter of Treviso of 1290, established that in order to satisfy the needs of the libraries and the friars, the convents could count on the presence of a permanent scribe.[100] Accordingly, one could argue that Franciscans were not only transcribing but also authoring many of the works studied in the convents. A careful approach to the matter is still nevertheless required. Indeed, recent research on the topic of book production in Franciscan convents carried out by Nicoletta Giovè Marchioli shows that there is as yet no satisfactory evidence to confirm the presence of permanent *scriptoria* in many Franciscan convents, including the convent of Sant'Antonio.[101]

In any case, the conception of the Franciscan book as a tool of study to be extensively used within the convents was only possible thanks to the complete reconstruction of the intentions of Francis through sophisticated

98 'Fratres tam clerici quam laici compellantur per suos superiores in scribendo et in aliis sibi competentibus exerceri.' Cenci, 'De fratrum minorum constitutionibus praenarbonensibus', p. 91.

99 'Cum Regula dicat quod "Fratres quibus dedit Dominus gratiam laborandi, laborent fideliter et devote" ordinamus quod fratres, tam clerici quam laici, compellantur per suos superiores in scribendo, studendo et aliis laboribus sibi competentibus exerceri.' Bihl, ed., 'Statuta generalia Ordinis', p. 69.

100 'Ordinat minister et diffinitores cum provinciali capitulo quod in conventu Padue et Veneciis et aliis conventibus, qui sustinere poterunt, teneatur continue unus scriptor, qui scribat libros necessarios et pro armario opportunos.' A. Little, 'Statuta provincialia', p. 460.

101 Giovè Marchioli, 'Codici francescani a Roma nel Duecento', p. 133; Giovè Marchioli, 'Scrivere e leggere il libro francescano', p. 185.

interpretation. A similar development could be observed in the type of manuscripts described by the regulations. The Franciscan rule mentioned biblical books and devotional texts in restrictive terms, and theological works or books for study were not even considered by Francis. Still, by the end of the thirteenth century the question was not whether theological books or books of study were to be allowed in the convents, but how to efficiently provide friars arriving at the universities with the intellectual tools they needed.[102]

The second feature of the ideal book conceived by the regulations is its role. The original purpose of books within the community was to be a support for the performance of the divine offices, for devotion and for pastoral care. The training of friars as preachers introduced the circulation of books destined to be tools in their education; but very soon Franciscans found themselves transcribing, authoring and collecting works on theology, philosophy, canon law, natural sciences, history and even literature.

A third feature of the book as outlined by the regulations regards its availability. As described by the rule, books should be available to those members of the order who were already able to use them at the moment of their arrival in the order. This disposition reflected the intention of keeping a balance in the presence of unlearned and learned members of the community. Yet, the situation changed dramatically with the active participation of friars in the scholastic culture of their time: the creation and development of a network of schools was a consequence, rather than the cause, of the 'intellectualization' of the order. Naturally, instead of restricting access to books, the order had to find ways to make them available within the convents, and very elaborate mechanisms for the production and circulation of volumes were found, as will be shown in the next chapter. A manuscript of restricted availability, produced outside the community and employed as a rudimentary device of devotion was not the ideal of the main tool of study for an order of intellectuals, and that helps us to understand the dramatic contrast between the ideal and the actual manuscripts written, studied and collected by Franciscan friars.

As a dimension of the Franciscan manuscript, the ideal, as expressed in the regulations, had to develop and adapt to the needs of a community with shared devotional, pastoral and intellectual expectations. The following chapter will explore another dimension of the Franciscan manuscript, namely the space or the places where this ideal was challenged by the actual practices of production and use of manuscripts.

102 Roest, *History of Franciscan Education*, p. 15.

2. The Space

Libraries and Franciscan Manuscripts in Padua

Introduction

In a passage of his *Cronica*, the Franciscan friar Salimbene of Adam describes a dispute between the Dominican lector Peter of Apulia and the Franciscan master Hugh of Digne. According to Salimbene, Peter, a learned and eloquent man, claimed that he could not care less about the doctrine of Joachim of Fiore, a statement that prompted a resolute answer from Hugh.[1] After persuading Peter by demonstrating the unquestionable truth of Joachim of Fiore's doctrine, Hugh addressed their audience, drawing attention to the fact that it was no longer possible to consider the Franciscan order a group of simple, unlearned men.[2]

The figure of Hugh, highly praised by Salimbene, was almost at the opposite end of the spectrum of the simple and unlearned members of the idealized first Franciscan brotherhood, and reflected the transformation of

---

1   'Cum autem vidissem quod in camera fratris Hugonis congregabantur iudices et notarii atque phisici et alii litterati, ad audiendum ipsum de doctrina abbatis Ioachym docentem [...] tunc supervenerunt etiam duo fratres Predicatores, qui redibant a suo generali capitulo quod Parisius fuerat celebratum; quorum unus dicebatur frater Petrus de Apulia, in Ordine eorum Neapolitanus lector et litteratus et magnus prolocutor [...] Huic quadam die post prandium dixit frater Ioanninus, Neapolitanus cantor, qui eum optime noverat: "Frater Petre, quid vobis videtur de doctrina abbatis Ioachim?" Respondit frater Petrus: "Tantum curo de Ioachym, quantum de quinta rota plaustri [...] Cui frater Hugo dixit: "Et quid ad me, si non credit? Sibi imputetur. Ipse viderit, cum vexatio dabit auditui intellectum. Verutamen vocate ipsum ad disputationem, et audiemus in quo dubitat." Salimbene of Adam, *Cronica*, I, pp. 343-44.
2   'Post quorum recesum dixit frater Hugo remanentibus litteratis hominibus qui disputationem audierant: "Isti boni homines semper de scientia gloriantur et dicunt quod in Ordine eorum fons sapientie invenitur, cum Ecclesiasticus dicat: *Fons sapientie verbum Dei in excelsis* [Ecclus. 1:7]. Dicunt etiam quod transierunt per homines ydiotas, quando transeunt per loca fratrum minorum. [...] Sed per Dei gratiam modo non potuerunt dicere quod per homines ydiotas transierint quia feci quod docet Sapiens in Proverbiis, dicens *Responde stulto iuxta stultitiam suam, ne sibi sapiens esse videatur* [Prov. 26:5]. Et iterum dicit: *Stude sapientie, fili mi, et letifica cor meum, ut possis exprobranti respondere sermonem* [Prov. 27:11]."' Salimbene of Adam, *Cronica*, I, p. 364.

Hernández Vera, R., *Franciscan Books and their Readers: Friars and Manuscripts in Late Medieval Italy*. Taylor & Francis Group, 2022
DOI 10.5117/9789463729512_CH02

the community into an order that could rival Benedictines and Dominicans in their devotion to study. In fact, the recruiting of master Alexander of Hales at the University of Paris in 1236 became the unquestionable proof of the swift success of the Franciscan order, which by the end of the thirteenth century had attracted many of the most influential and renowned intellectuals of the time: Peter Cattani, Caesarius of Speyer, John Pian del Carpine, John Parenti, Anthony of Padua and Haymo of Faversham, among others.[3]

At the origin of the intellectual eagerness of the order was the increasing need of theological education for the friars responsible for preaching.[4] The whole process was supported by an efficient network of schools that offered the possibility of reaching the highest levels of learning to the most talented students, who were expected to attend the *lectio* regularly.[5] Naturally, learning depended on the use of books, and therefore the Franciscan schools should be provided with book collections that guaranteed continuity in studies.[6] Consequently, very quickly the library, understood not only as a physical place but also as the collection of books, became one of the most important spaces in Franciscan convents.

---

3   Lawrence, *Friars*, p. 127; Roest, *History of Franciscan Education*, pp. 14-17, and Luigi Pellegrini, *L'Incontro tra due 'invenzioni' medievali*, pp. 116 and 129-31; see also Potestà, 'Maestri e dottrine', and Şenocak, *Poor and the Perfect*, pp. 66 and 171-83.

4   The general traits of the development of preaching in the Middle Ages are described in O'Malley, 'Introduction: Medieval Preaching'. A remarkably clear introduction to medieval sermon studies can be found in Bataillon, 'Approaches to the Study of Medieval Sermons', and in Kienzle, 'Typology of the Medieval Sermon'. The International Medieval Sermon Studies Society and its journal, *Medieval Sermon Studies*, have contributed significantly to the understanding of medieval sermons. A comprehensive description of the development of scholarship on sermon studies may be found in Roberts, 'Sermon Studies Scholarship'. Recent research also explores the performance of the medieval sermon using interdisciplinary tools, as shown by Berardini, 'Discovering Performance Indicators'; for an overview of the development of preaching in the mendicant context, see D'Avray, *Preaching of the Friars*. The link between preaching and study, particularly at the university, is explained by the Franciscan sources in terms of the acquisition of the knowledge of sacred scripture in order to preach properly. Neslihan Şenocak warns, however, that it is 'risky to accept the arguments of medieval friars at face value', and says that this argument does not explain satisfactorily the outstanding levels of variety and sophistication of the friars' involvement with learning. See Şenocak, *Poor and the Perfect*, pp. 144-88; see also Lombardo, 'La production homilétique franciscaine'. A comprehensive overview of preaching within the Franciscan order can be found in Johnson, ed., *Franciscans and Preaching*.

5   The obligation of attending school in the convent was established by the constitutions of Assisi in 1279: 'Arctentur autem omnes fratres clerici ad ingressum scholarum, cum non fuerint circa iniuncta sibi officia occupati.' See Bihl, ed., 'Statuta generalia Ordinis', p. 76; see also Bartoli Langeli, 'I libri dei frati', p. 284; Roest, *History of Franciscan Education*, pp. 67, 82-86 and 92-93; and Şenocak, *Poor and the Perfect*, pp. 215-37.

6   Roest, *History of Franciscan Education*, pp. 197-201.

As mentioned before, Franciscan libraries have been considered a topic of research within the study of Franciscan institutional history and Franciscan education.[7] Another area of research is devoted to edited sources, mainly inventories, complemented with the identification and description of the books registered in these documents.[8] A more recent set of studies has focused on processes such as the creation of specific regulations for the libraries and the acquisition and circulation of books within Franciscan houses.[9] Unexplored fields of study remain, nonetheless, and this chapter aims to explore at least two of them. First, after briefly describing the main features of medieval and mendicant libraries, this section will compare the book collections of two Franciscan houses from two different branches of the order – one unreformed, the other, reformed –, as they were during the second half of the fifteenth century. Second, and as a result of the comparison, it will identify differences in the types of manuscripts collected, as well as characteristic physical features of these volumes, according to the library of provenance in order to verify whether there is a relation between these characteristics and the needs of the community of users. In that way, it will be possible to explore the second significant dimension of the Franciscan manuscript: the space.

The Medieval Library

One of the most fascinating representations of writing embellishes the Codex Amiatinus of the Biblioteca Medicea Laurenziana of Florence.[10] On folio 2^r (formerly numbered 4^r and V^r), the prophet Ezra is depicted in the labour of rewriting the books of the Old Testament after their loss by fire.[11] Perhaps

---

7   Clark, *Care of Books*, pp. 199-207; Abate, 'Manoscritti e biblioteche'; Humphreys, *Book Provisions*; Humphreys, *Friars' Libraries*; Bartoli Langeli, 'I libri dei frati'; and Roest, *History of Franciscan Education*. For a general overview of the developments of book culture and librarianship in Italy during the Middle Ages, see Lombardi and Nebbiai-Dalla Guarda, eds., *Libri, lettori e biblioteche*.

8   Humphreys, *Library of the Franciscans of the Convent of St. Antony*; Humphreys, *Library of the Franciscans of Siena*; Cenci, ed., *Bibliotheca manuscripta*; Pantarotto, *La biblioteca manoscritta*; Somigli, 'Hoc est registrum omnium librorum'.

9   See Lombardi and Nebbiai-Dalla Guarda, eds., *Libri, biblioteche e letture*; Şenocak, 'Book Acquisition'; and Şenocak, 'Circulation of Books'.

10   Florence, Biblioteca Medicea Laurenziana, MS Amiat. 1. See Appendix 3, Plate 1.

11   As the couplet above the image informs the reader: 'Codicibus sacris hostilii clade perustis/ Esdra Deo fervens hoc reparavit opus.' Scholarship has debated the relation between Cassiodorus, Bede and the figure represented on fol. 2^r of the Codex Amiatinus. For further details, see Meyvaert, 'Date of Bede's *In Ezram*'; see also Weitzmann, *Late Antique and Early Christian Book Illumination*, pp. 24 and 126.

one of the most striking features of this miniature is the fact that it presents a privileged perspective to the readers, especially if their attention focuses on the splendid cupboard that opens its doors generously offering a view of its precious contents: books. The image of the open cupboard powerfully illustrates the complexity of the medieval conception of the library, that is, a process rather than a place.[12] Actually, the term *bibliotheca*, or its equivalent *armarium*, had a wide range of meanings and could be used for an actual repository of books, for a collection of volumes or for a collection of texts gathered in one codex, as usually happened with the Bible.[13] This multiplicity of meanings certainly represents a challenge to the study of any aspect of medieval librarianship and so it is necessary, first, to establish the concept of a medieval library.

For the purposes of this work, the medieval library will be understood to be a collection of written volumes, characterized by a principle of organization useful for the location and retrieval of books.[14] This approach offers a twofold advantage. In the first place, since it refers to the collection rather than the room where it is located, this definition of a library does not depend on the presence of a designated place for the gathering of volumes; and further, it allows us to consider a small book collection contained in one single cupboard to be just as significant as the most magnificent religious or university libraries of the late Middle Ages. To understand the role of the Franciscan libraries, and particularly the Paduan collections, a brief description of the development of libraries in the Middle Ages will be offered in the following.

In the aftermath of the collapse of the Western Roman empire, two models of intellectual work related to two different ways of conceiving and using

---

12   *CHLB*, I, p. 1; see also Bell, 'Libraries of Religious Houses'.

13   Isidore of Seville, for instance, defines the library as the place where books are collected: 'Bibliotheca a Graeco nomen accepit, eo quod ibi recordantur libri. Nam βιβλιων librorum, θηκη repositio interpretatur. Isidore of Seville, *Etymologiarum*, I, VI, III, 1. However, the term had a very wide range of meaning, as shown by Teeuwen, *Vocabulary of Intellectual Life*, p. 155.

14   See Stam, ed., *International Dictionary of Library Histories*, I, pp. xii-xiii. The significant variation in the terminology has led me to adopt the term 'volume' in its sense of a unit of the library cataloguing process. Therefore, a volume may contain one or more works. The term 'book' will be used in this sense, unless indicated otherwise. This terminology is compatible with the distinction between *liber, codex* and *volumen* that was already in use since the early Middle Ages, as shown by Isidore: 'Codex multorum librorum est; liber unius voluminis. [...] Volumen liber est a volvendo dictus, sicut apud Hebraeos volumina Legis, volumina Prophetarum.' Isidore of Seville, *Etymologiarum*, I, VI, III, XIII. However, there are some contexts in which the boundaries of meaning are unclear. For further details, see Teeuwen, *Vocabulary of Intellectual Life*, pp. 168 and 178, and Dolbeau, 'Noms de livres', p. 80.

the library appeared. These models were embodied by the figures of two Roman scholars: Boethius and Cassiodorus.[15] Boethius was one of the most influential figures in medieval Latin culture. His *Consolatio Philosophiae*, written in captivity shortly before his execution in 524/5, is an expression of a *religio grammatici*, that is, a strong devotion to knowledge and study as an individual's source of hope. In the whole of Boethius's work, there co-existed Greek Neoplatonism, Latin philosophical writing, Greek Christian literature, and the Latin church fathers. This synthesis was possible thanks to his extensive and profitable use of his personal library, as well as that of his father-in-law Symmachus.[16] This way of using one's own book collection reflected one specific conception of the library during late antiquity, that is, the library understood as a personal possession that reflected its owner's intellectual history and interests.

Although Cassiodorus received the same kind of education as Boethius, he followed a very different path. After having pursued a remarkable *cursus honorum*, Cassiodorus decided to establish a Christian school in Rome following the model of those of Alexandria and Nisibis. However, once he realized that political chaos would make it impossible to accomplish his task, he retired to Squillace, in southern Italy. There he founded Vivarium, a monastery organized around a library accessible to the community of monks. The core of the work at Vivarium was the care, preservation and careful copying of books.[17] Like Boethius, Cassiodorus embodied a distinctive model of conceiving of, and working in a library: for Cassiodorus, the library was a resource shared by the religious community and reflected the needs of that communal body.

While the personal working library practically disappeared with Boethius, Cassiodorus's choice established an archetype for the early medieval library: the collection should be linked to a *scriptorium*, that is, a centre for the production of books.[18] During the next three centuries the growth of *scriptoria* and their libraries continued and fully developed, especially under the Carolingians who, as rulers, followed a cultural programme aimed at

---

15   For an overview of Boethius's historical context, see Moorhead, 'Boethius' Life'; for a thorough consideration of the life, work and influence of Boethius in the cultural tradition, see Marenbon, *Boethius*, as well as Gibson, ed., *Boethius: His Life, Thought and Influence*; for an overview of the cultural context of Cassiodorus, see Garzya, 'Il modello della formazione'; and for a complete study on the life and work of Cassiodorus, see O'Donnell, *Cassiodorus*, as well as Cassiodorus, *Introduction to Divine and Human Readings*, ed. and trans. Jones, pp. 3-64.

16   Marenbon, *Boethius*, pp. 7-11, and Thompson, *Medieval Library*, pp. 34-35.

17   Thompson, *Medieval Library*, p. 37.

18   See Thompson, *Medieval Library*, p. 35, and Stam, ed., *International Dictionary of Library Histories*, I, p. 104.

connecting directly with the heritage of classical antiquity and the Christian church.[19] This cultural transformation was mainly accomplished through the flourishing of monastic foundations and their *scriptoria* such as those of Fulda, Reichenau, St. Gall and Lorsch, which were centres of production for magnificent codices.[20] The Carolingian world enhanced the role of the book as a physical object with strategic value, specific types of books became tokens of power with political impact, and as a consequence, libraries also acquired a strategic value.[21]

The eleventh century introduced a period of deep transformation that affected monastic culture.[22] The new millennium brought a renewal of urban culture and centres of intellectual activity developed outside the cloister. In the twelfth century the universities became the natural space for the dissemination of knowledge.[23] This process stimulated the growth of a written culture which required new types of books and libraries; for example, many university texts were produced through a system in which the books were broken up into *peciae*, that is, sections that could be rented by the students who needed to copy them.[24] As a result, a single book could be copied simultaneously by many scribes, who were, more often than not, their readers.[25] The libraries were also transformed by ingenious mechanisms such as the 'double collection', a system in which one collection was formed by books chained to the benches and available only for consultation, and a second collection was constituted by unchained copies, available for loan.

19   For a description of the changes in the conception of the book and libraries during this period, see Petrucci, 'La concezione cristiana del libro'; for the specific changes in the Merovingian and early Carolingian world, see Riché, *Éducation et culture*, as well as McKitterick, *Carolingians and the Written Word*, p. 166, and McKitterick, 'Scriptoria of the Merovingian Gaul', pp. 174 and 182-85. McKitterick observes: 'Such, indeed was the [Carolingians'] zeal, intelligence and sheer productiveness in so doing that the whole period is generally classified as a "Renaissance", despite the inevitable ambiguities and assumptions of such a term.' McKitterick, *Carolingians and the Written Word*, p. 165; see also McKitterick, 'Carolingian Renaissance'.

20   McKitterick, 'Le Rôle culturel des monastères'.

21   Thompson, *Medieval Library*, pp. 54-101; see also McKitterick, *Carolingians and the Written Word*, pp. 149 and 157-59, and McKitterick, 'Charles the Bald (823-877) and his Library'.

22   Luigi Pellegrini, *L'Incontro tra due 'invenzioni' medievali*, p. 8; see also Leclercq, *Love of Learning and the Desire for God*, pp. 153-90.

23   Luigi Pellegrini, *L'Incontro tra due 'invenzioni' medievali*, pp. 49-73.

24   See Nebbiai-Dalla Guarda, 'Modelli bibliotecari pre-mendicanti'.

25   Lovatt, 'College and University Book Collections and Libraries'. For the University of Paris, especially the College of Sorbonne, see Thompson, *Medieval Library*, pp. 255-58; for the libraries of Oxford and Cambridge, see Thompson, *Medieval Library*, pp. 393-401; and for the production of books for the medieval university, see Boyle, 'Peciae, apopeciae, epipeciae', pp. 39-40; Shooner, 'La production du livre'; and Fink-Errera, 'La produzione dei libri'.

This is the context in which the mendicant orders became involved with study and made intensive use of books and libraries.

Mendicant Orders and their Libraries

The flourishing and rapid spread of new religious movements from the second half of the twelfth century reflected a situation of crisis that is closely related to the appearance of the mendicant orders.[26] Like the heretical movements, the mendicants were the expression of a wish for renewal linked to the consolidation of the urban mercantile class. As well, they satisfied the spiritual expectations of a new society with their flexibility, mobility and declared devotion to poverty – all of which permitted them a remarkable adaptability.[27] The main mendicant orders were the Augustine Hermit Friars, or Augustinians; the Preachers, or Dominicans; the Friars Minor, or Franciscans; the Hermit Friars of Mount Carmel, or Carmelites; and to a lesser extent, the Sack Friars and the Pied Friars. In a general sense, the mendicant orders pursued their activity within urban society, established their houses among the people and were closely linked to the Holy See, which used them not only as a valuable, highly skilled resource for administrative roles but also as perhaps the main asset for fighting heretical movements, thanks to their dedication to study, pastoral care and preaching.[28] In order to accomplish their mission, the mendicants established an internal programme of study that soon led them to pursue higher-level studies at the universities. There the members of the new orders, especially Franciscans and Dominicans, became protagonists of the intellectual life of their time and contributed decisively to the development of scholarly practices, manuscript culture and librarianship.[29]

Along with the Preachers and Minors, the Augustinian Hermit Friars played a significant role from the second half of the thirteenth century. Like the Carmelites, the Augustinians were originally a group of hermits who adopted the distinctive way of life of mendicants in an attempt to reconcile an active apostolic vocation with the contemplative life of the desert, and did

26 Leff, *Heresy*, I, pp. 3-7; see also Dal Pino, *Rinnovamento monastico-clericale*; Vauchez, *Ordini mendicanti*; Bailey, 'Religious Poverty'.

27 A comprehensive study of the origins, role and impact of the mendicant orders on society can be found in Lawrence, *Friars*. See also L. Little, *Religious Poverty*; Merlo, 'Religiosità e cultura religiosa'; Marenbon, 'Imaginary Pagans'.

28 Manselli, *Studi sulle eresie del secolo XII*, p. vi; Andrews, *Other Friars*, pp. 1-4.

29 See Luigi Pellegrini, *L'Incontro tra due 'invenzioni' medievali*, pp. 115-31.

not have a charismatic founder, nor a specific date of foundation.[30] Augustinians emerged from groups of hermits distributed in Lombardy, Tuscany and the Romagna during the thirteenth century. In 1224, Pope Innocent IV instructed Cardinal Richard Annibaldi to organize the hermits of Tuscany and to appoint a superior general over them. At almost the same time, a group of hermits founded by John Buoni gathered in Mantua. After the canonization of Buoni in 1254, Annibaldi, under instruction of Innocent IV, summoned the head of these houses to a meeting in Rome in 1256 and proclaimed an act of union, merging the communities in a single mendicant order. The bull *Licet Ecclesiae Catholicae* ratified the union and founded the Order of Friar Hermits of St. Augustine.[31] The new order adapted and followed the rule of St. Augustine and modelled their constitutions on those of the Dominicans, devoting themselves to preaching and pastoral care.[32] By the time of the order's inception, Thomas Aquinas and Bonaventure of Bagnoregio were masters in Paris and the seeds of the dispute between secular masters and mendicants were already growing within the community of scholars.[33] Under the protection of the powerful cardinal Annibaldi, the Augustinians survived the reassessment of new religious orders at the Second Council of Lyon in 1272, by showing that somehow their existence pre-dated 1215. In 1303, the Augustinians achieved the same privileges as Franciscans and Dominicans.[34]

Learning and study were of paramount importance for Augustinians, in accordance with their commitment to preaching and pastoral care: one of the main criteria for recruitment into the order was the disposition and ability to learn.[35] By 1260, the Augustinians had a house of learning in Paris, and in 1264 they founded a *studium* in Bologna. In 1287, the general chapter ruled that there should be at least four *studia generalia* in Italy, at Rome, Bologna, Padua and Naples. With time, then, there were Augustinian friars among the most influential and renowned late medieval university masters, whose impact became even deeper with humanism.[36]

The intellectual profile of the Augustinians was outlined by friar Giles of Rome, the first master of the order educated in Paris. Giles' most important

30   Lawrence, *Medieval Monasticism*, p. 266.

31   Lawrence, *Medieval Monasticism*, pp. 268-69; Andrews, *Other Friars*, pp. 72, 84.

32   For a detailed description of the normative development of the order, see Ponesse, 'Augustinian Rules and Constitutions'.

33   Pini, 'Le letture', p. 81; see also Gutiérrez, *Gli Agostiniani nel medioevo*, I, pp. 54-84.

34   Andrews, *Other Friars*, pp. 91-92.

35   Andrews, *Other Friars*, pp. 121 and 148.

36   Gutiérrez, *Gli Agostiniani nel medioevo*, pp. 85-122, Andrews, *The Other Friars*, p. 165; see also Antonella Mazzon, 'Gli Eremitani tra normativa e prassi libraria'.

sources were, on the one hand, Thomas Aquinas's interpretation of Aristotle, and on the other, the figure of Augustine of Hippo, who was adopted by Giles as the pillar of the cultural identity of the order. Giles' work was fundamental to the 'revival' of Augustine as an authority of devotional and philosophical content from the fourteenth century. Hence, Giles' legacy could be understood as the careful harmonization of Aquinas and Augustine. The importance and impact of Giles' endeavour is shown by the fact that his writings became the core of the programme of learning for incoming friars.[37]

From the devotion to learning followed a special relationship with books and tools of learning, and accordingly, a body of dispositions emerged that reflected the Augustinians' dedication to study. For example, incoming friars assigned to become students should sell any property previously possessed, and the profits were to be used to buy books, bedding and clothing. The constitutions of 1290 established that new lectors should receive 40 *livres tournois* to buy books necessary to their teaching before leaving Paris. When they died, their books should revert to the province. Additionally, a library should be present in every *studium generale*, as well as a copyist assigned to transcribe books according to the needs of the community.[38] It is possible to trace Giles' contribution here also: the section of the constitutions of 1290 regarding the structure and role of libraries was written following his advice. Among the dispositions was a specific request for enhancing or, if necessary, building a new library when the convent became a *studium generale*. From the beginning, the set of regulations linked friars' books to the library of the convent of origin as a way to guarantee the growth of the collections.[39]

The Dominican order was founded in 1215 with the specific purpose of opposing heresy through preaching.[40] An intense discipline of study based on the extensive use of books was at the core of the Dominican programme of preaching, and therefore Dominicans needed very efficient libraries. They

37 Pini, 'Le letture', pp. 84-90 and 93-107; see also Saak, 'Augustine in the Later Middle Ages'; Saak, *Creating Augustine*; and Andrews, *Other Friars*, p. 149-50.

38 Andrews, *Other Friars*, p. 156. Regulations concerning the presence of *scriptoria* within the convents usually described an ideal to aim for, not necessarily the reality of every mendicant house, as discussed in Chapter 1.

39 Pini, 'Le letture', p. 108; see also Humphreys, *Book Provisions*, pp. 67-76.

40 'Notum sit omnibus presentibus et futuris quod nos. F.[oulques] Dei gratia Tolosane sedis minister humilis, ad extirpandam hereticam pravitatem et vicia expellenda et fidei regulam edocendam et homines sanis moribus inbuendos, instituimus predicatores in episcopatu nostro fratrem Dominicum et socios eius, qui, in paupertate evangelica, pedites religiose proposuerunt incedere et veritatis evangelice verbum predicare.' Laurent, *Monumenta Historica S. P. N. Dominici*, p. 66; see also Hinnebusch, *History of the Dominican Order*, I, pp. 39-43, and Galbraith, *Constitution of the Dominican Order*, pp. 6 and 31-34.

did not experience any conflict with book culture, since their constitutions established that friars should be devoted to study and pastoral care. Like Franciscans, Dominicans had a clear restriction on personal property of goods, but books were regarded as tools of personal use and so could be made available through purchase, donations and bequests, and friars could even buy books from other friars. It was forbidden for friars to copy texts to sell them, but it was allowed to copy texts for personal use.[41] In any case, books were considered as the property of the province or of the convent of provenance, and once the friar died or was awarded a special dignity, such as a bishopric, his books should be returned to his convent of origin.[42] Concerning the libraries of the order, it seems that the provisions of books and topics depended on whether or not the convents were centres of study, and hence substantial variation could be found in the presence of some topics or authors, such as the Fathers of the Church.[43]

By the second half of the thirteenth century, Humbert of Romans, the fifth general of the order, prepared a set of detailed instructions concerning libraries in his *De officiis ordinis*. In the chapters 'De officio cantoris', 'De officio librarii' and 'De officio gerente curam scriptorum', Humbert established the principles of the organization and functioning of Dominican libraries such as the classification of volumes, opening hours, regulations on consultation and loan of books, indispensable reference books that should be in the library and even provision of materials to carry out the work of copying.[44] The general purpose of these regulations was to guarantee the most rational and efficient possible use of libraries and books in the education of the preacher.[45]

The Franciscan order had a far more complex relationship with study, books and libraries than the Dominicans. The first community of apostles constituted the model of life that Francis wanted to follow, and that left little space for books, libraries or a culture of intellectual achievement in the early history of the Franciscan order. However, the purpose of preaching the Gospel implied some degree of education of the friars and consequently the use of books. The order tried to reconcile poverty, apostolic life and the use of books and libraries through regulations. As the first chapter of this book has

41   A master could ask others to copy some of the texts he needed, as shown by Vatican City, Biblioteca Apostolica Vaticana, MS Vat. Lat. 718, a selection of works by Albert the Great copied to be used by Thomas Aquinas. See Letizia Pellegrini, *I manoscritti dei Predicatori*, and Bataillon, 'Le letture'.

42   Bataillon, 'Le letture', pp. 120-21.

43   Bataillon, 'Le letture', p. 130.

44   Humbert of Romans, *Opera de vita regulari*, II, pp. 238-39 and 263.

45   Severino Polica, 'Libro, lettura, "lezione"', pp. 384-88; see also Humphreys, *Book Provisions*, pp. 44-45.

shown, the process of establishing a set of regulations was not smooth, but reflected the internal struggles of the Franciscan order between institutional life and the model established by its founder. If using books could be a problematic practice, collecting them could be even more so. Nevertheless, some books were necessary to the performance of the divine office, and this kind of manuscript should be part of the goods of the convents. From the second decade of the thirteenth century, the growth of schools in the convents led to the enhancement of the book collections. Still, libraries for study were not a distinctive feature of the early Franciscan community. The first Franciscan book collections were intended to gather liturgical manuscripts, while other arrived through donations and bequests.[46] These sets of books were complemented by reference books and preaching aids to be kept in repositories.[47] The collections of volumes started to grow as early as the first half of the thirteenth century, when certain educational needs arose and special provisions – like having two separate collections of manuscripts, one for consultation and one for loan – were adopted in order to guarantee that books were always available for the friars.[48]

The provision of two collections of books was not invented by the mendicants. In 1212, a diocesan synod summoned in Paris recommended that monasteries divide their books into two groups: one should remain in the house, while the other should be kept for lending.[49] In order to fulfil these dispositions, some monastic houses adopted the practice of chaining the most valuable volumes to benches.[50] Later, the more recent university colleges adopted the same practice. It has been argued, therefore, that the mendicants followed the example of the existing colleges and kept a chained collection of books, being careful to ensure that the most requested volumes were always available for loan. However, this assumption has been challenged, as evidence suggests that the colleges copied the strategy of book collection already employed by the mendicants. An assessment on the process of gathering of the library of the College of the Sorbonne shows that the setting up of a double collection within the college dates by the end of the thirteenth century, long after the arrival of the mendicants at the University of Paris.[51]

46   Gavinelli, 'Per una biblioteconomia', pp. 271-74; see also Bartoli Langeli, 'I libri dei frati', pp. 288-91.
47   Humphreys, *Book Provisions*, pp. 56-57; see also Roest, *History of Franciscan Education*, pp. 197-99, and Şenocak, 'Earliest Library Catalogue'.
48   Roest, *History of Franciscan Education*, p. 200.
49   Mansi, *Sacrorum conciliorum*, XXII, p. 832.
50   Clark, *Care of Books*, pp. 101-16.
51   Angotti, 'Les bibliothèques des couvents mendiants', pp. 44-49; see also R. Rouse, 'Early Library of the Sorbonne', pp. 68-69.

Also, the use of books for limited or short periods of time had some implications for the discipline of study. The normal practice of study, especially at
higher levels, implied long periods of time and, most importantly, physical
interaction with the book by writing personal comments, by identifying
passages of interest with the aid of small hands drawn in the margins,
or *maniculae*, by adding cross references to the same text or by adding
references to other works. It was necessary, therefore, to guarantee long
periods of work with books. It is in this context that long-term loans were
devised as a solution to the problem, and in some cases, even life-long loans
were to be granted.[52]

For Franciscans, the earliest evidence of the assignment of books on
long-term loan comes from the first general constitutions, dating from 1239.
These statutes made it possible for friars who held the office of preacher
to have books granted to them for life, or 'concessi ad vitam'. Neslihan
Şenocak has discussed the circulation of books in the medieval Franciscan
order and has considered some examples of long-term loans and loans of
books for life.[53] She provides examples of how some Franciscan lectors and
preachers received books in concession for life such as friar Monaldo of Todi,
who received three volumes on those terms in 1245: a commentary on the
Gospel of Luke by Bonaventure, the commentary of William de la Mare
on the first and second books of the *Sentences*, and a commentary on the
Gospel of Matthew by Nicholas Gorran. One of the manuscripts registered
the concession, indicating that the book was destined to be used by friar
Monaldo and that anyone who dared to take the books from him without
proper authorization would be under anathema. Here we find the expression
that typically indicates the concession of books on loan for long periods of
time, usually for life: 'Concessus ad usum.'[54]

Mendicant Libraries in Padua

Augustinians established their Paduan house in 1237. By 1264 they had built
a convent, and from 1287 on their convent became one of the most important
studia of the order in Italy.[55] Accordingly, the library of the convent was well

---

52　Şenocak, 'Circulation of Books', pp. 147-53; see also Frioli, 'Gli inventari delle biblioteche
degli ordini mendicanti', pp. 334-35.

53　Şenocak, 'Book Acquisition', and Şenocak, 'Circulation of Books'.

54　Şenocak, 'Circulation of Books', p. 151.

55　Gutiérrez, 'De antiquis ordinis eremitarum', p. 240.

provided for and its collection grew steadily. This growth was accompanied by a set of specific norms concerning the management of the collection and the circulation of books. For example, a disposition of 1422 established that there should be two sets of keys for the library: one should be in possession of the librarian, and the other should be made available to friars for the preparation of the cycles of preaching; as well, the disposition ordered the immediate return of all books in possession of anyone who was not a member of the order.[56]

In 1430, Michele Savonarola described in his *Libellus de magnificis ornamentis regie civitatis Padue* the splendour of the building, the distribution of the volumes and the size of the collection, which by that time had reached nearly 400 manuscripts. An important feature of Savonarola's description is the presence of chained volumes, which suggests that the organization of the collection followed the model of the double collection typical of mendicant *studia*.[57]

On 10 May 1432, the general prior Gerardus of Rimini wrote a letter offering a set of regulations to guarantee the integrity of the book collection in Padua. Among the dispositions there was a specific request to carry out inventories of the libraries. A similar disposition was drafted in a letter from 1467, underlining the importance of excluding the presence of *saeculares* from the library. During the sixteenth century, a project was conceived to enhance the library by building a new place for the collection; nevertheless, the plan was eventually delayed and abandoned. It seems that the availability and portability of printed volumes had a negative impact on the care of old vellum codices.[58]

The inventory of the Paduan libraries carried out by Iacopo Filippo Tomasini in 1639 shows that, at the time, the library preserved about

56 Gutiérrez, 'De antiquis ordinis eremitarum', p. 240.

57 'Alterum vero locum gloriosum, primo in aspectu iucundissimum nimis nominabo, quem bibliothecam Eremitarum appellant, cuius ingressus librorum pulchritudine eorumque multitudine homines in admiratione ducit; locus enim amplissimus est, vitreis fenestris et lucidis ornatus, cuius superiora scampna parte ad septemtrionem versa: quae grammaticae, quae rethoricae, quae loycae, quae philosophiae attinent libros speciosos cum catenis tenent. Hacque in parte in mechanica plurimi et in theologia collocantur. Altera vero ad meridiem versa: quae decretis, quae decretalibus, quae novo et veteri Testamento attinent. Eorum omnium summa sunt quadringenta gloriosa volumina.' Michaelis Savonarole, *Libellus*, p. 56; Gutiérrez, 'De antiquis ordinis eremitarum', p. 240.

58 'Fratres illius temporis, non solum Patavii sed fere ubique, de libris impressis praecipue habendis diligenter curabant, dum antiquos codices -utpote ad studium difficiles vel saltem minus commodos- saepe negligebant.' Gutiérrez, 'De antiquis ordinis eremitarum', pp. 241-42.

380 manuscripts produced before mid-sixteenth century.[59] According to Tomasini, by the seventeenth century only a fraction of the original manuscripts survived. Nevertheless, there were volumes on theology, collections of sermons – including those of the most important masters of the order – books on poetry such as the works of Virgil, and the Odes of Horace, books on history, the life of Francis of Assisi, followed by a collection of philosophical texts, mainly by Aristotle and commentaries on his works, and then a collection of books on law and canon law, decretals and summae, and finally, some books on mathematics, astronomy and medicine. This set of tools for learning survived more or less unaltered until the end of the eighteenth century when the Napoleonic suppressions resulted in the scattering of the collection. Some of the surviving manuscripts are currently available at the Biblioteca Universitaria of Padua.

Dominican friars arrived in Padua in 1226 and settled within the walls of the city, on the banks of the river Bacchiglione near the city centre. By 1229 they had completed a church dedicated to Sant'Agostino, and a small adjacent convent. According to sources, from the beginning, the convent had a collection of books devoted both to the performance of the divine office and to satisfying the needs of study and preparation for preaching. The fourteenth-century movement of reform that spread across the order had a limited impact on the Paduan community, and by 1397 the convent definitely passed under the jurisdiction of the unreformed province of Lower Lombardy. Eventually, the conventual school became part of the *universitas theologorum* instituted at the University of Padua through the aggregation of the theological schools of the mendicant orders active in the city, namely Franciscans, Dominicans, Augustinian friars and Carmelites.[60]

The library of the Dominicans in Padua was certainly contemporary to the construction of the convent, and, as was usual for mendicant orders, the original collection of books contained the tools necessary to the divine office and to the basic duties of preaching and pastoral care. The library was destroyed by a fire in 1352, and a second library was built soon after. The first inventory of the collection was carried out at the end of the fourteenth century. According to this inventory, the manuscripts were distributed in sixteen cupboards: eight 'versus claustrum', that is, to the left-hand side, and

---

59   'Ut ex inventario apparet, valde bonam saeculis XIV-XVII conventus Patavinus habuit bibliothecam, inter maiores Ordinis librarias eiusdem temporis certe annumerandam; nam, quamvis melior pars suorum codicum iam a. 1639 "temporum iniuria ab alienata esset", 380 volumina manuscripta -fere omnia saeculo XVI antiquiora- adhuc conservabat.' Gutiérrez, 'De antiquis ordinis eremitarum', p. 251.

60   Gargan, *Lo studio teologico*, pp. 3-6 and 13.

the others 'versus cementerium', namely to the right-hand side. The library kept the same structure until the sixteenth century, when it was enhanced in order to allocate room for the great number of arriving printed books.[61]

The three medieval inventories outline a collection that reflected the purpose of offering the necessary tools for preaching and pastoral care.[62] Nevertheless, the Dominican book collection in Padua was not as rich and complete as that of the Franciscan library of Sant'Antonio.[63] The library had the typical structure and composition of a Dominican collection of the time. Apart from exemplars of the Bible, the library gathered biblical comments, books on philosophy and theology, and additional tools useful for students. There were also some works of the Fathers of the Church and additional volumes such as texts on grammar and law. Sadly, no manuscripts of the original collection survived, and the loss of the volumes seems to be related to both the introduction of printed books and to sudden changes in the acquisition of books.[64] The period of transition to modernity was a time of struggle and difficulties within the order, as shown by the almost complete absence of institutional sources on books, libraries and written culture.[65] By the beginning of the eighteenth century, the library was all but lost and abandoned, and when the Napoleonic suppressions arrived in 1806, there were no manuscripts at all, and only very few early-printed volumes remained.[66]

The presence of the university contributed significantly to establishing the Franciscan convent of Sant'Antonio in Padua as a point of arrival for friars coming from many different places in search of high-level education. These Franciscans contributed significantly to the growth of the library collection with their work of study.[67] By the second half of the fifteenth century, the library of the convent held an impressive collection of more than a thousand volumes, as shown by an inventory carried out in 1449.[68] A few years earlier, in 1420-21, another Franciscan convent had been founded not very far from Sant'Antonio. This new convent, dedicated to Francis, belonged to the Observant reform and was conceived as a support for a hospital and house of pilgrimage. Very soon the convent of San Francesco

---

61 Gargan, *Lo studio teologico*, pp. 175-76.
62 Bataillon, 'Le letture', p. 128.
63 Gargan, *Lo studio teologico*, pp. 184-89.
64 Gargan, *Lo studio teologico*, pp. 186-87.
65 Giannini, 'Intellettuali militanti', pp. 329-31.
66 Gargan, *Lo studio teologico*, p. 188.
67 Giovè Marchioli, 'Circolazione libraria e cultura francescana', pp. 132-35.
68 The current Padova, Biblioteca Antoniana, MS 573.

Grande became an important centre for the Italian Observance as well as for high-level education for Observant preachers. Its library, although recent, was remarkable by the standards of the time.

The following section will explore these two Franciscan libraries' history and configuration and will compare them as functioning tools in the education of the members of their respective communities during the fifteenth century. The main sources of evidence are two inventories. For the library of the convent of Sant'Antonio, or Biblioteca Antoniana, a fifteenth-century inventory preserved in MS 573 is currently available in the library of the convent. For the Observant library, the earliest inventory available dates from the year 1600 and is the result of the dispositions of the Sacred Congregation of the Index.[69] The list reflects the size of the collection as it was during the fifteenth and sixteenth centuries, and it has been possible to identify and describe the volumes that were present at the library during the fifteenth century.[70] The presence of two sources describing the libraries of two different Franciscan houses in the same city is an exceptional circumstance that allows us to explore, with some detail, their similarities and differences.[71]

The Biblioteca Antoniana in Padua

The origin of the collection of the Biblioteca Antoniana in Padua has not been clearly established. However, it is almost certain that when the Franciscan friars arrived in Padua in 1229, they brought with them the books required to perform the divine offices properly.[72] It is possible that the most ancient volumes of the collection were read, studied and commented on by Anthony of Padua himself. In fact, among the earliest volumes of the collection were a Bible and copies of patristic and theological literature that were part of the collection of sources for the sermons and theological lessons of Anthony.[73]

One of the first documents concerning the history of the library is the last will of the canon of the cathedral, Egidius, who lent to the library of

---

69   The current Vatican City, Biblioteca Apostolica Vaticana, MS Vat. Lat. 11283, fols. 40^r-54^v.

70   See Pantarotto, *La biblioteca manoscritta*, pp. 14-17.

71   See Nebbiai-Dalla Guarda, 'Les inventaires des bibliothèques mèdiévales'; see also Nebbiai-Dalla Guarda, 'Le biblioteche degli ordini mendicanti'.

72   Sartori, *Archivio Sartori*, I, p. 1309; see also Abate, 'Manoscritti e biblioteche', pp. 87-88.

73   See Abate and Luisetto, *Codici e manoscritti*, I, xxiv.

the convent his books and a copy of the sermons of Anthony in 1237.[74] In 1240, Uguccione, another canon of the cathedral, donated to the convent a Bible in twenty-five volumes that he had probably acquired in Paris in 1214-20.[75] Further donations to the conventual library were registered in 1260. In this year, Nicolaus Clericus from the Benedictine monastery of San Pietro in Padua donated a book of sermons to the convent.[76] Later, in 1289, Zilborga, widow of the count of Vicenza, stated in her will that 200 pounds should be given to her son in order to buy books, but only if he joined the Franciscan order.[77] Among the most important donations to the library during the fourteenth century were those of Beatrice Tolomei, who in 1300 donated to the Paduan provincial minister the sum of 25 lire to repair the books in the library. Another significant donation to the conventual library was the legacy of Bishop Ildebrandino de' Conti in 1352, as well as that of the professor of natural philosophy at the University of Padua, Gaetano of Thiene, in 1461.[78] Two inventories carried out in 1396 (the current Padua Biblioteca Antoniana MS 572) and in 1449 (the current Padua, Biblioteca Antoniana, MS 573) provide information about the remarkable growth in the quantity of volumes during the brief period between them, as well as about some significant losses.[79] The arrival of printing was also an opportunity to enhance the book collection.[80] In 1477, the minister general Francesco Sansone created a fund of 200 pounds for the acquisition of books for the library. This sum was used exclusively for the acquisition of printed books, among which were the *Rationale divinorum officiorum* (printed in Mainz in 1459) and the decretals of Boniface VIII (in a printed edition of 1465).[81]

Emanuele Fontana's research on the medieval Franciscan province of Sant'Antonio has shown that apart from donations and bequests, other

---

74 'Conventui fratrum minorum de Padua et ad eorum utilitatem et usum reliquit libros suos, qui sunt aput dictos fratres, et sermones quondam fratris Antonii, qui sunt aput magistrum Patavinum.' See Sambin, 'Tre notizie', p. 2.

75 It is the current Padua, Biblioteca Antoniana, MS 285. In an internal note it is written: 'Iste liber est de conventu Padue et in eodem conventu debet permanere, qui fuit quondam magistri Ugutionis de voluntate ipsius. Si quis autem eum alienaverit anathema sit; et est Genesis de littera et apparatu Parisiensi, cum multis aliis quorum scripta sunt inferius, quos magister Ugutio dedit fratribus Minoribus de conventu Padue, ut ibi debeant stare.' See Cassandro et al., eds., *I manoscritti*, p. 53; see also Abate and Luisetto, *Codici e manoscritti*, I, xxvii.

76 Sambin, 'Tre notizie', p. 4.

77 'Libras ducentas pro libris si ordinem fratrum Minorum intraverit; alias non.' Abate and Luisetto, *Codici e manoscritti*, I, xxvii.

78 See Sartori, *Archivio Sartori*, I, p. 1309.

79 See Humphreys, *Book Provisions*, p. 7; see also Baldissin Molli, *La sacrestia del Santo*.

80 Abate and Luisetto, *Codici e manoscritti*, I, xxxvii.

81 Abate and Luisetto, *Codici e manoscritti*, I, xxxviii.

significant modalities for the acquisition of books for the library included the purchase of books from other convents or even from friars from other orders.[82] Additionally, the regulations of the provincial chapter gathered at Treviso in 1290 established that a scribe should be appointed in the convents of the Venetian province to copy the books required. Therefore, it has been assumed that the Biblioteca Antoniana was among those that could count on its own *scriptorium*. This assumption has been challenged by Nicoletta Giovè Marchioli, who argues that there is no satisfactory evidence to confirm the presence of a permanent *scriptorium* in many of the Franciscan convents, including the convent of Sant'Antonio.[83]

The designation of the Paduan convent as a site for a theological college with the prerogative of awarding degrees in 1630 represented a considerable increase in the collection of the library. In 1772, professor Alessandro Burgos brought to the convent his remarkable personal library.[84] In 1806 and 1810, the Napoleonic laws separated the library from the convent. However, the library was not affected by the suppressions and/or confiscations, because the rights of ownership and the duties of administration had been transferred since the Middle Ages to a lay entity, the Arca del Santo. As a consequence, the Biblioteca Antoniana became an exceptional case of a Franciscan library in Italy that remained in its original location and that did not suffer the complete loss or dispersion of its collection.[85]

The Book Collection of the Biblioteca Antoniana in the Fifteenth Century

In 1449 the Arca del Santo decided to carry out an inventory of all the goods of the sacristy and the library, as stated in the *incipit* of the document that registered it.[86] The original programme was never completed, and only the volumes collected in the conventual library were counted, omitting the

---

82 Fontana, *Frati, libri e insegnamento*, pp. 92-108; see also Fontana, 'La bibliothèque du convent'.
83 See Chapter 1; see also Little, 'Statuta provincialia', p. 460; Giovè Marchioli, 'Codici francescani a Roma nel Duecento', p. 133; and Giovè Marchioli, 'Scrivere e leggere il libro francescano', p. 185.
84 Sartori, *Archivio Sartori*, I, p. 1310.
85 See Manselli, 'Due biblioteche'.
86 MS 573, fol. 1ʳ: '[H]ic liber presens continet inventarium omnium librorum existentium in libraria huius sacri conventus fratrum Minorum Padue tam cum chatena quam sine chatena; insuper et inventarium omnium rerum existentium in sacristia predicti sacri conventus, videlicet reliquiarum, tabernaculorum, calicum, patenarum, turibolorum, ampularum et alliarum argenteriarum generis cuiuscumque; insuper omnium apparamentorum aureorum argenteorum, sericorum, telle cum omnibus ad illa spectantibus, item palliorum, perlarum, vellutorum et sericorum; item et missalium ceterorumque librorum divinorum offitiorum, item et aliarum rerum et ornamentorum in dicta sacristia existentium [...] Currentibus annis a

books contained in the sacristy. The inventory of the library was written in a parchment volume, MS 573 of the Biblioteca Antoniana. After MS 572, this manuscript is the oldest evidence of the organization and composition of the book collection at the library. The parchment volume of 314 × 225 mm and sixty-six leaves was written in an elegant script, a variation of the *rotunda bononiensis*. Its formal character was underlined by a set of three miniatures in gold and other colours.[87]

The 1449 inventory registered the books of the collection in two main parts. The first concerned the books present in the library for consultation or loan. The second part listed books on loan at the time of the writing of the inventory. In order to register the books present in the library, the 1449 inventory followed their location in the room: it began with the chained books on the first bench on the right-hand side, moved towards the left and then turned back, registering the unchained books kept in cupboards.

At the time of composition of the inventory, the books on loan were divided between those that could be retrieved and those that had been on loan since 1423 and therefore considered missing or lost. The registration proceeded by indicating the name of the person who had requested the book, followed by the title of the volume. In some cases, notes indicating the return of the volume can be found beside the title. For those books on loan since 1423, the inventory showed an understandable lack of hope, since most of those who had kept the books on loan were already dead.[88]

As to the recording of the volumes, the inventory provided a summary and a concise description that would help to identify the items quickly.[89] The inventory also revealed awareness of the distinction between *volumen* and *liber*, that is, between the compilation of different works in a single codex and the text of a single work.[90] The first element of importance for the identification of a volume was its location in a specific bench or cupboard. The inventory followed the distinction between *bancha*, or bench, and *scaffa*, or cupboard. The first were used to keep the chained books, while

Nativitate Domini nostri Yesu Christi 1449, de mense marcii, et pontificatus beatissimi domini nostri pape Nicolai quinti anno secundo.' See also Humphreys, *Book Provisions*, pp. 70-71.

87   See Appendix 3, Plate 2; see also Abate and Luisetto, *Codici e manoscritti*, II, p. 595.

88   Fol. 66ᵛ declared: 'Suprascripti nominati in dicto libro antiquo pro maiori parte sunt mortui et tamen non sunt depenati in ipso libro.' See Appendix 1 for a full transcription of the section.

89   Monfrin, 'Le Catalogue et l'inventaire', p. 135.

90   Frioli, 'Gli antichi inventari della Biblioteca Antoniana di Padova', p. 81. A clear example is item no. 224: in a *Summa super Sententias*, there is, *interpoxitus*, a *Tractatus de quatuor cardinalibus virtutibus*. The scribe registered for each one of the works the *incipit* and *explicit* but put them together in one item, preserving the unity of the *volumen*.

the latter were used as the repository for the books available for loan.[91] Then the inventory registered the title of the work or the name of the author, followed by a description of the binding.[92] Next there was the *incipit* of the work, usually introduced by the formula 'It begins with' (*cuius principium*) and, to better identify the book described, there followed the *incipit* of an internal leaf, usually the first folio of the second quire, with the formula 'The second quire begins with' (*secundus quinternus incipit*). Finally, the *explicit* of the volume was transcribed, usually introduced by the formula 'It ends with' (*finis vero ultimus*).

The Organization of the Book Collection in the Biblioteca Antoniana

Including the eighty-four books on loan, and the thirty-five lent since 1423, the Biblioteca Antoniana in 1449 had a collection of 1,024 volumes, distributed among fifty-three depositories. A swift comparison with the fourteenth-century inventory shows that during the intervening fifty-three years the Biblioteca Antoniana increased its collection by 71 per cent, which constituted a remarkable rate of growth.[93] Thus, the Paduan library was at the level of the most important libraries of the order, such as those of Assisi, Bologna, Florence and Siena. The latter was the only one with a higher number of volumes.[94]

MS 573 reveals that there were twenty-one copies of the Bible plus eighty-three glossed biblical books.[95] There were also copies of postils by Thomas Aquinas, Philip of Moncalieri, Peter of Tarantaise, Francis Abatis, Stephen Langton, Jacob of Alexandria, William of Antona and William of Saint-Amour. This set was complemented by a collection of patristic commentaries on the Bible by Augustine, Ambrose and Gregory the Great,

91   Genest, 'Le mobilier des bibliothèques', pp. 152-53; see also Frioli, 'Gli antichi inventari della Biblioteca Antoniana di Padova', p. 70.

92   Frequently the title of the work included the name of the author or the work was known only by the author's name. See Sharpe, *Titulus*, pp. 22 and 30-32; see also Frioli, 'Gli antichi inventari della Biblioteca Antoniana di Padova', pp. 74-76.

93   Bartoli Langeli, 'I libri dei frati', pp. 286-87; see also Frioli, 'Gli antichi inventari della Biblioteca Antoniana di Padova', pp. 75-76, and Humphreys, *Library of the Franciscans of the Convent of St. Anthony*, p. 7.

94   Cenci, ed., *Bibliotheca manuscripta*, I, pp. 29-34; Humphreys, *Book Provisions*, pp. 111-15; Grauso, 'La biblioteca francescana medievale di Assisi', pp. 13-79; Humphreys, *Library of the Franciscans of Siena*, p. 24.

95   Five of the twenty-one copies of the Bible went missing while on loan.

plus more recent commentaries by Nicholas of Lyra, Peter Lombard, Thomas Aquinas and Alexander of Alexandria.

Apart from the biblical commentaries, the patristic literature included works from Augustine, Gregory the Great, Jerome, John of Damascus, Isidore, Rabanus Maurus and Pseudo-Dionysius the Areopagite. The collections of the lives of the saints were important tools of study, and consequently a fair number of copies, all anonymous, were available.[96] Apart from these collections there were volumes dedicated to the most important Franciscan saints: Francis and Anthony of Padua.

Peter Lombard's *Sentences*, a compilation of theological questions systematically arranged around major topics, was perhaps the most influential theological text of the Middle Ages.[97] Accordingly, the Biblioteca Antoniana had several copies of this work plus a remarkable set of commentaries. The best known were those of Bonaventure, Alexander of Hales, John Duns Scotus, William of Ockham, Francis of Meyronnes, Peter Auriol, Landolfus Caracciolus and John of Ripa. There was also a complete collection of influential theological works such as the *Summa theologiae* and the *Summa contra gentiles* of Thomas Aquinas, and the summae of Alexander of Hales and Henry of Ghent. There was also a remarkable collection of compilations of disputes on specific topics, or *quaestiones*. Only two of these volumes were identified by the name of the authors, Thomas Aquinas and William Almoinus, while the others remained anonymous. The compilations of answers to a great variety of different questions, or *quodlibeta*, were very important in the programme of training in universities and in the convent, as shown by the presence of copies of *quodlibetales* by Duns Scotus, Thomas Aquinas and Henry of Ghent in the collection. Among the philosophical literature were copies of the Aristotelian *Metaphysica*, *De anima*, *Physica* and *Ethica*. The collection of Aristotelian commentaries included those of the most renowned masters such as Duns Scotus, Albertus Magnus, Thomas Aquinas and Averroes.[98] Other important philosophers present in the

---

96 According to Kenneth W. Humphreys, Jacobus de Voragine is the author of eight of the volumes. See Humphreys, *Library of the Franciscans of the Convent of St. Anthony*, p. 15.

97 See Rosemann, *Peter Lombard*, pp. 8-70; Colish, *Peter Lombard*, I, pp. 33-154; and Friedman, '*Sentences* Commentary'. Monika Asztaloz summarizes the reasons for the appreciation of the *Sentences* in these terms: 'The lasting success of this work of compilation has been ascribed to its lack of originality, its relative orthodoxy, its complete coverage of the debated issues of the day and the author's unwillingness to give final solutions to difficult questions.' See Asztalos, 'Faculty of Theology', p. 412; for further detail, see Chapter 3.

98 On fol. 26ᵛ, the inventory describes a commentary on Aristotle's *Metaphysics* as follows: 'Scriptum Allexandri super Methaphisica in volumine mediocri coperto coreo sanguineo per totum cum claviculis de metallo, cuius principium "Sicud dicit Philosophus [...]"'. Humphreys

library were Boethius, Porphyry and masters such as William of Ockham, Walter Burley and William of Heytesbury.[99]

Perhaps the most important section of the library was its collection of sermons. There were 230 volumes, of which 180 were anonymous. This constituted a remarkable number, even in the context of the Franciscan libraries.[100] There were several volumes of sermons by Jacobus de Voragine, as well as works by the best-known Franciscan masters such as Luke of Bitonto, Bonaventure of Iseo, Francis of Meyronnes, Servasanctus of Faenza, Bertrand of Turre and Anthony of Padua, including the renowned 'Codice del Tesoro'.[101]

The book collection also included works on canon law such as the *Decretals*, and their commentaries; and there was even a copy of the *Institutes* of Justinian, the most important work of Roman, or civil, law. To guarantee proper instruction in grammar, the library had copies of works such as the *Institutiones* of Priscian, the *Derivationes* of Hugh of Pisa and the *Summa* by Guglielmus Britonis. There were also some classical treatises such as *De officiis* by Cicero, and the *Rhetorica ad Herennium* by pseudo-Cicero and *De beneficiis* by Seneca, along with works by Sallust, Lucan, Martianus Capella and Orosius, and the library could also count among its holdings a copy of Dante's *Commedia*.[102] The scientific literature was limited to the treatises *De natura animalium* by Aristotle, *De sphera* of John of Sacrobosco, Boethius's *De arithmetica*, two anonymous volumes of astrology, a miscellany entitled *Liber diversarum scientiarum*, four copies of *De proprietatibus rerum* by Bartholomeus Anglicus and one copy of the *Speculum historiale* by Vincent of Beauvais. Finally, there was a fair collection of works of reference, among which were the *Historia scholastica* by Peter Comestor, a set of *Concordantie*

identifies the manuscript with the current Padua, Biblioteca Antoniana, MS 386, and attributes the authorship to Alexander of Alexandria. Humphreys, *Library of the Franciscans of the Convent of St. Anthony*, pp. 17 and 115. Although Alexander of Alexandria was not a commentator on Aristotle, the evidence suggests that Humphreys' identification and attribution are correct. See Abate and Luisetto, *Codici e manoscritti*, I, pp. 323-24.

99   Roest, *History of Franciscan Education*, pp. 123-46.

100 See Humphreys, *Book Provisions*, pp. 103, 105-7, 111 and 115, and Humphreys, *Library of the Franciscans of Siena*, pp. 22, 27; for a swift comparison with a Dominican house, see Gargan, *Lo studio teologico*, pp. 234-38 and 248-49.

101 The sermons of Anthony were item nos. 95 and 96 of the fifteenth-century inventory. The first is the 'Codice del Tesoro', Padua, Biblioteca Antoniana, MS 720. See Abate and Luisetto, *Codici e manoscritti*, I, xxvi-xxvii, and II, p. 656; see also Frasson et al., eds., *In nome di Antonio*, pp. 10-19, and Giovè Marchioli, 'Mitologia di un manoscritto'.

102 On fol. 16^r: 'Item est in bancha suprascripta est uno Dante coperto corio rubeo cum claviculis. Incipit "Nel mezo" et secundus quinternus incipit "partiti vestie". Finit "Deo gratias".' See also Pasquini, 'San Francesco e i frati Minori in Dante', and Ragazzini, 'Presenza di Dante al Santo'.

Biblie and copies of the *Distinctiones*, *Capitula Bibliae* and *Correctiones Bibliae*, plus several copies of the *Mammotrectus* of John Marchesinus, a popular encyclopaedic guide to the Bible.

This brief overview of the composition of the book collection shows that the Biblioteca Antoniana was an impressive library, not only in terms of the number of volumes, but also in terms of the extent of the topics and authors available. These observations suggest that the collection aimed to satisfy the needs of a programme of study at the highest levels and that it offered the required resources to successfully complete such a programme: from the basic manuals and tools of reference to the most sophisticated commentaries and treatises on theology and philosophy. At the same time, since the declared main purpose of the Franciscan intellectual training was preaching, the library of the convent of Sant'Antonio made the collection of sermons and preaching tools the section with the highest number of items.

The Organization of the Books in the Space of the Library

The order of registration adopted by MS 573 followed the organization of the space and the distribution of volumes in the Biblioteca Antoniana. In this respect, the inventory was also a map of the library. The collection was located in a wide room whose area was divided into two sides. On the right-hand side were fourteen benches and twelve cupboards, while on the left-hand side there were fourteen benches and thirteen cupboards. As mentioned above, the books for consultation were chained to the benches, while the books available for loan were kept in the cupboards.

On the right-hand side, the first two benches kept copies of the Bible and biblical texts. From the third bench on, and until the ninth bench, there was a complete collection of specific commentaries on biblical texts.[103] Among them, on the seventh bench, was a copy of Joachim of Fiore's *Psalterium decem chordarum*, one of the sources for the controversial interpretation of the role and purpose of the order adopted by some Franciscans during the thirteenth century.[104] From the ninth to the fourteenth bench there was a collection of sermons on biblical books.

---

103 Some of the commentaries were Augustine's on the book of Genesis, the commentary of Nicholas of Lyra on the Psalms and the treatises of Thomas Aquinas on the Gospels.
104 The manuscript is the current Padua, Biblioteca Antoniana, MS 322. See Abate and Luisetto, *Codici e manoscritti*, I, pp. 290-92; for a description of the influence of the Joachite ideas in the Franciscan spirituality, see Chapter 1.

The theological section began on the left-hand side. The first bench held copies of the *Sentences*, a Bible and a copy of Dante's *Comedy*.[105] The second and third benches had theological treatises like the *Summa* of Henry of Ghent, but were mainly occupied by commentaries on the *Sentences*.[106] The fourth bench had mainly summae, *quodlibetales* and *questiones,* while works on logic and commentaries on the *Sentences* occupied the fifth bench.[107] The sixth and seventh benches were dedicated to the literature of the Fathers of the Church.[108] Treatises on canon law and philosophy were available on the eighth and ninth benches, while the volumes on moral theology were chained to the tenth bench.[109] The eleventh bench was dedicated to Aristotle and the commentaries on his works, a set that was complemented by the books kept on the twelfth bench, dedicated to the treatises on natural philosophy and logic.[110] Finally, the thirteenth and fourteenth benches kept treatises on mathematics, rhetoric, history and manuals of grammar.[111]

---

105 See above note 102.

106 For example, the commentaries of Alexander of Hales, Bonaventure, Duns Scotus, Peter Auriol, Francis of Meyronnes, Landolfus Caracciolus and Richard of Middleton.

107 Such as the *Summa theologiae* and *Quodlibetales* by Thomas Aquinas, and two volumes of *quaestiones* on the *Sentences* by Landolfus Caracciolus and Giles of Rome. Some of the works on the fifth bench were the *Dialogus* and the *Summa logicae* by William of Ockham, accompanied by volumes of the *Quaestiones* by Henry of Ghent, other works by Giles of Rome, the *Summa super Sententias* by Philip the Chancellor and the commentary on the fourth book of the *Sentences* by Duns Scotus.

108 The sixth bench was dedicated almost exclusively to Augustine, with copies of *De civitate Dei*, *Milleloquium*, *Confessiones* and a volume containing *De vera religione, De libero arbitrio* and *De conflictu vitiorum*. The seventh bench was mainly dedicated to treatises by Fathers of the Church with works by Jerome, Augustine, John of Damascus, Isidore of Seville and Pseudo-Dionysius the Aeropagite. This bench also contained the *Breviloquium* of Bonavenure, the treatise *De miseria humanae conditionis* by Innocent III and copies of the *Ordinarium vite religiose* by John of Wales.

109 The eighth and ninth benches had copies of the *Decretales* and commentaries such as the *Summa super titulos decretalium* by Geoffrey of Trani, the *Summa super titulos decretalium* by Henry of Segusio and the *Summa casuum* by John of Erfordia (de Saxonia). On the tenth bench were treatises such as the *Summa de penitentia* by Servasanctus of Faenza, the *Summa* on the same subject by Peter Cantor and several treatises on virtues and vices.

110 There were copies of the *Metaphysica, De anima*, the *Physica* and other major works by Aristotle. Among the commentaries were copies of the *Super methaphysicam* by Duns Scotus, the *Expositio in librum de Anima Aristotelis* by Gaetano of Thiene and the commentaries by Averroes. The twelfth bench contained the *In quatuor libros metheorum* by Albert of Cologne and the *De caelo et mundo* by Gaetano of Thiene. The works on logic comprised the *Summa logicae* or *Loyca guallis* by William of Ockham, the *Logica* by William Burley and a copy of the *Quaestiones* of Rudolf Brito. There was also a copy of the *Ethics* by Aristotle, one volume containing *De officiis* by Cicero, and *De beneficiis* by Seneca.

111 There was one copy of Boethius's *De arithmetica* and one miscellany with encyclopaedic works by Rabanus Maurus, Isidore of Seville, Macrobius and Bede, as registered on fol. 29ʳ of

The cupboards with the copies for loan were behind the benches. On the left-hand side, the first four cupboards contained the Bible, biblical books and concordances to the biblical text. The fifth and sixth cupboards were occupied by commentaries on biblical books. From the seventh cupboard on, and until the eleventh, more than 150 volumes of sermons were available. The twelfth cupboard contained glossed volumes of biblical books, especially the Psalms, as well as commentaries on the Gospels, the prophets and the book of Revelation. The thirteenth cupboard contained useless, unidentified material.[112]

The first cupboard on the right-hand side contained copies of the *Sentences* and the commentaries by Thomas Aquinas. The second cupboard contained fourteen volumes of commentaries on the *Sentences*, all by Bonaventure, while the third cupboard was dedicated to the commentaries on the *Sentences* and to summae by other influential Franciscan masters.[113] The series of commentaries on the *Sentences* continued through the fourth cupboard and was complemented by volumes of *quaestiones* in theology composed by renowned masters.[114] The fifth and sixth cupboards kept the volumes on canon law and the commentaries on the subject as well as tools of reference.[115] The volumes on the lives of saints filled the seventh cupboard, while the eighth cupboard had a more heterogeneous content.[116] The ninth

MS 573: 'Rabanus De computo in aseribus et coreo viridi et blavo ad ligaturas, cuius principium "Dilecto fratri" et est in antiqua littera et incipit secundus quaternus "dianum et nocturnum" et habet in finem novem folia circulis et signis de zodaico [sic].' It is the current Padua, Biblioteca Antoniana, MS 27. See Abate and Luisetto, *Codici e manoscritti*, I, pp. 28-33. On the same bench was also a copy of the *Rhetorica ad Herennium* by Pseudo-Cicero, two miscellanies of historical works by Sallust and the treatise *De sphera* by John of Sacrobosco. The fourteenth bench was devoted to works on grammar and reference such as the *Derivationes* by Hughes of Pisa, a manual on grammar by the same author, a miscellany of works of William Brito that included the *Expositio vocabulorum Bibliae*, and *De accentu* by Priscian.

112 On fol. 49[r-v]: 'Tertia decima scaffa sinistra. Quedam scartafacia inordinata et quasi inutilia.'

113 There were copies of the commentaries by Alexander of Hales, Duns Scotus, William of Ware, Peter Auriol and Francis of Meyronnes.

114 Apart from the *questiones* written by the authors of the commentaries kept in the third cupboard, there were the compilations of Henry of Ghent and Hannibal of Hannibaldis, a disciple of Thomas Aquinas.

115 There were six copies of the *Decretales,* thirty summae and commentaries, plus one copy of the *Institutiones* of Justinian.

116 Apart from the general hagiographical compilations such as the *Legenda aurea*, the seventh cupboard contained four copies of Bonaventure's *Legenda* of Francis and two of the *Legenda* of Anthony of Padua. This series was complemented by six copies of the *Mammotrectus Biblie*, a very popular encyclopaedic guide to understanding the text of the Bible, composed by John Marchesinus. On the other hand, apart from a copy of *De proprietatibus rerum* and a missal, one could say that the eighth cupboard was dedicated to treatises on virtues and vices, including

cupboard contained volumes concerning theological questions, including those related to the *Sentences*.[117] Many volumes on natural sciences were placed in the tenth cupboard with topics such as arithmetic and astrology, while the eleventh cupboard kept works on logic.[118] Finally, the twelfth cupboard had only eight volumes on different topics.[119]

A schematic summary of the organization of the volumes is shown in Fig. 1.

Left-hand side				Right-hand side			
Scaffae (Cupboards)		*Banchae* (Benches)		*Banchae* (Benches)		*Scaffae* (Cupboards)	
		-Bible -Book of *Sentences, Divine Comedy*	1				
		-Commentaries on the *Sentences* -Theological treatises (mainly *Summae*)	2-3			1	-Book of *Sentences* -Thomas Aquinas' commentaries on the *Sentences*
1-4	-Bible, biblical texts -Concordances	-Thomas Aquinas -*Summae* and *Quodlibetales*	4	-Bible	1	2-4	-Commentaries on the *Sentences* -*Quaestiones*
5-6	-Postils -Commentaries	-William of Ockham -*Quaestiones*	5	-Bible -Biblical texts	2	5-6	-Canon law and reference
7-11	-Sermons	-Augustine	6	-Commentaries on biblical texts	3-9	7	-Hagiography, Mammotrectus
12	-Glossed biblical books -Postils	-Fathers of the Church	7	-Sermons on biblical texts	9-14	8	-Treatises on vices and virtues
13	-Additional, scattered materials	-Canon law and Philosophy	8-9			9	-Theological questions
		-Moral theology	10			10	-Natural science
		-Aristotle, commentaries on Aristotle	11			11	-Logic
		-Natural philosophy -Logic	12			12	-Miscellany
		-Mathematics -Rhetoric, history, grammar	13				
		-Grammar, reference	14				

Fig. 1: Distribution of volumes in the Biblioteca Antoniana of Padua, 1449.

the homilies and the *Dialogi* of Gregory the Great and the popular *Diadema monachorum* by Smaragdus.

117 There were also copies of the *Summa theologica* by Alexander of Hales, the *Quaestiones* by Francis of Meyronnes and the *Quodlibetales* by Duns Scotus.

118 On the tenth bench were treatises like *De sphera*, as well as works by Aristotle such as the *De historia animalium*, the *Ethica*, the *De anima*, the *Physica* and the *Metaphysica*. The eleventh bench mainly had copies of the *Summa logicae* by William of Ockham.

119 There were two copies of the *Expositiones vocabulorum scripturae* by William Brito, one volume of *De bello civili* by Lucan, one exemplar of an anonymous *Ars dictandi*, one copy of the *De nuptiis Philologiae et Mercurii* by Martianus Capella and one volume described as a 'Pirtimanus sine principio'. It is worth noting that there were also two choir books available for loan, as registered on fol. 64ᵛ: 'Liber Cantus in magno volumine in papiro in aseribus et coreo rubeo per totum. Incipit in secundo quinterno "Ave maris stella" cum A magno laborato in medio cum figuris beate Virginis et aliis. Finis ultimus "CCCLXXXII". Liber in quinternis CC in cantu in papiro, cuius principium "Sanctus". Finis "seculi amen".'

The Library of San Francesco Grande in Padua

In the first half of the fifteenth century, Baldo Bonafari and his wife Sibila de Cetto founded an institution to receive the poor, the sick and pilgrims in the city of Padua.[120] In 1407 Baldo and his wife asked permission to carry out the project, and work began in October 1414.[121] Meanwhile, the idea of associating a church dedicated to St. Francis with the hospital took shape, and they obtained a licence for the foundation of a church and a small convent from the bishop of Padua in December 1416, and the right to perform divine offices in the church was granted to the Franciscans who depended exclusively from alms, that is 'viventes ex elemosinis'.[122] However, the spiritual care of the sick in the hospital and the rights of burial were to be allocated to the parish church, according to a bull issued by the pope in 1420. In the following year, Sibila died. In her last will she established that the convent should be occupied exclusively by Franciscan Observant friars, while the administration and government of the hospital should be the responsibility of a college of jurists.[123] The Franciscan community grew swiftly, and in a short time there were nearly fifty friars at the convent who formed an active international community. From 1444, the friars of the convent asked for and obtained the right to provide spiritual assistance to the sick and pilgrims in the hospital.[124]

The convent became one of the most important centres of the Observance in northern Italy and received Bernardino of Siena as a visiting master in 1423. In 1441, 1443, 1450 and 1451, the convent received John of Capistrano, Robert of Lecce and John Marchesinus. Usually, the visiting masters preached a cycle of sermons, many of which were transcribed in volumes destined to become part of the library collection.[125] The importance of the convent as a

---

120 Collodo, *Una società in trasformazione*, p. 473; see also Pantarotto, *La biblioteca manoscritta*, p. 8.

121 Collodo, *Una società in trasformazione*, pp. 481-84.

122 Collodo, *Una società in trasformazione*, p. 487. It is very probable that Baldo had known the Franciscan Observance during his stay in Venice during 1405-13, through the Venetian convent of San Francesco della Vigna. See F. Ferrari, *Il francescanesimo nel Veneto*, pp. 305-7. Silvana Collodo, however, argues that Bonafari's relation with the Observance began in 1413, when Bernardino of Siena visited the city for the first time. Collodo, *Una società in trasformazione*, p. 485.

123 Collodo, *Una società in trasformazione*, pp. 490-91.

124 Collodo, *Una società in trasformazione*, p. 520, and Pantarotto, *La biblioteca manoscritta*, p. 10.

125 Pantarotto, *La biblioteca manoscritta*, p. 11; see also Silvana Collodo, 'Il convento di S. Francesco'.

centre of education also grew steadily. Very soon it was able to offer not only basic levels of education but also the instruction required to gain access to the university, and by 1470 the convent became a *studium* of the Observant Venetian province. Consequently, at the end of the fifteenth century, the city of Padua could count on two Franciscan *studia* to support the training of the growing community of friars, many of whom had arrived in Padua as students of the university.[126]

During the early modern period, the convent grew as the needs of the hospital increased. By the beginning of the seventeenth century, the convent was the seat of the archive of the Observant province, and in 1634 it became a *studium generale*. During the seventeenth century, Augustine Macedo became the first Observant to hold a teaching position at the University of Padua. Another influential figure in the history of the convent was Michelangelo Carmeli, a scholar who carried out the project of the construction of a great library for the convent. The project included a detailed inventory that was finished in 1776.[127] By the end of the century the republic of Venice obtained control of the convent, and the Napoleonic invasion meant the suppression of the convent, the expropriation of all goods and the transfer of the books to a public library. The cloister was transformed into a military storehouse, and the Franciscan friars returned to the convent only in 1914.

During the fifteenth century, the Observant convent received gifts or bequests to allow the acquisition of books. The library also enriched its collection with the donations of books from students and visitors who lived in the hospital.[128] There are, therefore, good grounds to suppose the presence of a book collection contemporary with the early institutional life of the convent. Nevertheless, the earliest available document that describes the composition of the book collection dates from 10 January 1600. It is an inventory made during a search of the Congregation of the Index of Prohibited Books.[129] This inventory registered 193 manuscripts, giving their title and author and in some cases including a brief description of the contents if the work was a miscellany. The inventory distinguished manuscripts and printed volumes. A second inventory was made thirty-nine years later in the context of the compilation of the inventories of the libraries in Padua

---

126 Pantarotto, *La biblioteca manoscritta*, pp. 11 and 13; Collodo, *Una società in trasformazione*, pp. 527-28 and 553.

127 Pantarotto, *La biblioteca manoscritta*, p. 13.

128 Pantarotto, *La biblioteca manoscritta*, p. 12.

129 It is the current Vatican City, Biblioteca Apostolica Vaticana, MS Vat. Lat. 11283, fols. 40^r-54^v. See Lebreton and Fioriani, eds., *Codices Vaticani Latini*, pp. 112-13, and Pantarotto, *La biblioteca manoscritta*, p. 14.

under the direction of Iacopo Filippo Tomasini.[130] This was a list of the volumes available in the convent, and registered 128 volumes plus 17 from the convent of St. Ursula. This second inventory offered additional information on other aspects of the volumes such as the *incipit* and *explicit*, the date of the book and the works that formed part of a single volume, although the information was not always accurate. A third inventory was carried out in 1776, and is part of a miscellaneous manuscript currently in the Biblioteca Civica of Padua.[131] This inventory registered 346 manuscripts described with a great level of detail. This precision has permitted a secure identification of many volumes as books belonging to the library of the convent.

Recent research has made an important contribution to the reconstruction of the medieval book collection. Martina Pantarotto edited the three inventories of the library and identified the surviving medieval volumes.[132] She has also established, from codicological and philological evidence, a large corpus of manuscripts that undoubtedly were in the library before the year 1525. The main evidence is the enumeration of the leaves, completed on all the volumes of the collection during the late sixteenth century, plus the registration at the end of each volume of the total number of leaves and in some cases of quires. Moreover, there are traces of a precedent numeric system of reference, which was modified by the scribe of the sixteenth-century inventory.[133] Finally, she completed a careful and detailed description of each of the surviving volumes. This catalogue has been the principal resource for the following analysis of the main features of the fifteenth-century book collection of the convent of San Francesco Grande.

The Book Collection of the Convent of San Francesco Grande

It is not possible to assert beyond any doubt that there was a double library at the convent of San Francesco Grande in Padua during the fifteenth century. The earliest inventories available do not register the presence of chained and/or unchained books, and the absence of the original bindings makes it difficult to establish if the volumes were chained or not. Most probably the

---

130 Tomasini, *Bibliothecae Patavinae*.
131 Padua, Biblioteca Civica, MS B.P. 929. The inventory, which occupies thirty-nine leaves, is the sixth work of the miscellany. The volume lacks numeration. See Pantarotto, *La biblioteca manoscritta*, p. 16.
132 Pantarotto, *La biblioteca manoscritta*.
133 Pantarotto, *La biblioteca manoscritta*, p. 98. Additional evidence is provided by the absence of ownership inscriptions from later periods. This feature has been instrumental in establishing the presence of the volume in the convent during the fifteenth century.

books were available for consultation and loan without distinction, and in this perhaps characteristic feature of Observant collections had a decisive influence their being 'recent' libraries. In fact, only 5 out of 170 volumes were produced before the fifteenth century, and in the early stages of the life of the convent the dynamics of circulation, use and production of books were probably not clearly established.

On the nature of the collection, although it is not possible to reconstruct the distribution of the books in the space of the library, it is possible to identify the main thematic groups around which the library was organized. First, it is necessary to consider the presence of the Bible and biblical texts. Surprisingly, there are only two of these volumes in the corpus established by Pantarotto.[134] The first is a copy of the Bible from the thirteenth century. The second is a copy of the Epistles of Paul, included in a miscellany. Most probably, the circulating copies of the Bible were part of the collection of the sacristy and were therefore not registered in the inventories.

The most important part of the collection consisted of tools useful for the training of the preachers, including fifty-three volumes of postils, commentaries, compilations, treatises on the vices and virtues, and miscellanies of treatises on various topics. The authors were the leading masters of the order, especially the two main Observant preachers, Bernardino of Siena and John of Capistrano. However, the Dominican masters had an important place as well: there were works by Thomas Aquinas, and the library had a good number of copies of the works of the fourteenth-century Dominican master Antonino of Florence.[135] A copy of extracts from the *Divina Commedia* was included in a volume of treatises on moral subjects, which seems to be a personal copy prepared by friar Francis of Padua, who left it to the convent after his death.[136]

As we might expect from an Observant library, sermons constituted an important part of the collection. There were at least twenty-eight volumes of sermons, especially miscellanies including Fathers of the Church, Dominican masters such as Jacobus de Voragine, and the main Observant masters, especially Bernardino of Siena. Works such as the treatise *De ornatu et habitu mulierum* by Antonino of Florence were included in miscellanies of diverse subjects. There were just two copies of volumes of the lives of

134 Pantarotto, *La biblioteca manoscritta*, pp. 111 and 154.
135 See Kaeppeli, *Scriptores Ordinis Praedicatorum*, I, p. 80.
136 On fol. II[v] of Padua, Biblioteca Universitaria, MS 1030, there is a note: 'Hic liber est ad usum fratris Francisci minorite de civitate Patavii quem propria manu conscripsit et post mortem ipsius pertinet ad locum Padue.' See Pantarotto, *La biblioteca manoscritta*, p. 138.

saints, one of which was the *Legenda aurea* of Jacobus de Voragine. Among the six volumes on canon law were volumes of the *Decretals*, their tables of concordances, and treatises on the nature of the power of the pope. The theological treatises were important for the convent, as is shown by the number of volumes available. The main category was that of commentaries on the *Sentences* and the theological contents of the *Decretals*. The treatise *Compendium theologicae veritatis* by Hugo Ripelin de Argentina should be mentioned because it was available in a single copy of its vernacular version under the title *Spina e rosa*.[137] Then again, the literature of the Fathers was present with volumes concerning commentaries on biblical books or treatises on Christian spirituality such as the *Scala Paradisi* of John Climacus. An important section of the collection dealt with Franciscan institutional life. There were copies of the constitutions, of the bulls of the popes Nicholas III and Clement V, of the Franciscan rule and commentaries on the rule and the founder's *Testamentum*.

The presence of ten manuals of logic, grammar and similar works of reference illustrates the importance of these subjects of study in the Paduan convent. There were works such as the *Grammatica* of Gaspare of Verona, the *Summae grammaticae* of Petrus de Isolella, a copy of the *Orthographia* by Gasparino Barzizza and the *Sophismata* by William of Heytesbury. Although it did not constitute a big section of the library, classical literature was represented by works such as the *Achilleid*, the *Satires* of Juvenal, works by Cicero and a commentary by Nicholas Trivet on the tragedies of Seneca.[138] The library had a few books on natural sciences, particularly on astronomy and astrology, plus a treatise on natural philosophy known as the *Mare magnum*.[139] There were also volumes on Roman history, including a catalogue of the Roman emperors, and some philosophical treatises, especially the commentaries on Aristotle's works.

The library's earliest volume currently available was produced during the thirteenth century, with a very small number of works produced before the fifteenth century. The analysis of the traces left behind by the scribes suggests that a significant part of the collection was produced by the friars themselves, and so a clear choice in production favoured tools of study and

---

137 Pantarotto, *La biblioteca manoscritta*, p. 162.

138 The *Achilleid* is an unfinished epic poem by Statius that was intended to celebrate the life and deeds of Achilles. See Statius, *Achilleid*, ed. Dilke.

139 It is the current Padua, Biblioteca Universitaria, MS 1110, a paper manuscript in folio written during the fifteenth century, titled: *Theorica in lapide philosophico quae intitulatur Mare magnum*. See Pantarotto, *La biblioteca manoscritta*, pp. 30, 76 and 143; see also Thorndike and Kibre, *Catalogue of Incipits*, p. 305.

placed other genres, such as lives of saints, in a secondary role. From this description of the book collection of the library of San Francesco Grande it is possible to outline its profile as a working library focused on the education and training of preachers. This feature is consistent with the fact that *studia* among the Observance are prior to the process of affirmation of their libraries and hence it seems that the Observants arrived to the convent with their books and then, later, they bequeathed the volumes to the library.[140]

At this point, the profiles of the two main Franciscan libraries in Padua in the fifteenth century have been outlined. Both libraries were part of the order's system of *studia*, each coming from a different tradition with a particular interpretation of the rule and the role of learning and books within the community, as shown in Chapter 1. Although a 'topographical' inventory is not available for the Observant library, it is possible to propose a comparison between the two book collections in terms of their working methods, their size, their main orientation and the types of manuscripts available in each of them.

If the Biblioteca Antoniana applied the model of the double collection of books, that is, a division between chained and unchained volumes according to the needs of reading and study, there is no indication of a similar situation for the library of San Francesco Grande. The few surviving original bindings do not suggest the presence of chained books, and the earliest inventories of the Observant library show no trace of a double collection. Moreover, it is possible that in the Observant library there was a single collection of books, all unchained, available for loan and copy. This means that the model of the double library was not always followed by mendicants and that its application depended on the particular circumstances of the convent and could be linked to specific practices of reading and study, as will be discussed below.

A second feature of comparison and contrast is the size of the libraries. By the end of the fifteenth century, the Biblioteca Antoniana was a firmly established library with almost three centuries of history and one of the biggest book collections of the order, which had grown remarkably between the fourteenth and the fifteenth century, and this situation certainly reflected the importance of the convent as a centre of spirituality and study.[141] In contrast, the library of the convent of San Francesco Grande had existed for only seventy years, and although the number of volumes available was far smaller than that of the Biblioteca Antoniana, the size of its collection

---

140 See Letizia Pellegrini, 'Cultura del libro e pratiche', p. 197.
141 Hernández Vera, 'Space in the Cupboard'.

was, proportionally speaking, remarkable. The importance of the convent as an Observant centre and the high profile of its *studium* were strong incentives for the growth of the library collection. Certainly, there was a close relationship with the students who stayed as permanent guests in the hospital, to the extent that it was not uncommon for a student to abandon his course in favour of the religious life under the habit of an Observant friar.

Conclusion

This overview of the development and main features of the two Franciscan libraries allows us to formulate a few observations. After presenting a set of conclusions for each of the Paduan libraries, a set of general observations on the role of Franciscan libraries as the space for the Franciscan book will be offered.

The analysis of the fifteenth-century inventory of the Biblioteca Antoniana shows that, by the end of the Middle Ages, the library was firmly established with more than a thousand volumes available. An overview of the contents of the library shows that it offered a complete set of tools for study, from reference books to volumes on devotional, theological, philosophical and scientific subjects. However, the strength of the collection relied on its impressive set of sermons. This means that the Biblioteca Antoniana was mainly a space devoted to the intellectual training of the preacher through individual study. This conception of study and use of books made loans, even life-long loans, necessary.[142]

The description of the location of the books confirms that the main purpose of the Biblioteca Antoniana during the fifteenth century was to offer the necessary tools for the education of the preacher in complete accordance with the general programme of the order.[143] This is particularly clear for the Bible, the biblical texts and the biblical commentaries: the chained volumes were located on the first ten benches on the right-hand side. The copies for loan were available in the first six cupboards on the left-hand side. The chained manuscripts of the *Sentences* were on the first two benches on the left-hand side, and their copies were available for loan in the first four cupboards on the right-hand side. In another case, five cupboards with volumes of sermons corresponded to five benches of chained volumes on the right-hand side.

142 Şenocak, 'Circulation of Books', pp. 153-54.
143 Roest, *History of Franciscan Education*, pp. 276-90.

This particular arrangement leads to a second observation. To place the books for loan on the opposite side of their respective chained volumes may seem an unusual pattern of organization.[144] It would in fact be more practical to locate all the copies of one chained work on the same side, keeping the volumes for loan stored in the adjacent cupboards. The systematic distribution of the volumes on opposite sides suggests that this arrangement of the space was deliberate. Most probably, it had the purpose of achieving a homogeneous distribution of the volumes in the repositories, avoiding an imbalance in the layout of the library and simultaneously securing a quick, efficient way to verify the availability of copies for loan.[145]

The third observation regards the topics. The compilation of the inventory followed the layout of the library, allowing us to identify the order in which the topics were located. In the case of the chained books, the most significant part of the collection was formed by the Bible and biblical texts, the commentaries on the biblical text, a complete collection of sermons on biblical topics, the *Sentences* and its commentaries. These were followed by volumes on philosophy, the works of the Fathers of the Church, the books on canon law, moral theology, the works of Aristotle and the treatises on natural philosophy, sciences and grammar. The organization of the topics in the cupboards was very similar. First came the Bible and biblical texts, followed by concordances, postils and sermons – then, the glossed books of the Bible, the *Sentences* and its commentaries. This set was complemented by books on canon law, hagiography, theology, natural sciences and logic. This arrangement reflected a hierarchy of the sources of authority and knowledge, a practice that was not unusual in the mendicant libraries.[146]

In the library of Sant'Antonio the Bible, the supreme source of authority, was followed by the writings of the masters of the order, the Fathers of

144 A similar practice was not followed in the Franciscan libraries of Assisi, Florence or Siena. In Assisi, the chained books and those for loan were located in different rooms. See Cenci, ed., *Bibliotheca manuscripta*, I, p. 33; see also Grauso, 'La biblioteca francescana medievale di Assisi', pp. 40-79. In the case of the Franciscan library of Santa Croce in Florence, the whole collection was chained to two rows of benches. See Humphreys, *Book Provisions*, p. 112; Davis, 'Early Collection of Books of S. Croce in Florence'; and O'Gorman, *Architecture of the Monastic Library*, pp. 52-53. In the case of the library of the convent of Siena, the inventory did not provide information on the specific location of the cupboards in relation to the benches. See Humphreys, *Library of the Franciscans of Siena*, pp. 15-16.

145 See Hernández Vera, 'From Chained Books to Portable Collections', pp. 91-97.

146 The hierarchy of the topics was established following the criterion of importance. Usually, this principle appeared more clearly in the collection of books for loan, mainly because they were used for individual study after becoming part of the collection through more informal and complex processes. See Bassetti, 'I libri "degli antichi"', pp. 432-33 and 444-45.

the Church and the tools of reference. This would mean that the Fathers of the Church had a secondary role in relation to the Franciscan masters. In effect, the works of the Fathers were usually part of the intellectual training of the student, but they were not a principal subject of study or commentary by the Franciscan friars.[147] As a result of the mendicant approach to reading and learning, the Fathers of the Church played a complementary role and were limited, apart from Augustine, to supporting the innovative reflections and discussions of the masters.[148] By reflecting the order's new approach to the sources of intellectual authority, the organization of the library offers further evidence of its role as a space devoted to providing, as effectively as possible, the required tools for the education of the Franciscan preacher.

At first sight, the two libraries seem very similar: both were working libraries strongly focused on education and training, and both catered to the concrete needs of study. However, there were significant differences. First, a remarkable difference was apparent in the number of available copies of the Bible. While the collection of the Biblioteca Antoniana could offer a magnificent Bible in several volumes of large size, nothing similar seems to be listed in the Observant library, or if it was, it did not leave any trace of its presence. On the other hand, if it is true that both of the libraries were focused on study and the training of preachers, it is also true that they differed significantly in their exact interests. While the Biblioteca Antoniana had a strong emphasis on collections of sermons and theological and philosophical literature, the main part of the collection of the library of San Francesco Grande was dedicated to biblical commentaries, postils and treatises. This difference is reflected in the proportion of philosophical literature in each collection: it is high in the Biblioteca Antoniana and barely perceptible in the library of San Francesco Grande. Another point of difference is the importance of the manuscripts dedicated to lives of saints. Their presence in the Biblioteca Antoniana is significant, while in the library of San Francesco Grande there are only two copies of the best-known works on the topic. This apparent lack of interest could be explained by the fact that the commentaries and postils could provide the required hagiographical knowledge. A great difference also appears in the literature containing regulations, constitutions and dispositions regarding the Franciscan order. While there is almost no trace of these works in the Biblioteca

---

147 Roest, *History of Franciscan Education*, pp. 123-32 and 250-58.
148 Hamesse, 'Scholastic Model of Reading', pp. 103-6.

Antoniana, apart from a few works lost on loan, there are at least ten volumes on the subject in the Observant library, reflecting the strong interest of the Observance in emphasizing the legitimacy of their way of life within the Franciscan order.[149]

This brief overview of the libraries' inventories also offers a glimpse of the system of production and growth of the collections of books. In both collections, donations, legacies and internal production played a significant part in their rate of growth. However, according to codicological evidence, such as the notes from scribes, it seems that by the end of the fifteenth century the rate of production of personal copies for study was significantly higher in the Observant library.[150] Those copies were meant for personal use and were normally left to the convent on the death of the possessor. Perhaps the libraries represented two different ways of understanding the discipline of study at the end of the fifteenth century: it seems that while the Biblioteca Antoniana strongly focused on reading and studying, the Observant friars 'kept the quill in hand', that is, they were deeply committed to the continuous production of books.[151]

At this point it will be helpful to recall the figures of Boethius and Cassiodorus as personifications of two different models of development for book collections. Medieval libraries are usually seen as strictly 'Cassiodorean', that is, as book collections devoted to satisfying the needs of a community. The 'Boethian' library, that is, the personal library, is seen as a characteristic feature of modern humanism. Nevertheless, as will be seen in the following chapters, some examples of Franciscan manuscripts suggest they played the role of personal, portable libraries that reflected the expectations, needs and intellectual background of their owners who, as users of the libraries, were no longer the simple, unlearned Franciscan friars of the origins of the order, but friars devoted to writing and reading, that is 'fratres rescribentes vel legentes', as described by Bonaventure.[152] As it has been shown, Franciscan book collections were organized to satisfy the needs of readers capable of using more than one book at a time, that is, of scholars who followed a programme of training that aimed at intellectual achievement, even if

---

149 The inventory of the Biblioteca Antoniana shows that a master Francis of Belluno had on loan a set of volumes among which were the general and provincial constitutions of the order, the constitutions of Pope Benedict XI, the privileges of the order and the rule of the Poor Claires. See Appendix 1.

150 Pantarotto, *La biblioteca manoscritta*, pp. 98-100.

151 Giovè Marchioli, 'La cultura scritta al Santo', pp. 386-88; Hernández Vera, 'From Chained Books to Portable Collections'.

152 Bonaventure of Bagnoregio, *Opera Omnia*, VIII, p. 350.

formally subordinated to preaching.[153] In other words, and according to Salimbene of Adam, Franciscan libraries were a place where the enthusiastic and intellectually proud friar Hugh of Digne could feel perfectly at home.

After exploring the development, organization, role and significance of *space* as the dimension of the Franciscan book that represents the places where Franciscan books were collected, organized and made available for their readers, it is time to take a closer look at the manuscripts themselves.

---

153 Roest, *History of Franciscan Education*, pp. 278-81; see also Robson, *Greyfriars of England*, pp. 219-24 and 229-34. The practice of reading more than one book simultaneously is illustrated by the list of books on loan of the inventory of the Biblioteca Antoniana, MS 573, on fols. 64ᵛ-66ᵛ. See Appendix 1; see also Humphreys, *Library of the Franciscans of the Convent of St. Antony*, pp. 177-84.

3. The Form

The Manuscripts

Introduction

By the middle of thirteenth century, the English Benedictine monk Matthew Paris described, with a hint of praise, an interesting group of newcomers. In his *Historia Anglorum*, he wrote how these men carried a great number of books, practically entire libraries, in sacks hanging from their necks and how over time 'they built schools, cloisters and lofty churches and how within their confines they established schools of theology and fervently talked to the people, bringing back no small crop to the barn of Christ, where the harvest was rich, but the labourers so few.'[1]

These peculiar characters were Franciscan friars, members of a community whose main elements of identity were, at the time, engagement in pastoral care, preaching and books, despite the fact that, according to their founder, books were not required for the friars to live in the simplicity of the first Christian group of apostles.[2] Still, by the second half of the thirteenth century, Franciscans had transformed themselves from a brotherhood of simple laypeople into an order of masters of theology, science and philosophy. Of course, the main tools of that transformation were their books, which leads one to ask: What were the contents of these books? How were they constructed physically? How were they employed? Furthermore, can these volumes provide us with clues on the friars' conception of the book? These questions will guide the discussion in this chapter.

---

1 'Libros continue suos, videlicet bibliotecas, in forulis a collo dependentes baiulantes. Tandem scholas edificaverunt, deinde domos et claustra, denuo, magnatibus sumptus sufficienter administrantibus, ecclesias et officinas amplias et excelsas fabricaverunt [...] Tandem scholas theologie infra septa sua constituentes, legentes et disputantes et populo predicantes, fructum ad horrea Christi, quia messis multa et operarii pauci fuerant, non modicum reportarunt.' Mattheus Parisiensis, *Historia Anglorum*, p. 397.
2 For further detail, see Chapter 1.

Hernández Vera, R., *Franciscan Books and their Readers: Friars and Manuscripts in Late Medieval Italy*. Taylor & Francis Group, 2022
DOI 10.5117/9789463729512_CH03

After exploring aspects of the Franciscan manuscript such as the relation between its ideal and its reality, as well as the space where it was collected and read, it will be useful to assess the relation between the manuscripts' physical characteristics and purpose according to their contents and use. This is the sense that the dimension of the 'form' of the manuscripts will assume within this study. The first chapter of this book discussed the set of regulations on the use of books within the Franciscan order, as well as how these regulations were followed in the convents of Sant'Antonio and San Francesco Grande in Padua. Chapter 2 explored and compared the libraries of these Paduan convents and established significant differences that reflected the particular interests and the nature of each of them. Taking the comparative approach further, the current chapter will examine a corpus of manuscripts in order to identify distinctive characteristics that could reflect, not only a typology of manuscripts, but also of their readers during the fifteenth century. This typology plays an important role in the discussion of Franciscan readership. The analysis will show that there are substantial differences between the books collected and read in each of the convents. These differences regard not only their contents but, more profoundly, their physical characteristics and especially their composition as volumes, which suggests the presence of distinct practices of reading, a topic that will be explored further in the last chapter.

In order to proceed with the analysis, two sets of manuscripts have been established, one from the library of the convent of Sant'Antonio, namely the Biblioteca Antoniana, and one from the library of San Francesco Grande. The manuscripts selected are representative of the most important genres collected in each library. Accordingly, the set for the Biblioteca Antoniana consists of several copies of a theological treatise and a collection of sermons, while the set from the library of San Francesco Grande is constituted by tools for the composition of sermons and collections of sermons. The study of the manuscripts proceeds, first, by examining and comparing the volumes from the same set, and then by comparing the two sets.

Manuscripts from the Library of the Convent of Sant'Antonio

As shown in the first chapter, the history of the Biblioteca Antoniana practically starts with the arrival of Franciscan friars in Padua in 1229. During the late thirteenth and the fourteenth centuries the convent followed different strategies to improve the book collection to meet the expectations and needs of the education of the friars.[3] The library received donations to buy books for one particular friar or for the library, as shown, for example, by the last will of Zilio Teco, who in 1253 left 100 lire to the convents of Vicenza and Padua for the acquisition of books, or the last will of Ziborga, who left 200 lire to her son in order to buy books, but only if he became a friar.[4] As a result, the library collection grew steadily and by the late fourteenth century it had a remarkable collection.[5]

Although there is no specific study dedicated to the typology of texts collected in the library, the information provided by the early inventories reveals that there were copies of the Bible, works useful for pastoral care, works of theology, reference books, collections and tools for the composition of sermons, and texts of law and philosophy.[6] As discussed in Chapter 2, the main purpose of Franciscan education was to provide the friars with the tools essential to fulfilling the duty of preaching, and the libraries of the convents reflected that purpose.[7] The most important of these tools were theological treatises and collections of sermons, which had the role of providing models for the composition of new sermons.[8] Therefore, in order to have representative volumes for the analysis, the corpus of selected manuscripts consists of four copies of a theological treatise and four copies of a collection of sermons, both written by influential masters of the order and

3   See Fontana, 'La bibliothèque du convent', pp. 13-24.
4   'Legavit et dari iusit centum libras denariorum veronensium pro facere libros conventui et fratribus de sancto Francisco de Vicentia de ordine fratrum minorum. [...] Item legavit centum libras denariorum veronensium pro facere libro conventui et fratribus minoribus de Padua de Sancto Antonio.' See Sartori, *Archivio Sartori*, II, p. 2313; see also Fontana, *Frati, libri e insegnamento*, pp. 94-98; for Ziborga's last will, see Chapter 2, note 77.
5   Bartoli Langeli, 'I libri dei frati', pp. 286-87; see also Frioli, 'Gli antichi inventari della Biblioteca Antoniana di Padova', pp. 75-76, and Humphreys, *Library of the Franciscans of the Convent of St. Anthony*, p. 7.
6   A consistent typology of the texts *used* by the Franciscan friars would be a helpful tool for the description of Franciscan intellectual history. In the specific case of the Biblioteca Antoniana, Emanuele Fontana identifies the following main genres: texts for study and the *cura animarum*, the Bible and texts of theology, complete works and collections of authorities, lexicographical tools, collections of sermons and *artes praedicandi*, collections of *legendae*, collections of exempla, and texts of law and philosophy. This typology reproduces the classification of books established by the librarians who compiled the inventories. Therefore, only the direct examination of the manuscripts would provide the information necessary to establish different levels of use and a more accurate image of texts actually read and studied by the friars. See Fontana, *Frati, libri e insegnamento*, pp. 109-43.
7   Roest, *History of Franciscan Education*, pp. 277-79.
8   Roest, *History of Franciscan Education*, pp. 80-81 and 85-87, and D'Avray, *Preaching of the Friars*, pp. 64-65, and particularly 78-81.

studied during the fourteenth and fifteenth centuries, when the convent of Sant'Antonio became one of the most prestigious *studia generalia* in Italy.[9]

A Theological Treatise: The Commentary on the First Book of the Sentences *by Bonaventure of Bagnoregio*

An increasing tendency towards the exhaustive codification of knowledge produced fundamental works for medieval scholastic culture such as the *Glossa ordinaria*. In 1155-57 Peter Lombard, a canon of the cathedral school of Notre Dame in Paris, composed a compilation of theological questions systematically arranged around major topics in four volumes. His work, known as the *Sentences*, became the most influential theological treatise of the Middle Ages. The first book considered God and the Trinity; the second, the creation; the third, the Incarnation and the virtues; and the fourth, the sacraments and the Last Judgement. By 1215, the *Sentences* was recognized by the Fourth Council Lateran as a text that should be used in the schools, and it became an undisputed source of written authority from the second half of the thirteenth century.[10] With the development of universities, it was required that candidates for the highest degrees in theology produce their own commentary on the *Sentences*. This process of commenting became so influential that Peter Lombard's treatise was often studied through the commentaries rather than directly through the original text.

One of the most important commentaries on the *Sentences* was written by the Franciscan master Bonaventure of Bagnoregio.[11] The Biblioteca Antoniana had several copies of this work, as shown by the 1449 inventory: there were copies available for consultation chained to the second bench on the left-hand side, and more than fourteen volumes for loan located in the second cupboard on the right-hand side.[12] Currently the Biblioteca Antoniana holds fourteen manuscripts of Bonaventure's commentary on the *Sentences*, four of which – MSS 120, 123, 124 and 125 – are copies of the commentary on the first book.[13]

---

9   Fontana, *Frati, libri e insegnamento*, pp. 64-67.

10   Rosemann, *Peter Lombard*, pp. 8-70; Colish, *Peter Lombard*, I, pp. 33-154; Friedman, *'Sentences Commentary'*, pp. 41-128; and Asztaloz, 'Faculty of Theology', pp. 412-15.

11   Cullen, *Bonaventure*, pp. 15-16, and Bougerol, *Introduction to the Works of Bonaventure*, pp. 99-108.

12   Padua, Biblioteca Antoniana, MS 573, fols. 16^v and 50^v-51^r.

13   There are four copies of the commentary on the first book; three copies of the commentary on the second book: MSS 121, 126 and 127; three copies of the commentary on the third book:

MS 120 is a parchment volume of 332 × 232 mm, produced during the fourteenth century.[14] Its binding consists of wooden boards covered in leather. On the inside of the front plate there are traces of the clasp that held the ring connected to the chain.[15] The 153 leaves of the manuscript are organized into thirteen quires. The text is written in a formal gothic book hand, distributed in two columns with decoration limited to initials in red, accompanied by coloured paragraph marks, or paraphs, in red and turquoise. There are some notes that do not comment on the text but had the purpose of confirming that the manuscript belonged to the library of Sant'Antonio, according to the dispositions of the chapter of Verona.[16]

Readers left three types of written traces of their interaction with MS 120: marginal references, useful to 'navigate' through the text; marginal additions or corrections; and marginal comments. Some examples of references employed by readers of the MS can be found especially at the beginning of the volume, as in fols. 1^r-2^r, where there is a system of marginal lines drawn to the left of each column, useful for identifying the main divisions of the text. Each line is accompanied by a number, which corresponds to a heading of the paragraph.[17] Another set of marginal notes, written in a late hand, most probably from the fifteenth century, provides complementary references such as 'Primus liber' or 'Secundus liber', but these go no further than fol. 1^v. A third form of reference consists of short marginal references commonly introduced by the word 'Nota', and used to indicate a passage

MSS 119, 128 and 129; and four copies of the commentary on the fourth book: MSS 122, 130, 131 and 213.

14 See Appendix 3, Plate 3. For a detailed description, see Abate and Luisetto, *Codici e manoscritti*, I, pp. 161-62; see also Humphreys, *Library of the Franciscans of the Convent of St. Anthony*, p. 152.

15 Some examples of this system of chaining are available in Clark, *Care of Books*, pp. 159 and 175.

16 On fol. II^r: 'Iste liber primus Bonaventure deputatus est conventui padue ordinis minorum per capitulum provinciale celebratum Veronae. Ad voluntatem ministri pro exemplari ad tempus, propter studentes provinciales, tamen provinciae est liber iste'; on fol. I^r, there is a prayer: 'Domina sancta Maria que oratis pro omnibus orate per famulo vestro ad sanctum regem glorie, quia tanta sunt peccata nostra quod non possumus avere misericordiam [...]'; and on fol. II^v, there is a note: 'Conventus Padue est Bonaventure super sententias iste primus.' See Abate and Luisetto, *Codici e manoscritti*, I, p. 161; Fontana, *Frati, libri e insegnamento*, pp. 118-19. Many marginal notes in the manuscripts of the Biblioteca Antoniana were transcribed in Padua, Biblioteca Antoniana, MS 590, Paulus Franciscus Munegatus, *Collectio rerum ante initium et post finem Codicum scriptarum*. It is an autograph paper manuscript from the nineteenth century, of 285 × 195 mm and ninety-two leaves. It gathers together the notes on many of the flyleaves.

17 Accordingly, the number 1 corresponds to 'Primo propter prehemptionem'; 2, to 'Secundo, propter spaciositatem'; 3, to 'Tercio propter circulationem denaru fluvii'; 4, to 'Quarto propter emendationem' – and so on.

worthy of attention. Similarly, there are marginal references to indicate the place where the word 'Respondeo' introduces an answer to a question or where the words 'Contra' or 'Opinio' introduce arguments to be discussed by the author. An example of this type of reference may be found on fol. 25^r, where Bonaventure discusses a question by explaining three different arguments. These arguments are indicated by a fifteenth-century annotator, who wrote in a marginal note '1^a oppinio [sic]', to indicate the first argument; '2^a Opinio', to locate the second argument; and finally, 'Opinio Magistri', to indicate the doctrine of Peter Lombard, according to the interpretation of Bonaventure.[18]

Short summaries of the contents, written in the margins of the manuscript, constitute another form of reference. For example, on fol. 3^r, a fourteenth-century hand wrote: 'Three types of men'.[19] The same hand added the following words on fol. 3^v: 'writer, compiler, commenter, author' to indicate the place where Bonaventure discussed the different forms of authorship.[20] Further, a fifteenth-century hand wrote a simple scheme in the margin of fol. 23^r as a quick reference to summarize the types of necessity: 'Necessity of violence/ necessity of coercion; necessity of want/ necessity unavoidable; necessity of exigence/ necessity unchanged.'[21] A similar type of summary is found on fol. 94^r. In the margin, a fifteenth-century hand wrote, 'Threefold relation', to locate the beginning of Bonaventure's argumentation on the relation between reality and names of God.[22] Another example may be found on fol. 131^v, where the forty-second distinction considers the

---

18   Bonaventure of Bagnoregio, *Opera Omnia*, I, pp. 135-36.

19   'Tria genera hominum.'

20   'Scriptor, compilator, comentator, auctor.'

21   'Necessitas violentie/ necessitas coactionis, necessitas indigentie/ necessitas inevitabilis, necessitas exigentie/ necessitas inmutatis [sic].' This typology of necessity is treated in the sixth distinction of the *Sentences*. Specifically, Bonaventure discusses whether or not the generation of the Son, the second person of the Trinity, is to be attributed to a rational necessity, as is stated in the heading of the first question on fol. 23^r: 'Utrum generatio Filii sit secundum rationem necessitatis'. Bonaventure explains that necessity could arise from one of three principles: 'Disconveniente', 'Deficiente' or 'Conveniente et Sufficiente'. If necessity comes from the principle 'Disconveniente', it could be 'violentie' or 'coactionis'; if it comes from the principle 'Deficiente', it could be 'indigentie' or 'inevitabilis'; and finally if necessity comes from the principle 'Conveniente et sufficiente', it could be 'exigentie' or 'immutabilitatis'. See Bonaventure of Bagnoregio, *Opera Omnia*, I, pp. 125-26.

22   'Relatio triplex.' The passage is part of the third question of the thirtieth distinction. It considers whether the names convey any real relation in God. Bonaventure answers that there is a threefold relation between names and reality: 'Respondeo ad hoc intelligendum est, quod dici secundum relationem est dupliciter: aut secundum rem, aut secundum modum. Realis autem relatio triplex est.'

power of God. In the first question, Bonaventure discusses whether God can be other than himself. An insertion mark leads to the end of the leaf, where a fifteenth-century hand summarizes the contents of the answer: by and towards himself, God can be considered other than himself either as distinct, according to essences, and remote, according to distance; or, according to forms and essences, as unitary and not remote but rather within distance.[23] On fol. 152^v, there is another example of the summaries employed by the readers of the manuscript. A fourteenth-century hand wrote in the margin 'On threefold will', to identify the passage of distinction 48 where Bonaventure uses the authority of Hugh of St. Victor to support his account of the human will.[24]

Marginal comments were also used to correct or to add missing parts of the text. For example, the text of the *proemium* is corrected by a marginal addition on fol. 1^v.[25] Something similar happens on fol. 2^v, where Bonaventure answers a question concerning theological knowledge.[26] On fol. 7^r, there is another significant addition to the text, under the question of whether God is the most perfect source of joy.[27] Small additions and corrections of this type were made by a set of at least four different hands from the fourteenth to the early fifteenth century, and may be found all over the manuscript,

23 The transcription of the passage is as follows: 'Respondeo ad hoc intelligendum notandum est quod posse aliud sive in aliud a se hoc est dupliciter [*Insertion mark*]: aut in aliud sicut in distinctum secundum essentiam.' The insertion mark corresponds to a summary of the answer written on the bottom of the leaf: 'Posse in ad a se essere dividitur aut in/ -pro sicut in distinctum secundum essentias et remotum secundo distantiam./ -pro sicut in divisum secundum formas et essentias non tamen in remotum sed aliquam distantiam.'

24 'Voluntate triplex.' Bonaventure discusses the conformity of human will to divine will in distinction 48. In the second question of the second article, he reflects on whether human will is bound to conform to divine will regarding the object of the will itself, and answers affirmatively, using as part of his argument the authority of Hugh of St. Victor: 'Unde Hugo distinguit in nobis triplicitem voluntatem scilicet rationis, pietatis et carnis, et in Christo quadruplicem, extendens nomen voluntatis.' See Cullen, *Bonaventure*, pp. 92-96.

25 'Profundum creationis est vanitas esse creati. Creatur enim quanto magis evanescit [*Insertion mark, and in the margin, a fifteenth-century hand adds in formal gothic script*: tanto magis in profundum tenit, sive evanescat] per culpam sive per poenam.'

26 The introduction to the answer is as follows: 'Respondeo dicendum quod subiectum in aliqua scientia vel doctrina tripliciter potest accipi. Uno modo dicitur subiectum in scientia [*Insertion mark, and in the margin, a later hand adds in formal gothic script*: ad quod omnia reducuntur tamquam ad primum radicale. Alio modo] ad quae omnia reducuntur sicud ad totum integrale.'

27 Bonaventure answers that only God is the source of joy in the second question of the third article of the first distinction: 'Respondeo dicendum quod solo domino est fruendum proprie accepto frui pro ut dicim motum [*Insertion mark, and in the margin a fourteenth-century hand adds*: cum dilectatione et quietatione sed convenitur accepto frui pro ut dicim motum] cum dilectatione tantum omnibus.'

which suggests that the volume was used intensively and more importantly that it was carefully revised and corrected by its readers.[28]

Another purpose of the marginal notes was to keep a record of personal comments. Among examples is one on fol. 26^r, where a note indicates the lack of understanding of a passage of the seventh distinction.[29] The reader, however, did not provide any correction, most probably because the available copies of the work had the same unclear version of the text.[30] Another example may be found on fol. 55^r. In the introduction to the commentary on the sixteenth distinction, Bonaventure explains the topics to be considered. However, a marginal note, written by a fourteenth-century hand, warns of the master's lack of understanding, most probably as a way of underlining an inconsistency in the transcription, since the second part of the question is discussed in the following distinction.[31] On fol. 148^v, a third example of a comment may be found, where Bonaventure clarifies some doubts at the end of the forty-sixth distinction. The consideration of the doctrine of Ambrose concerning the different grades of truth in relation to the Spirit prompts a fourteenth-century hand to write in the margin that the argument reveals a higher form of truth: 'Nota de veritate superiore', both as a dramatic synthesis of the argument and as a personal reflection on the topic.

The second copy of Bonaventure's commentary is MS 123, a parchment manuscript of 315 × 228 mm produced during the fourteenth century.[32] Its

---

28   Some of the most significant additions can be found on fols. 5^r, 6^v, 9^v, 12^r, 13^r, 18^v, 47^r and 129^r.

29   'Et sic non intelligitur'.

30   The excerpt of the answer to the second question of the seventh distinction appears in MS 120 as follows: 'Unde secundum artem distinguendum est quando dicitur Filius non potuit generare, quia non potest tenere privative; et tunc est sensus, non potuit, id est impotens fuit; et tunc negatur potentia, et relinquitur aptitudo, sicud de truncato dicitur, quod non potest gradi [*Insertion mark.*] de filio quia non habet ad hoc aptitudinem [*In the margin, in a fourteenth-century hand*: Et sic non intelligitur].' MSS 123 and 124 have the same text, with a slight variant, in italics in the following transcription: 'non potest gradi *hec modo non potest dici* de filio quia non habet ad hoc aptitudinem.' MS 125 has a late marginal correction as follows: 'Et tunc negatur potentia et relinquitur aptitudo sicud de truncato dicitur quod non potest gradi [*Insertion mark, and in the margin, by a fifteenth-century hand*: quia aptus natus est ad contradicendi et generandi non potest hoc modo non potest dici] de filio quia non habet ad hoc aptitudinem.' The established version of the text is as follows: 'Unde secundum artem distinguendum est, quando dicitur, Filius non potuit generare: quia non potest tenere privative; et tunc est sensus, non potuit, id est, impotens fuit; et tunc negatur potentia, et relinquitur aptitudo, sicud de truncato dicitur, quod non potest gradi quia aptus natus est ad gradiendum et non potest gradi; hoc modo non potest dici de filio, quia non habet ad hoc aptitudinem.' See Bonaventure of Bagnoregio, *Opera Omnia*, I, pp. 140.

31   'Nota que hic Magister non tenetur.'

32   Abate and Luisetto, *Codici e manoscritti*, I, pp. 163-64.

binding consists of wooden boards covered in leather. The back cover and fol. 154 have traces left by the support for the clasp linked to a chain. The manuscript has 154 leaves, organized in thirteen quires, written in two main scripts: fols. 1 to 36 are written by a late fourteenth-century gothic cursive hand with strong signs of a notarial training, while from fol. 37 the script shifts to a more formal, gothic book hand, most probably Italian and highly abbreviated.[33] The text is organized in two columns, decorated with coloured titles in red and blue with the initials of the chapters in blue, and paraphs.

MS 123 also has three types of marginal comment. The first are references to locate some passages and to summarize contents. For example, on fol. 1[v] a late hand wrote three references in order to locate the summary of three books of the work in the introduction.[34] On fol. 12[r], there is another example of this type of reference. In order to indicate the passage of the third distinction where Bonaventure explains the three types of memory, a fifteenth-century hand writes in the margin: 'memoria triplex'.[35] Further, on fol. 18[v], another reader elaborated a complex scheme in the margin of the text to summarize the contents of the passage, specifically the types of necessity according to the first question of the sixth distinction.[36] These marginal references are very frequent throughout the first half of the volume.[37] Corrections to the text are also frequent in MS 123. For example, on fol. 19[r] there is a marginal correction to the third question of the sixth distinction, where Bonaventure considers the generation of the Son as part of the Trinity.[38] There is another example on fol. 38[r], in the second question under the first article of the fourteenth distinction. Bonaventure concludes that it is appropriate to attribute a twofold process to the Spirit, eternal and

33 See Appendix 3, Plate 4.

34 'Nota hoc primi liber sententiarum/ Nota hoc secundi liber/ Nota hoc tercii liber.'

35 Bonaventure discusses whether the reckoning of the image is attained in the memory, intelligence and will in the first question of the first article of the second part. He explains that one type of memory is receptive and retentive of past and sensitive things, the second kind of memory is merely retentive of past things, either sensitive or intelligible, while the third memory is retentive of the species, that is, of the abstract qualities: 'Memoria accipitur tripliciter: uno modo prout est receptiva et retentiva sensibilium et praeteritorum; alio modo prout est retentiva praeteritorium, sive sensibilium sive intelligibilium; et tertio modo prout est retentiva specierum, abstraendo ab omni differentia temporis, utpote specierum innatarum.' See Cullen, *Bonaventure*, p. 56.

36 See the description of MS 120, fol. 23[r] above.

37 Some examples on fols. 19[v], 20[r], 16[v], 20[v], 23[v], 24[r], 40[v], 41[r], 41[v], 42[v], 44[v] and so on. Their frequency decreases on the second half of the manuscript.

38 The text is corrected as follows: 'sed quos fit vel datur ex liberalitate [*Insertion mark, and in the margin, in another hand*: et sic creaturae procedunt a Deo; alio modo sicut illud quod est ratio liberalitatis] ut amor et sic procedit.'

temporal. Part of his argumentation was revised and corrected by a reader of the fifteenth century.[39]

Comments can also be found in the margins of MS 123. One example is fol. 14[r], where a fifteenth-century reader comments on the subject of having knowledge of God by referring to another source of authority, master Richard of St. Victor.[40] On fol. 15[r], a marginal reference comments on the third question of distinction 4, where Bonaventure discusses whether according to the rules of grammar, that is, logically, it could be said that there are many gods. Bonaventure mentions the words 'phoenix' and 'sun' as examples in one of his arguments. These examples prompted a reflection on the relation between potency and act, according to what a reader wrote at the bottom of the leaf.[41] On fol. 37[v], there is another comment, this time on the second question under the first article of the sixteenth distinction. There, Bonaventure discusses whether the eternal and temporal processions of the Spirit should be considered as two different processions.[42] The consideration of the arguments against the proposition includes an analysis of the nature and origin of such processions.[43] One reader wrote in a fifteenth-century script a complementary marginal comment on the same subject.[44] Another example of personal comments may be found on fol. 46[v], where there is a marginal comment on distinction 17, question 2. Bonaventure discusses whether charity is to be loved out of charity.[45] A fifteenth-century hand followed the argument and commented on the first forms and the reflection

---

39 The correction states that a twofold way of calling things is not equivocal but analogical, and proceeds as follows: 'Scilicet aut quia duplex modus dicendi numquid equivocus [*Insertion mark, and in the margin, in a late hand*: non univocus sed analogicus] et per hoc pars sequens de homine picto et vero quia illi non est analogia sed equivocacio pura.'

40 'Ricardus de sancto V[ictore] dicet quod est vera essentiam graciam, sed vero tenetur in hic capi.'

41 'The form is multiple: in potency and act, as in the form of a man. In potency, but not in act, like in the form of the phoenix. In potency of the form but not in act, due to lack of material potency, like in the form of the Sun. And finally, neither in potency nor in act but only in the intellect like the form of the Chimera.' The reference was composed as follows: 'quodam est forma multiplex/ -potentia et actu, ut forma hominis./ -potentia sed non actum ut forma fenicis./ -potenti forme sed non actu propter defficiens potentie materiali ut forma solis./ -nec potentia ne actu sed solo intelleri [sic] ut forma chimere.'

42 'Secundo queritur, utrum processio temporalis ponat in numerum cum aeterna. Et quod sic videtur.'

43 'Item. Processio temporalis et aeterna si differunt, aut hoc est ex hoc, quod sunt diversae emanationes, aut quia diversus modus emanandi.'

44 'Ad hoc qui aliquod numerentur requiritur distinctio <…> cum participatione eiusdem nature.'

45 'Utrum caritas diligenda sit ex caritate.'

of their properties on themselves.[46] A final example is found on fol. 66^r, where the third question of the twenty-third distinction discusses whether the term 'essentia' is properly employed to describe the divine, as well as the differences between essence, subsistence, substance and person. To comment on the introduction to the question, a fifteenth-century hand corrected the text and wrote a personal reflection on the relation between the names and the communicability of the essence of things.[47]

The third copy of Bonaventure's commentary on the *Sentences* is MS 124, a parchment volume of 306 × 215 mm, written during the early fifteenth century.[48] Like the former volumes, this manuscript has a binding of wooden boards covered in leather with traces of having been a chained volume. It is composed of 156 leaves gathered in thirteen quires plus two separate leaves. This manuscript was written in a more formal gothic script than the former, certainly a non-Italian script, with a significantly high proportion of abbreviations. The text is organized in two columns, with spaces for initial letters decorated in red and blue and with paraphs in red and blue.

Compared with the other copies of the commentary, this manuscript has two main distinctive characteristics. Firstly, this copy has remarkably high-quality parchment and manufacture; and, secondly, it has fewer traces of interactive reading.[49] In addition to references such as 'Nota' or the use of numbers in the margins to indicate subdivisions in selected arguments, there are also marginal corrections and comments. Some of the corrections consist of the insertion of capital letters or of missing words.[50] Other corrections are more extensive, as happens on fol. 55^r, where, in the introduction to the first question under the second part of the seventeenth distinction, the author explains how he intends to explore whether charity is the Holy Spirit and whether spirit increases with charity.[51]

---

46 'Nota quod prime forme seu intentiones sunt hec scilicet veritas, bonitas, unitas et entitas et reflectuntur super se nam bonum dicens veritas est vera, unitas est una et sicud significatis.'

47 'Utrum nomen essentie [*Insertion mark, and in the margin:* vere dici] debeat in divinis.' The same hand that corrects writes a comment: 'Nam communicabile potest signum in abstractione et sic dicitur esentialiter vel in concretione.'

48 Abate and Luisetto argue that the book was written during fourteenth century. Abate and Luisetto, *Codici e manoscritti*, I, p. 164.

49 Abate and Luisetto propose an unspecified high-level atelier as the centre of production. See Abate and Luisetto, *Codici e manoscritti*, I, p. 164.

50 For example, on fol. 17^v: '[*Inserted*: quarto et] ultimo'; or on fol. 18^r: '[*Inserted*: tercio queritur utrum hoc sive utrum congrue po]ssit.'

51 See Appendix 3, Plate 5. 'In order to understand this part, there is the consideration of the increasing of charity and on that matter four questions will be considered: first, whether charity might [increase; second, of the form of increase of this charity; third, there is the consideration

The manuscript has a disruption in the transcription of the text. On fol. 71^v, in the twenty-third distinction, a marginal reference warns of a problem of legibility, and suggests that the reader should locate on the following folio the sign + in order to find the missing part of an argument on how, when considering the divine, the substance is equivalent to the underlying subsistence.[52] The proper continuation of the text is to be found on fol. 72^v, col. b. The portion of text from fol. 71^v to fol. 72^v belongs to a further section, as is shown by the marginal reference on fol. 73^v, indicating that the reader should go to the rear of the third folio under the + sign, where the continuation should be found.[53] All the revisions and corrections of this type were made by a cursive hand from late fourteenth or early fifteenth century.

Comments on the text may be found, for example, on fol. 3^v, where a reader notes that the sources of Bonaventure's prologue are patristic, namely the *De Trinitate* by Augustine and Hilarius of Poitiers.[54] On fol. 8^v, a marginal comment is given on the negative answer to the question whether there could be many gods. The reader uses as a source the Arabic philosopher Abu Masar; nevertheless, his works were not among the books held in the Biblioteca Antoniana, which suggests that the comment was written before the arrival of the manuscript in Padua, and in an academic context, maybe Paris, which would be consistent with the script of the text.[55] Another comment is found on fol. 22^r in the context of the sixth distinction, where consideration of the nature and types of necessity establishes that there are three types of necessity, depending on which principle necessity comes from. Thus, necessity can be inadequate, deficient or convenient and sufficient.[56]

of the opposite increase of charity, that is, the decrease, or whether charity can decrease].' The text is corrected as follows: 'Ad intelligentiam hoc partis est hic quo de augmento [sic] caritatis et circa hoc quaeruntur quatuor. Primo queruntur utrum caritas possit [*Cancelled*: 'diminuiri', and *above the word*: 'augeri'; *insertion mark, and in the margin, in an early fifteenth-century cursive*: Secundo de modo augmenti ipsius caritatis. Tertio queritur de opposito augmenti ipsius, scilicet diminutione utrum caritas possit diminui].' See Bonaventure of Bagnoregio, *Opera Omnia*, I, p. 307.

52 '[...] Autem ille rationes et precedentes et sequentes loquntur de substantia pro ut equivalet ypostasi sui supponito [*Insertion mark*] non dependet. [*In the margin*: Hic deficit. Quere in sequenti folio ad hoc signum: +]'

53 'Quere retro tertio folio de XXIII ad hoc signum: +'.

54 'Nota que qui totus iste prologus trahitur ex prologo Augustinus III De Trinitati vel ex prologo Hilari X De Trinitade [sic] propter illa quod summetur de Biblia.'

55 'Ad hoc est facit que dicit Asbumassar in libro de Magisterio astrologicum: Laus Deo celi qui creavit celum et terram cum omnibus qui in eis sunt ex mirabilium suis et posuit stellas et sequitur unde igitur alius deus propter eum solum et nullus modo habet principium.'

56 See the description of MS 120, fol. 23^r, and MS 123, fol. 18^v, above. The text of the comment is as follows: 'Necessitas triplex/ -quedam eius est perveniens ex principio disconveniente/ -quedam ex principio deficiente./ -quedam ex principio conveniente et sufficiente.'

The final copy of Bonaventure's commentary on the first book of the *Sentences* is MS 125, a parchment manuscript of 348 × 232 mm, produced during the fourteenth century. Its binding consists of wooden boards covered in red leather that has traces of having been chained. The manuscript has 143 leaves organized in twelve quires, but lacks the first leaf, containing the prologue. The text was written in a gothic book hand, organized in two columns with initial letters coloured in red and turquoise. The paragraphs are easily identified thanks to paraphs in alternate red and blue.[57]

The manuscript has a significant number of notes, marks, *maniculae* and other signs to quickly locate specific contents. The references are mainly marginal comments on the contents or cross references. For example, on fols. 1[r] and 2[r] there are a couple of marginal comments written by a fourteenth-century hand that identifies Aristotle as the source for the writer's remarks.[58] The text has also several comments that complement the discussion or indicate sources or cross references. For example, on fol. 2[v], a marginal comment on the third question of the *proemium* discusses theological science as both speculative and practical knowledge. The comment, written in a cursive Italian script from the fifteenth century, refers to the relationship between measure and symmetry.[59] On fol. 4[r], a marginal reference is made to Aristotle and Augustine as sources for the part concerning the second question of the first distinction, namely whether everything created is susceptible to being used.[60] On fol. 5[v], there is the first question under the third article of the first distinction, and its subject is whether God is to be enjoyed. Bonaventure answers affirmatively, and during his exposition he explores the relation between convenience and reason. As a result, a fifteenth-century hand wrote a complementary comment on the multiplicity of convenience.[61]

---

57 See Appendix 3, Plate 6.

58 On fol. 1[r]: 'Philosopus [sic] tertio *De anima*', and: 'Philosopho X *De problematis*'; on fol. 2r: '*Secundo philosophicorum* philosophus'.

59 'Assimetrens non est commensurabili coste, hoc ad rationem quia quadrate quod debet essere commensurabilia [*Insertion mark, above the line*: summa quatuor latera debent essere commensurabilia] debent se habere.'

60 'Philosophus in secundo quarto methaphisice [*Above*: et commentator eius] et Augustinus in liber de 28 c. 73 *De libero arbitrio*.'

61 The fifteenth-century reader states that convenience, or better, adequateness is multiple because even when stating its absence there is a form of attribution of adequateness, and adds afterwards that the intellect is not altered by external observation, due to a threefold reason. The comment was written as follows: 'Nota quod conveniencia multiplex est etiam quoniam intelligit quamdiu ad dicendum nulla est conveniencia quo modo est conveniencia.' Further added: 'Nota quod intellectus non corrumpitur ab observatione exterioris ratione triplici.'

Another feature of MS 125 are the ownership inscriptions. One of them, written in a barely legible fifteenth-century hand, appears on fol. 141^v and attributes the use of the manuscript to a brother Francis.[62] Moreover, two almost identical ownership inscriptions raise a question. On fol. 127^v, an inscription states that the manuscript was conceded *ad usum*, that is, on a life-long loan, to friar Guido in 1283.[63] Further, on fol. 143^r, another ownership inscription apparently confirms the former, followed by some excerpts from the *Summa theologiae* of Thomas Aquinas.[64] The notes describe with almost identical wording the manuscript's loan for life to a friar. However, while the script of the first note is late thirteenth century, the script of the second is a cursive of the late fourteenth century. There are two possible interpretations. First, the note on fol. 143 may simply be a copy of the former note, in which case there would be only one Guido, reader of the commentary during the thirteenth century. It remains a mystery, however, why a second hand would have copied just that single note almost a hundred years later.[65] The second interpretation suggests that two friars, both named Guido, borrowed the manuscript in different periods. In this case, the first note would confirm that MS 125 was an early copy of Bonaventure's treatise and that, as such, it would have been swiftly made available for loan as soon as newer copies were acquired.

When one considers the question of the practices of reading for the set of copies of Bonaventure's commentary on the first book of the *Sentences*, it becomes clear that all the books were used for study. However, not all the volumes were available at the same time. An analysis of the corrections of the manuscripts can reveal the dynamics of circulation of these copies of the commentary. MS 125 was the first volume to arrive in the library, and it is not unreasonable to think it was produced internally. Naturally, the volume was chained to a bench, and it was available for consultation only. Afterwards, MS 120 arrived, and it was immediately corrected using MS 125 as a model. Then MS 125 was 'released' for loan, and MS 120 was left for consultation only. Later, MS 123 arrived in the library, and it was corrected using MS 125 as a model and was chained. Most probably MS 120 was made available for loan at that moment. Finally, a high-quality copy of the commentary, MS 124, arrived. Apparently, it was swiftly revised and

---

62   'Liber fratris Francixi de Ordine Minorum'
63   'Iste liber datus est ad usum fratis [sic] Guidonis anno MCCLXXXIII.' See Appendix 3, Plate 7.
64   'Iste liber est concessus ad usum fratris Guidonis de Padua ordinis fratrum minorum.' See Appendix 3, Plate 8.
65   As proposed by Fontana, *Frati, libri e insegnamento*, pp. 119-20.

was chained immediately. This dynamic suggests that from a group of four copies of one fundamental work for the Franciscan discipline of study, possibly only one, the first, was produced internally. This is consistent with the increasing importance of bequests, donations and external acquisitions of books during the fourteenth and fifteenth centuries.[66]

There are grounds to propose a second period of revision and correction of this set of copies. In fact, there is a common hand that revises and inserts corrections in all the manuscripts of this set. This hand, an Italian gothic book hand from the late fourteenth or early fifteenth century, is remarkably similar to the hand that wrote MS 573, that is, the 1449 inventory of the library. This suggests that the hand that swiftly revised and corrected the set of copies was that of the fifteenth-century librarian of the Antoniana, perhaps as part of the preparation of the inventory of the library.

The Collection of Sermons of Luke of Bitonto

The twelfth-century theologian Alan de Lille described preaching as public instruction in faith and morals, straight from the source of authority. This definition underlined the public nature of preaching, as well as its purpose of reforming humanity and contributed decisively to the development of the conception of preaching as the highest calling of a priest.[67]

Although the first Franciscan preaching was a call to penance, it developed into complex forms and adapted to very different audiences, especially after the friars' engagement with scholastic culture in the universities, which was justified, at least formally, by the need of having the best preparation for preaching.[68] Indeed, a master of theology should be capable of discussing

---

66 For a detailed summary of the process of textual verification and correction of the copies of the commentary, see Appendix 2.

67 'Praedicatio est, manifesta et publica instructio morum et fidei, informationi hominum deserviens, ex rationum semita, at auctoritatum fonte proveniens.' Alanus de Insulis, *Summa De arte praedicatoria*, col. 111. See Briscoe, 'Artes Praedicandi', p. 21. Recent studies discuss medieval preaching as a communication event whose contents were delivered to the audience through an oral or written text which could have two forms: the homily or the sermon. While the homily had its roots in patristic culture and survived in monastic environments, the sermon was linked to scholastic culture and was mainly developed by the mendicant orders. The study of the medieval sermon, its definition, its development and its typology is based on evidence that, in some cases, was a memory-based reconstruction of speech or even the transcription of a speech that never took place. See Kienzle, 'Typology of the Medieval Sermon'.

68 Şenocak, *Poor and the Perfect*, pp. 144-88; see also Johnson, 'Introduction: The Franciscan Fascination with the Word'.

passages of the Bible using proper tools of interpretation, and thus preaching was supported by the medieval university.[69] Usually, sermons produced in the universities had a deep theological meaning and were addressed mainly to an audience of university students or masters.[70] There was, however, another kind of sermon, whose main purpose was to instruct and persuade the laity, instead of discussing deep theological questions with university scholars. These sermons took place in public spaces and were addressed to a wide and mixed audience, and mendicant friars played a fundamental role in their development. A third kind of sermon, an intermediate type, was designed to be addressed to neither an audience of masters in theology nor the public in general, but to fellow friars, and was used mainly as a tool for education within the convents. While not having the deep complexity of university sermons, they were sound enough to guarantee a proper preparation for preaching.[71] Some representative examples of this type of sermon were composed by the Franciscan friar Luke of Bitonto. His figure, influence and legacy in the convent of Sant'Antonio will be considered in what follows.

Luke of Bitonto and his Controversial Legacy

Luke of Bitonto was one of the most influential authors of sermons within the Franciscan order, as the *Cronica* of Salimbene of Adam testifies.[72] Despite his fame and influence, there is little available information on his life. It is known that he was born in the thirteenth century in Bitonto, near Bari in the south of Italy, and it can be assumed that he followed the normal programme of education for his time, that is, that he pursued studies in one of the cathedral schools of his city.[73]

---

69   Peter Cantor summarized the duties of a master of theology in terms of reading, discussing and preaching: 'In tribus igitur consistit exercitium sacrae Scripturae: circa lectionem, disputationem et praedicationem. Cuilibet istorum mater oblivionis et noverca memoriae est nimia prolixitas.' Petrus Cantorus, *Verbum abbreviatum*, col. 25; see Roberts, 'Medieval University Preaching', p. 318.

70   O'Malley, 'Introduction: Medieval Preaching', pp. 7-11, and Roberts, 'Medieval University Preaching', p. 320.

71   Lombardo, 'La production homilétique franciscaine', pp. 85-87, and O'Malley, 'Introduction: Medieval Preaching', p. 10; Robson, 'Sermons Preached to the Friars Minor'.

72   'Et tunc vivebat frater Lucas Apulus ex Ordine Fratrum Minorum, cuius est sermonum memoria, qui fuit scholasticus et ecclesiasticus et litteratus homo et in Apulia in theologia eximius doctor, nominatus, sollemnis atque famosus; cuius anima per misericordiam Dei requiescat in pace! Amen.' Salimbene of Adam, *Cronica*, I, p. 262.

73   Two manuscripts, Vienna Österreichische Nationalbibliothek, MS 1349 and MS 1364, identify him as 'Parisiensis' and 'Parisinus', and a third one identifies him as 'eximii sacrae theologiae doctoris Lucae de Bitonto'. These references have laid the grounds for assuming that Luke received

It is certain that Luke became a friar before 1220, when Francis appointed him as minister for the eastern province, succeeding Elias.[74] After a while, he went to Rome and moved to his native province, becoming the *lector* of the local convent. His sermons became renowned within the order, so much so that they were apparently better known and more studied than those of Anthony of Padua.[75] The fact that he was appointed to deliver a sermon at the funeral of the son of emperor Frederick II suggests that Luke was a respected and famous preacher.[76] Very soon his works became part of the collection of the most important libraries of the order. For example, the library of the convent in Assisi had at least seven different volumes of his sermons distributed between the *libraria publica*, that is, the collection available for consultation, and the *libraria secreta*, that is, the volumes available for loan.[77] This swift popularity of Luke's sermons is consistent with their use as a tool in the training of preachers from the thirteenth to the fifteenth centuries.[78]

Luke composed a very influential cycle of sermons, known as 'Narraverunt', after its *incipit:* 'Iniquitous tales came to my ears [...]'.[79] Apparently, due to Luke's fame as theologian and preacher, the minister general, probably Aymo of Faversham, asked him to compose this set of sermons to be used in the training of the friars.[80] Unfortunately, the *Sermones narraverunt*

---

the title of magister at the University of Paris, as proposed in Moretti, *Luca Apulus*, and in Moretti, 'I sermoni di Luca da Bitonto'. However, it seems that the attribution of 'Parisiensis' could be the result of a scribal error if it is assumed that the title 'Doctor' was equivalent to 'Magister'. 'Doctor' was a title employed mainly in Italy to address those who had completed theological studies, but not necessarily to the highest levels in the university, while in the Transalpine region 'Magister' implied completion of the highest levels of theological learning, especially in the University of Paris. See Rasolofoarimanana, 'Luc de Bitonto, OMIN, et ses sermons', p. 240.

74 Golubovich, *Biblioteca bio-bibliografica*, I, p. 97.

75 Golubovich, *Biblioteca bio-bibliografica*, I, pp. 128-29, and II, pp. 283-84; see also D'Avray, *Preaching of the Friars*, p. 156.

76 Salimbene of Adam, *Cronica*, I, pp. 122-23.

77 The *libraria publica* had two manuscripts of sermons *Super epistolas et evangelia dominicalia*. The *libraria secreta*, on the other hand, had two collections of sermons *Super epistolas et evangelia*, two collections of sermons *Dominicales, quadragesimales et festivi*, and a volume on loan to friar Iacobus de Bictonio. See Cenci, ed., *Bibliotheca manuscripta*, I, pp. 91-92, 144, 329-30 and 378.

78 Rasolofoarimanana, 'La tradition manuscrite', pt. 1 (2004), p. 272, and pt. 2 (2006); and Rasolofoarimanana, 'Un sermon anonyme'.

79 'Narraverunt mihi iniqui fabulationes.'

80 In the prologue, Luke declares: 'Nolite plures ingrati effici fratres mei quare cum imperitiam meam videam et insufficientiam recognoscam, ad insipientiam mihi mandato superioris urgente, nec non quorundam fratrum desiderio impellente, opusculum sermonum dominicalium coactus sum annotare. Et licet super hoc multorum preclara opera iam sint edita, dignum duxi eorum satisfacere voluntati, ne viderer subterfugere cum possem proficere, non de meo confisus ingenio,

were very soon attributed to others. The accusation that Elias was an ally of the emperor, his deposition and his later excommunication seem to have a decisive impact in the perception of Luke of Bitonto and could have been powerful reasons for a deliberate confusion concerning the authorship of the sermons in favour of Luca Belludi or Luca Lector, both friars of the Paduan convent. Nevertheless, recent scholarship has established beyond doubt that Luke of Bitonto was the rightful author of the *Narraverunt* cycle.[81] The set of copies of this cycle preserved in the Biblioteca Antoniana will be described in the following section.

Manuscripts of Luke of Bitonto in Padua

The fifteenth-century inventory of the Biblioteca Antoniana of Padua reports that there were six copies of the sermons of Luke of Bitonto: four were chained, one was available for loan and one had already been on loan for at least twenty-five years.[82] Four of these manuscripts have survived and are extant in the current collection of the library as MSS 417, 418, 419 and 527. These volumes constitute the second set of manuscripts that will be considered in the analysis.

MS 417 is a collection of *Sermones dominicales*. It is a parchment manuscript of 303 × 208 mm produced in the second half of the thirteenth century. It still has its original binding of wood plates covered in leather, with traces of the clasp, which suggests it was a chained volume. It has 218 leaves organized in eighteen quires. The sermons were copied using a gothic book-hand script, in two columns.[83] The only notes of decoration are the

sed de gratie celestis auxilio, de obedientie merito, de fraterne suffragio caritatis. Suscipe, digne pater totius ordinis minorum minister, auctoris tui licet inculti operis rudimenta, paternaque benevolentia quod minus est supple, quod plus est rade, quod hirtum come, quod obscurum declara, quod vitiosum emenda; sic tibi opus per te sine menda.' See Moretti, *Luca Apulus*, p. 166; see also Lombardo, 'Ecclesia huius temporis', pp. 123-24.

81   Rasolofoarimanana, 'La tradition manuscrite', and Fontana, *Frati, libri e insegnamento*, pp. 147-49. However, the attribution has not always been accurate, as shown by the case of some anonymous sermons *Sermones de sanctis* found in Assisi, Biblioteca Comunale, MS 505, and Rome, Biblioteca del Pontificio Ateneo Antonianum, MS 24; see Rasolofoarimanana, 'Sermons anonymes'.

82   The volumes were distributed as follows: on the ninth right-hand bench, two chained copies of the *Sermones dominicales*; on the tenth right-hand bench, one chained copy of his sermons, attributed to Luca Lector; on the eleventh right-hand bench, a chained collection of sermons on the Gospels and the *Sermones narraverunt*; on the eight left-hand cupboard, there was a copy of a collection of sermons available for loan, and there was another copy of his sermons already on loan, at least from 1423. See Humphreys, *Library of the Franciscans of the Convent of St. Anthony*, pp. 84, 85, 88, 138 and 183.

83   The script seems to be more fourteenth-century than a thirteenth.

initials of the main chapters in red, and the coloured number of the sermons in the running heading.

A note on fol. 1^r, written by a later hand, attributes the sermons to Luca Lector of Padua, but the *incipit* of the manuscript, 'Narraverunt mihi iniqui fabulationes', shows that these are the sermons of Luke of Bitonto.[84] On the other hand, along with the heavy presence of marginal comments and corrections, another type of note links the topics of a specific sermon with other sections, creating internal cross references between the different sermons.[85] A set of lines is also drawn to identify the connections between the main topics in the different paragraphs revealing the hierarchy of concepts in the text.[86] This reading resource suggests an intensive practice of study and underlines the usefulness of the manuscript as a tool to develop skills for argumentation. The final *tabula* on fols. 213^r-215^r, composed by a late fourteenth- or early fifteenth-century hand and organized alphabetically, was a complementary resource to locate the sermons quickly within the volume.

The traces of use are also interesting testimonies of the practices of learning in the convent. For instance, the system of lines used to identify the structure of the sermon reveals that not only the contents but the way they were organized were the subject of study and practice, since Luke was particularly effective in adapting complex theological questions to the structure of sermons for didactic purposes.[87]

The second manuscript with the sermons of Luke of Bitonto is MS 418, a parchment volume of 293 × 204 mm produced during the second half of the thirteenth century.[88] The binding consists of plates of wood covered in leather, with traces of being a chained volume.[89] The manuscript has 176

84 'Sermones beati Luce de Padua ordini minori conventuali qui fuit lector'. This attribution was reproduced by the ancient inventories of the library. For instance, the 1396 inventory registers on fol. 11^v: 'Item sermones fratris Luce lectoris Padue dominicales cum tabulis et corio çallo ad ligaturas cum cathena'; and the inventory of 1449 quotes: 'Sermones dominicales fratris Luce lectoris de Padua cum tabulis copertis coreo nigro et claviculis. Cuius principium Ecce veniet. Secundus quinternus incipit primum dicit. Finis vero ultimus eternam. Amen.' See Humphreys, *Library of the Franciscans of the Convent of St. Anthony*, pp. 31 and 85.

85 For example, on fol. 2^r, 'Sermo 3 adventus', a note that links the topics of the first and third sermons.

86 Rasolofoarimanana, 'La tradition manuscrite', p. 252.

87 Lombardo, 'Ecclesia huius temporis', pp. 126-32.

88 Abate and Luisetto, *Codici e manoscritti*, I, p. 347; see also Rasolofoarimanana, 'La tradition manuscrite', p. 253.

89 According to a note written on the inside of the front plate, the binding was restored in 1926 by the 'Officina di restauro della Biblioteca Vaticana'.

leaves organized in twenty-six quires and is written in a gothic hand-book script. There are some variations in the distribution of the script: from fol. 1[r] to fol. 16[v] the text is distributed across the page, but from fol. 17[r] on the distribution of the script shifts into a two-column pattern, and the dimensions of the quire also change.[90] Two hands are visible in the transcription of the sermons.[91] The manuscript lacks decoration, although some spaces are reserved for capital letters that were not intended to be very elaborate.

The text has corrections and comments written by a later hand employing a very light, minuscule cursive script. Some of the comments are simply corrections to the text, as on fols. 5[r], 6[v] and 9[r], where the word 'cheerfulness' (*hylaritas*) is cancelled and replaced by 'humility' (*humilitas*) in the margin, or on fol. 9[v] where 'scriptures' (*scriptas*) is followed by an insertion mark that leads to the marginal annotation 'on divine books' (*in divinis libris*), or on fol. 10[r] where 'set down' (*deponit*) is changed to 'arrange' (*disponit*) and 'insertive' (*insertiva*) changed to 'matter' (*materia*). There are other marginal references, such as the word 'Nota', to identify a particular passage. However, the marginal commentaries do not contain cross references or theological reflections. Perhaps this was a copy destined to be read and used by its own scribe, who bequeathed it to the convent. This hypothesis is supported by the low quality of the parchment, and thus it could be an example of the ideal Franciscan book proposed by Nicoletta Giovè: it was produced with a low level of sophistication in a Franciscan place by a Franciscan scribe; it contained a Franciscan work, was preserved in a Franciscan library and was used as a tool in preparation for preaching.[92]

MS 419 is the third volume that will be described in this section. It is a parchment volume of 221 × 167 mm produced during the thirteenth century.[93] The volume has a modern binding in wood covered in leather.[94] The ancient binding has been preserved apart, and a close examination reveals that it has traces of the supporting device for the chain. The MS has 224 leaves, organized in nineteen quires, and it was written in a gothic script by, at least, two different hands: the first hand, probably German, transcribed from fol. 1[r] to fol. 122[v].[95] The second is an Italian hand that transcribed from

---

90 See Appendix 3, Plate 9.

91 The second hand appears from fol. 175[r].

92 See the Introduction to this book; see also Giovè Marchioli, 'Il Codice Francescano'.

93 Abate and Luisetto, *Codici e manoscritti*, I, p. 348; see also Rasolofoarimanana, 'La tradition manuscrite', pp. 254-55.

94 The binding was restored in the late nineteenth century by a 'Gabinetto di Restauro del libro'.

95 See Appendix 3, Plate 10.

fol. 123ʳ. The decoration of the volume consists of rubrics at the beginning of the main sections and some initials.

As happened with MS 417, a fourteenth-century hand attributed the text to a different author.[96] However, the presence of the *Sermones narraverunt* confirms that the text is certainly by Luke of Bitonto. Concerning the presence of notes and commentaries, the manuscript has two parts: the first has a small number of notes and commentaries, mostly corrections to the text, while in the second, particularly from fol. 110ʳ, commentaries and notes are more frequent. The volume ends with a *tabula* on fols. 210-218. Although the catalogue of Abate and Luisetto describes the manuscript as having traces of heavy use, apart from the few commentaries described above, the manuscript has no traces of intensive interaction with the reader. This is consistent with the higher quality of the parchment employed in the making of the manuscript: MS 419 seems to be a copy of a corrected original, most probably MS 417.

MS 527 is the last of the surviving volumes containing the sermons of Luke of Bitonto. It is a parchment volume of 198 × 145 mm produced during the fourteenth century.[97] It has a modern binding with wood plates covered in leather, but the last leaves of the MS have traces of a clasp, which suggests the volume was chained at a certain point. Its 364 leaves are distributed into thirty-three quires. It was written by two different hands, probably German, due to the characteristic angular form of the gothic script.[98] The text is arranged into two columns of script, and its decoration consists of initial letters in red and rubrics at the beginning of the sections.[99]

The manuscript has few marginal notes, most of them are spelling corrections or references, complemented by a few *maniculae* to point out some of the most important passages. There is an almost total absence of marginal commentaries, cross references or similar forms of interaction. The few traces suggest that, as happened with MS 419, this was a later copy of another manuscript, previously corrected. It is difficult to establish unequivocally whether MS 527 was produced in the convent, although the

---

96 On fol. 224ᵛ, it wrote: 'Isti sermones fratris Lucae lectoris paduani sunt sacri conventus Paduae, videlicet fratrum minorum de Padua.'

97 Abate and Luisetto, *Codici e manoscritti*, I, pp. 547-48; see also Rasolofoarimanana, 'La tradition', pp. 255-56.

98 The hands, probably German, alternate as follows: the first hand wrote fols. 1-6, 11-12, 143-148, 307-15 and 358-362; the second hand wrote the other parts of the manuscript. See Abate and Luisetto, *Codici e manoscritti*, II, p. 547.

99 See Appendix 3, Plate 11.

presence of an international community of friars supports the possibility of the intervention of a non-Italian hand in the writing of the volume.[100]

In summary, this set of manuscripts of the sermons of Luke of Bitonto is composed of one heavily used and annotated manuscript, and three more copies with relatively few traces of commentaries or intensive interaction with the text. There are two possible explanations. The first assumes that the volumes were independent, and arrived as finished manuscripts in the convent at different times. In this case, MS 417 became the model for the correction of the others. The second hypothesis is that MS 417 was the model for the transcription and correction of the other books. If so, and it being the earliest of the manuscripts of the set, it should have arrived first to the library. The absence of traces of interaction on the remaining three volumes and the notes of possession present there suggest that they shared the same place of production, namely the Paduan convent. This possibility seems consistent with the intensive practice of study and writing within the community. In any case, the set is composed of two distinct types of manuscripts: a volume used to establish the text, the structure and the quality of the transcription; and a group of 'fair copies'.

Manuscripts from the Library of the Convent of San Francesco Grande

As discussed in Chapter 2, the Observant convent of San Francesco Grande was founded by the family Bonafari in Padua. When Sibila Bonafari made her last will, she established that the convent should be occupied exclusively by Observant friars.[101] The convent became one of the most important centres of the Observance in northern Italy and offered education at high levels. However, we lack specific information regarding San Francesco Grande's library; for example, there is not enough evidence to allow us to confirm whether or not the library had a double collection of books.[102] The earliest inventories available do not register the presence of chained and/or unchained books, and the absence of the original bindings makes it difficult to establish whether or not the volumes were chained. Most probably, all the books were available for consultation and loan.

---

100 See Fontana, *Frati, libri e insegnamento*, p. 66, and Sartori, 'La "Ratio Studiorum"', p. 135.
101 Collodo, *Una società in trasformazione*, pp. 490-91 and 520, and Pantarotto, *La biblioteca manoscritta*, p. 10.
102 See Chapter 2.

As with the Biblioteca Antoniana, apart from general thematic descriptions, there are no studies of the typology of the manuscripts contained in the library of San Francesco Grande. Therefore, it is possible only to confirm that the main groups around which the library was organized were the Bible, the tools useful for the education of the preacher such as postils, commentaries, compilations, treatises on the vices and virtues, and miscellanies that included Dominican masters such as Thomas Aquinas or Antonino of Florence, as well as collections of sermons.[103] There were also other materials such as lives of saints, treatises on canon law and copies of the *Decretals*, as well as theological treatises important to the education of the friars. The writings of the Fathers were present mainly in volumes containing commentaries on biblical books or treatises on Christian spirituality such as the *Scala Paradisi* of John Climacus. There were also copies of the constitutions, of the bulls of the popes Nicholas III and Clement V, of the Franciscan rule and commentaries on the rule and the founder's *Testamentum*. Apart from these works, there were reference books and manuals of grammar, rhetoric, a few classical texts and books on natural sciences.

It is important to note that a thematic description of the manuscripts in the library may be misleading because it may give the idea that the book collection was composed mainly of volumes containing single works or anthologies of works arranged by topic. In reality, a preliminary exploration of the surviving manuscripts suggests that most of the volumes were produced according to particular needs, reflecting the experiences, requirements and expectations of the scribes and therefore more often than not they were miscellanies of works of different genres, both in Latin and the vernacular. Consequently, the set of manuscripts selected for the comparison should reflect the purpose of these anthologies, as shown by the fact that there are two main groups of manuscripts to explore: tools for confession and tools for the composition of sermons. A closer examination of the tools for confession allows one to classify them into two further groups: anthologies on moral subjects and practical anthologies of cases and prescriptive excerpts focused mainly on the practice of confession.

A Selection of Treatises on Morality

The first volume to be described is Padua, Biblioteca Universitaria, MS 1030, an anthology of excerpts and moral treatises.[104] It is a paper volume

---

103 Kaeppeli, *Scriptores Ordinis Praedicatorum*, I, pp. 80-100.
104 Pantarotto, *La biblioteca manoscritta*, p. 138.

in quarto of 211 × 153 mm, produced during the second half of the fifteenth century. It has a modern stiff binding and shows no traces of being a chained volume. The 109 leaves of the manuscript were written by a single hand using a minuscule cursive script, strongly influenced by the Florentine style, distributed into two columns on the page. The decoration is limited to capital letters coloured in red.

The manuscript contains a selection of authorities.[105] According to an ownership inscription, the manuscript was conceded on long-term loan to friar Francis of Padua, who wrote it by his own hand and who intended to bequeath it to the convent.[106] It is worth noting the absence of comments in the text, apart from a few corrections, which suggests a careful revision by the reader, who shows particular interest in identifying St. Dominic in a marginal note to a passage of the eleventh canto of *Paradiso*, on fol. 78[r]. The comment describes Dominic as a companion of Francis in the task of supporting the pastoral care of the pope.[107]

The inscription 'ad usum' by friar Franciscus on fol. II[v] confirms that the manuscript was a personal volume. Additionally, the absence of comments suggests that this was not a volume of study but rather a tool of reference. The anthology gathers together a collection of texts on moral matters, but no excerpts discussing theological, or even 'Franciscan', topics such as poverty and humility. The selection reflects the intention of having an efficient personal tool of reference containing a collection of authoritative sources, in which there is a place for contemporary masters like Bernardino of Siena, Dante's *Commedia* or the *Laude* of Jacopone da Todi.[108] Another feature of interest is how texts written in vernacular share the same level

105 The selection includes the treatise of Albert de Brixia *De amore et dilectione Dei*; the *Epistola consolatoria ad patrem et ad madrem* and *De oboedientia* of Bernardino of Siena; the *Soliloquium* of Hugh of Saint Victor; *De vita Christiana* by Augustine; excerpts from the *Commedia* by Dante, specifically from *Paradiso* XI, 28-39, and *Inferno* IV, 121-47; excerpts from various authorities; and the *Prophetia de beato Francisco* of Joachim of Fiore. From fol. 83[r] to fol. 113[v], there is a selection under the title *Flores auctoritates*, among which are excerpts from Jerome, Augustine, Bernard, Anselm and Innocent, followed by the *Constitutio basiliensis de conceptione Virginis Marie*, the *Concordia maiori di septem ordinibus sic scribit de beato Francisco* by Joachim of Fiore and the treatise *Super Matheum* by Chrysostom.
106 Fol. II[v]: 'Hic liber est ad usum fratris Francisci minorite de civitate Patavii quem propria manu conscripsit et post mortem ipsius pertinet ad locum Padue.'
107 The lines are *Paradiso*, XI, 118-20: 'Pensa oramai qual fu colui che degno/ collega fu a mantener la barca/ di Pietro in alto mar per dritto segno.' On this passage, the scribe comments in the right-hand margin: 'Hic loquitur de beato Domenico qui fuit collega beati Francisci et in eodem tempore.' See Appendix 3, Plate 12.
108 The poems of Jacopone da Todi were registered in the *tabula* of contents, but that section of the manuscript is lost.

of importance as those written in Latin. Usually works in the vernacular such as the *Commedia* or the *Laude* of Jacopone of Todi were considered of lower status than Latin treatises, but in this manuscript they have the same level of authority as the Fathers and their reflections on Christian life. This suggests that the compilation was employed as a source for preaching to the laity, a feature reinforced by the portability of the volume (as confirmed by its dimensions), in contrast to materials for preaching such as those present in the library of Sant'Antonio that were heavier, bigger and written in Latin.

As a tool for pastoral care, the selection of texts focused on moral topics, taking a descriptive approach instead of a prescriptive one centred on practical questions concerning confession, penitence or the absolution of sins. This is suggested by the absence of normative or prescriptive texts such as treatises on specific sins, on confession or even popular works such as Antonino of Florence's or Bernardino of Siena's versions of the treatise *De restitutionibus*. Therefore, MS 1030 was employed rather as a manual of reference, instead of being a tool for the preparation of sermons.

Padua, Biblioteca Universitaria, MS 548, is the second example of a selection of texts on moral topics. It is an anthology of moral treatises contained in a paper volume in quarto of 214 × 142 mm, produced in the first half of the fifteenth century. It has a modern stiff binding, and there are no visible traces suggesting that the volume was chained. The 106 leaves of the manuscript were written in a fifteenth-century minuscule cursive script, and the whole decoration could be described as basic, limited to some capital letters coloured in red and green.[109]

The manuscript contains a group of treatises on moral questions and hagiography. The main section reproduces the vernacular translation by Gentile da Foligno of the *Scala Paradisi* of John Climacus, a sixth-century monk from the region of the Sinai.[110] The second work is also a vernacular version of another treatise by John Climacus, the *Sermo ad pastorem*, followed by Daniel Monacus' *Vita Iohannis Climaci*, also in its vernacular version. The compilation ends with excerpts from the *Actus S. Francisci et sociorum eius* in Latin.

There are few textual notes, comments or references, most of them are corrections made by the same hand that wrote the main text. The only

109 Pantarotto, *La biblioteca manoscritta*, p. 110.
110 The *Scala Paradisi* was a popular treatise on the ascending degrees required to reach spiritual perfection, as explained in the introduction on fol. 1ʳ: 'Lauto nome sia sancta scala, perciò che in eso se demostrano tucti li gradi per li qualiter l'anima sali pervenire alla sumità et alteza dela perfectione spirituale ordenatamente componendo uno grado sopra l'altro, ad modo della scala.' See John Climacus, *Ladder of Divine Ascent*, pp. 1-6.

additional note appears on fol. 43^v, where a *manicula* was drawn to identify a passage of the *Scala Paradisi*. The excerpt from the *Actus S. Francisci* focuses on the figure of Bernard of Quintavalle, his conversion after listening to Francis's preaching, his exemplary devotion and commitment to Francis's example, and his role in the first community.[111] The 'Bernardian' perspective certainly underlines the closeness of Bernard to Francis and suggests that the *Actus* could have been easily interpreted as a prefiguration of Bernardino of Siena, one of the pillars of the Observance. The excerpt fits perfectly its use in pastoral care within the convent, since its topics were directly related to the identity of the community. In more general terms, the anthology reflects the intention of assembling a group of texts with a substantial moral and devotional content, instead of a selection of specific cases for confession and advice. As with MS 1030, it may be inferred this anthology was an alternative type of aid to pastoral care. Additionally, the predominant presence of non-Latin versions in the arrangement of the works transcribed should be underlined, since three out of four works were written in vernacular. This use of different levels of the language underlines the flexibility of these manuscripts that could be used to undertake pastoral care within or outside the convent.

A Selection of Tools for Confession

The first apostolic activity of the early Franciscan community was preaching, but very soon the effort for the salvation of others evolved into institutionalized forms of care such as offering advice, listening to confessions and absolving sins. Thus, pastoral care became one of the main tasks of the Franciscan community.[112] The library of San Francesco Grande offers some interesting examples of the tools employed by Observants in the fifteenth century to perform their duty efficiently.

The first example is Padua, Biblioteca Universitaria, MS 586, an anthology of treatises and cases. It is a paper manuscript in quarto of 217 × 156 mm, produced during the second half of the fifteenth century. The volume has a modern stiff binding from the nineteenth century and does not have traces of being chained. The manuscript has 195 leaves written by two different hands in a cursive script, close to the *corsiva notarile* employed

---

111 Bernard of Quintavalle, a wealthy man from Assisi, is commonly acknowledged as the first disciple and companion of Francis. See Moorman, *History of the Franciscan Order*, pp. 10-11, and Merlo, *Nel nome di san Francesco*, pp. 21-22.

112 Merlo, 'Storia di Frate Francesco', pp. 8-27, and Merlo, *Nel nome di san Francesco*, pp. 31-52.

in northern Italy, distributed in two columns, and its decoration is limited to red paraphs.[113] Most probably, the volume was left to the library by friar Francis of Sacco, who received it in concession thanks to the authorization of friar Ludovicus of Vicenza.[114]

The volume contains an anthology of treatises of very different natures, ranging from cases of commercial affairs to theological treatises on the nature of the Trinity or the answers of John of Capistrano to important questions regarding the observance of the Franciscan rule.[115] This apparent discordance in the selection of topics is the result of the practical nature of the volume; in fact, although there is a remarkable diversity, all the works are arranged around confession. The works that form the compilation could be classified into two types: authorities and cases. One might expect the authorities to be the writings of the masters of the order transcribed in Latin. However, it is worth noting the presence of treatises written in the vernacular such as the *Spetii di busie*, or *Mirror of Lies*, and the *De la sanctisima trinitade* that share the same level of authority as works of masters such as John of Capistrano, Antonino of Florence, Alexander of Alexandria or Thomas Aquinas. The cases are of a practical nature, for example commercial interactions of buying, selling and giving things on loan. This type of treatise had the purpose of providing practical guidance for confession, particularly to accurately identify usury.[116] MS 586 includes one of the most popular works

113 See Appendix 3, Plate 13; Pantarotto, *La biblioteca manoscritta*, p. 112.

114 A late nineteenth-century inventory of the Biblioteca Universitaria reports an ownership inscription written on an unspecified *in principio*, most probably the ancient binding, now lost: 'Hic liber concessus est per me fratrem Lodovicum de Vincentia [...] S. Antonii vicarium et servum indignum ad usus fratris Francisci a Sacco de eadem provincia confessore, et post cum pertinet loco S. Lodovici apud Rever die XVII iunii 1509.' See Pantarotto, *La biblioteca manoscritta*, p. 113.

115 The manuscript contains the following works: Angelus of Clavasio, *Opus contractuum venditiones*; *De restitutionis* [sic] and *De ornatu et habitu mulierum* by Antonino of Florence; a collection of excerpts presented as *Additiones in supplemento*; a selection of *Extracta de restitutionibus*; the treatise *De livellis*; *Casus* by Clarus de Florentia; a vernacular treatise under the title *Spetii de Busie*; the treatise *De la sanctissima Trinitade*; *Confessionale 'Defecerunt'* by Antonino of Florence; *Tractatus excommunicationum* by Francis of Platea; *Dubia,* by John of Capistrano; excerpts from the *Summa Monaldi*; *Casus* by Angelus de Castro; a selection of *Casus in quibus potest sacerdos defficere per negligentiam*; an excerpt from the case 'De sepulturis', which is part of the *Summa* by Antonino of Florence; an excerpt from the *Summa Astensis*; a collection of excerpts from different authorities on commercial affairs under the title *Qualiter potest vendi ad credentiam*; a collection of excerpts from different masters; a *Tabula definitiones* [sic] *peccatorum*; and the manual of reference *Brevis per confessionem*.

116 On the scholastic reflection on usury and the role of manuals for confession, see Noonan, *Scholastic Analysis of Usure*; Turrini, *La coscienza e le leggi*; Langholm, *Economics in the Medieval Schools*; and Langholm, *Merchant in the Confessional*.

on the subject, the *Opus contractuum* by Angelus of Clavasio, an Observant friar renowned by his *Summa de casibus conscientiae*, a compilation of articles on moral theology from which the *Interrogationes in confessione* was used extensively by the end of the fifteenth century.[117] The presence of additional tools such as a table of sins and their definition at the end of the volume underlines the purpose of this manuscript, and, as happens with MS 548, the selection of mixed materials suggests the flexibility of the book as a tool for internal and external pastoral care. Additionally, the almost total absence of marginal notes or comments, except for a few corrections, is consistent with its not being a volume whose main purpose was to support intensive study. Nevertheless, there is a specific excerpt on the use of books, on fol. 164[r], where the answer of John of Capistrano to a question concerning books may be found.[118] He established that friars should not sell books by themselves without the intervention of the order's procurators. They were allowed, instead, to exchange their books according to the principles of the rule.[119] This suggests that books were part of the daily life of Observant friars and that despite the Observants' purpose of keeping a strict adherence to the rule, the prescription concerning the friars *nescientes litteras* was no longer applicable.

The second example of a volume focused on pastoral care is Padua, Biblioteca Universitaria, MS 736, an anthology of treatises and cases. This is a paper manuscript in octavo of 143 × 107 mm, produced in the mid-fifteenth century.[120] The volume has an ancient stiff binding and has no traces of being

117 Deutscher, 'Angelo Carletti'; see also Todeschini, 'Credito ed economia della civitas'.
118 See Appendix 3, Plate 13.
119 'Whether the friars of our order can sell, alienate or exchange goods by themselves within or outside the order without the [intervention of the] procurator of the order. I answer that friars cannot sell by themselves within the order or outside from it, unless through the procurator; exchange, nevertheless, [is allowed] with the permission from the prelates, as for example is the case of exchanging one book for another without adding or lessening any price, and anything else they do, do it according to the rule.' The text is as follows: 'Utrum fratres nostri ordinis possint vendere alienare vel commutare aliquid in ordine vel extra ordinem per se ipsos absque procuratore ordinis. Respondeo quod fratres non possunt aliquid vendere per se ipsos in ordine vel extra, nisi per procuratore commutare autem sic sed de licentia prelatorum sicut esset commutare unum librum in alium non addere vel minuere aliquid pretium et qui aliter facit facit secundum regulam.'
120 The manuscript was produced between 1454 and 1462. The *Summa* of Antonino of Florence was completed in 1454, while on fol. 117[v] there is an ownership inscription that declares that the volume was given 'ad usum' by the Observant convent of Padua to friar Simon of Parma: 'Hic liber pertinet ad locum S. Francisci apud hospitale Paduae concessum ad usum fratris Simonis de Parma ordinis Minorum die X iuli 1462.' See Kaeppeli, *Scriptores Ordinis Praedicatorum*, I, p. 92.

chained. The 118 leaves are written in a form of cursive minuscule script, whose decoration is limited to coloured capital letters.[121]

The anthology is a collection of excerpts and treatises concerning pastoral care, focused entirely on confession. There is one normative text, John of Capistrano's *Dubia*, a set of answers to dubious cases of the proper interpretation of the Franciscan rule, such as the legitimacy of trading, especially books. Even in this case, the prescriptions of Capistrano had an illustrative value as reference cases. The exemplary nature of the anthology is reinforced by the description of more than 240 sins under the title *Peccata cordis, oris et oneris et obmissionis*.[122]

The manuscript has a remarkable consistency in terms of its palaeographical and codicological features. A distinctive characteristic is the small size of the handwriting if compared with similar volumes produced during the same period and held in the library. Another interesting feature appears on fol. 117^r, where the scribe left a significant space blank for further writing without additional comments. This is consistent with the case of a volume written to be used exclusively by its scribe and bequeathed afterwards to the convent to be lent, as the ownership inscription shows.

As a personal volume, there is no doubt that MS 736 was a tool of reference in the performance of pastoral care, supported by cases of a distinctly practical nature as shown by sections such as the *Dubia circa confessionem*, *De debito coniugali* and *De impedimentis matrimonii* and based on the dispositions of canons and the discussion of masters. The presence of the Dominican master Antonino of Florence is worth mentioning, especially because he has the role of a definitive source of authority for a reformed Franciscan practice.

The third example of a tool for confession is Padua, Biblioteca Universitaria, MS 1159, an anthology of treatises, questions and cases. It is a paper manuscript in octavo of 154 × 102 mm, produced during the fifteenth century. The volume has a modern rigid binding, and no traces of being chained. The manuscript has 188 leaves written in a minuscule cursive script, while the decoration consists of rubrics and capital letters coloured in red.[123]

---

121 See Appendix 3, Plate 14; Pantarotto, *La biblioteca manoscritta*, p. 123.

122 The works contained in the manuscript are John Peckham, *Summa confessionum*; Clarus de Florentia, *Casus*; an anthology of cases under the title *Utrumque sit lecitum vendere ad credentiam*; John of Capistrano's *Dubia*; Antonino of Florence, *Confessionale defecerunt*; a list and a description of sins under the title *Peccata cordis, oris et operis et obmissionis* and a selection of excerpts of Antonino of Florence under the title *Excerpta summa Antonini*. For the *Dubia* of Capistrano and concerning the exchange of books, the manuscript reproduces exactly the same prescriptions as those of MS 586 on its fol. 71^r.

123 See Appendix 3, Plate 15; see also Pantarotto, *La biblioteca manoscritta*, p. 149.

The manuscript contains a great number of cases and excerpts from authorities, and a note on fol. 188ʳ reveals that the volume was conceded on a life-long loan to friar Anthony of Padua.[124] The text does not have any corrections, marginal additions or comments, which is consistent with its character as a reference manual instead of a tool of doctrinal study. As with MS 736, the selection of texts reflects a very practical approach to the performance of pastoral care, especially confession. The anthology is carefully crafted in the selection of excerpts where the authors discuss particular cases. This approach, centred on the cases but strongly supported by the doctrine of the masters, makes this manuscript a more prescriptive tool than the former ones, even though it keeps its functional nature. The influence of Antonino of Florence as the main source for the cases in light of an authoritative view in this manuscript is worth underlining.

This brief exploration of five examples of manuscripts from the library of the convent of San Francesco Grande centred on pastoral care is useful for formulating some observations. The first regards the role of the vernacular. Apparently, it is linked to non-prescriptive works on morality and devotion, such as the *Commedia* and the *Laude* of Jacopone da Todi, but there are instances where it becomes equivalent to Latin in the manuscripts concerning practical cases.

The second question concerns two elements shared by the manuals on pastoral care. The first is the presence of works by Antonino of Florence. The

124 'Ad usum fratris Antonii de Padua.' On fols. Iʳ and IIʳ, there is a *tabula materiae* with a wide range of cases. The main topics are: De absolutione, De electione, De vicariatu et de subdiaconatu, De baptesimo, Dubia circa confessionem, De contrictione, De concubitu matrimoniali, De tribus casibus Capistrani, De debito coniugali, De decimis, De indulgentiis, De ignorantia, De itineratione, De ieiunio, De mendatio, De ornatu mulierum, De voto obiedientiae, De voto castitatis, De voto professionis, De voto paupertatis, De uxore fornicaria, De diffinitione matrimonii, De papalibus excommunicationibus, De episcopalibus excommunicationibus, De audientia confessionis, De ignorantia, De usura, De obligatione voti, De sumaria omnium contractuum, De venditione ad credentiam, De symonia – and so on. The works transcribed in the volume are an anonymous treatise under the title *Merchatum*; Clarus of Florence, *Casus*; Thomas Aquinas, *De secreto*; Jacobus de Marchia, *De impedimentis matrimoni*; Antonino of Florence, *De ornatu et habitu mulierum, De castitate, De professione* and *De paupertatis*; Alexander de Bologna, *Additiones in supplemento*; Francis de Mayronis, *De iuramento et periurio*; John de Prato, *Additiones in supplemento*; a treatise entitled *De emptione et venditione*; another treatise under the title *De usura*, followed by *De contractibus societatis*; Alexander de Alexandria, *De usura* (excerpta); Antonino of Florence, *Extracta ex Summa*; the treatise *Qualiter potest vendi ad credentiam ex dictis Alexandri de Alexandria, Iohannis Duns Scoti, Landulfi Caracioli, Thomae Aquinatis, Richardi de S. Victore, Bernardi Senensis et Francisci de Platea*; the treatise *De livellis*; Alexander de Nievo, *Casus*; Francis of Nardo, *Determinatio*; and Francis de Platea, *Quesitum de ornatu mulierum*.

constant presence of the Dominican master in the tools used as a reference for a practical approach to pastoral care exemplifies the Observants' flexibility in integrating Dominican masters as a legitimate source of authority on the same level as John of Capistrano, Bernardino of Siena or Duns Scotus. The second element in common is the prescriptive work of John of Capistrano on the Franciscan rule, especially in the passages concerning the trade in books. The reiteration of the prescriptions concerning buying and selling books suggests that these were common practices of Observants, despite their best intentions of following the rule in a stricter form. A third observation regards the authorities. There are two types of authoritative sources in the anthologies: the Fathers of the Church and the Franciscan masters, who provide moral advice; and the Observant masters, the Dominican masters and the cases in their own right, which provide practical suggestions for pastoral care.

A Selection of Tools for the Preparation of Sermons

The Franciscan Observance embraced preaching as one of its distinctive activities. Preaching, confession and penitence were understood by Observants as three inseparable features of pastoral care, since penitence and confession were seen as the natural outcome of proper preaching.[125] Preaching was of fundamental importance to the 'pillars' of the Observance, especially to Bernardino of Siena and John of Capistrano, whose activities as preachers had a significant impact on the cities where their pastoral activities took place.[126] The importance of preaching was also reflected in the constitutions of 1443, composed by John of Capistrano. He proceeded to define preaching as one of the fundamentals of the Christian faith, the light of truth, the school of virtues, the door of heaven and ultimately as the instruction of all rational souls.[127]

---

125 Roest, *History of Franciscan Education*, pp. 315-16; see also L. Little, 'Les techniques de la confession et la confession comme technique', pp. 88-89.

126 Roest, *History of Franciscan Education*, pp. 303-5; see also Moorman, *History of the Franciscan Order*, pp. 458-72; Merlo, *Nel nome di san Francesco*, pp. 336 and 354-62; and Roest, '*Ne Effluat in Multiloquium Et Habeatur Honerosus*'. On the importance and influence of Bernardino of Siena, see Origo, *World of San Bernardino*; Manselli, 'L'Osservanza francescana'; Nimmo, 'Franciscan Regular Observance'; Dickinson, 'Revivalism and Populism'; and Delcorno, '*Quasi quidam cantus*', pp. 291-326.

127 'Praedicationis officium est substentamentum fidei christianae, lumen veritatis, schola virtutum, ruina vitiorum, via salutis, doctrina orum, camera sanctitatis, tribunal iudicii, cruciatus daemonum, clausura infernorum, ianua coelorum, confirmatio iustorum, reductio peccatorum et instructio omnium rationabilium animarum.' *CHL*, p. 106.

The main purpose of Observant preaching was to reach the widest audience possible, and therefore Observant friars privileged effectiveness in their sermons. However, the characteristic simplicity of their preaching did not mean lack of theological depth.[128] The Observant preparation for preaching included the development of the skill of presenting the complexities of dogmatic questions in forms, normally in the vernacular, understandable to a lay audience, and whenever preachers had not already learned the local language, they used interpreters, as happened with the friars who preached in Germany.[129]

Some scholars think that Observants were disinclined to rely on the rules of the *artes praedicandi* in order to develop their preaching skills, since they were sceptical regarding the *sermo modernus*, that is, the type of sermon developed in the universities and characterized by a thorough division and further subdivision of the main topic, a technique useful in persuading learned audiences. Observants, instead, preferred to use models taken from their most renowned masters.[130] However, it has also been shown that under the apparent simplicity of the Observant masters' sermons there was a complex structure of thought characteristic of the university sermon.[131] In any case, by the second half of the fifteenth century, Observants produced a remarkable number of their own collections of sermons and materials useful to preaching. The following section will consider three examples of these materials, taken from the library of San Francesco Grande in Padua.

The first example to be discussed is the volume Padua, Biblioteca Universitaria, MS 1789, an anthology of materials useful for the composition of sermons. It is a paper manuscript in quarto of 169 × 120 mm, produced during the second half of the fifteenth century. The manuscript has a modern binding and has no signs of being a chained volume. It has 238 leaves, written in a minuscule *corsiva veloce*, one of the typical forms of cursive script from northern Italy, with the intervention of two main hands. The first hand writes until fol. 152^v, while the second starts on fol. 153^r. Although the two hands are similar, the first has a characteristic notarial, swift stroke, while the second has a higher level of sophistication. A section with an anthology of sermons starts on fol. 176^r.[132] This section has significant variation in the hands of the scribes, although all of them employed the characteristic

---

128 Roest, *History of Franciscan Education*, pp. 307 and 309-10; see also Delcorno, 'L'"Ars predicandi" di Bernardino da Siena'.

129 Roest, *History of Franciscan Education*, pp. 311-13; see also Delcorno, 'La lingua dei predicatori'.

130 Roest, *History of Franciscan Education*, p. 309.

131 Delcorno, 'L'"Ars predicandi" di Bernardino da Siena'.

132 See Appendix 3, Plate 16.

cursive script from the second half of the fifteenth century. The most evident variation is found in the scribe's tendency to write more or less rapidly, depending on each particular case. The decoration of the manuscript is limited to highlighting very modestly some capitals, while in the anthology of sermons there are rubrics, capital letters decorated in red and some passages underlined also in red.

The text starts with a list of the contents and a heading informing the reader that they will find sermons already performed in the proper time and place: 'Iste sunt predicationes facte in loco'. An anthology of treatises on devotional topics begins on fol. 3^r and continues until fol. 37^r.[133] This anthology constitutes the first section of the manuscript and could be described as a gathering of notes on penitence and moral edification.[134]

An excerpt from the *Distinctiones* of Alexander of Hales that explores cases and questions starts on fol. 38^r. This section is followed by an extract from a work on the virtuous fear of God on fol. 42^r. On the same folio a marginal reference suggests reading the treatise on the fear of God by friar Robert for excellent additional insight on the topic.[135] Most probably the reader refers to one of the most popular works on the subject among Observants: *De timore iudicio dei* by friar Robert of Lecce.[136]

A section with a selection of excerpts clearly focused on the preparation of sermons starts on fol. 43^v, where the manuscript offers a treatise on the topic of death and a detailed description of its features: deceitful, powerful and most cruel.[137] The purpose of assuming a more practical approach for the composition of sermons is illustrated by a dramatic resource employed to describe the most cruel death, the 'crudelissima mors': a dialogue between man and death. Death comes to meet a man. When he reveals that he is afraid of dying and asks important questions trying to buy some time, Death answers leaving no space for doubt.[138] Finally, the man acknowledges the

---

133 Some of the treatises are incomplete or partially developed. For example, on fol. 33^r: 'Scripture comminatio'; on fol. 33^v: 'Mortalitatis nostre conditio' and 'Proximi edificatio'; on fol. 34^r: 'Sanctorum intercessio' and 'Vite eterne expectatio'.

134 Some of the topics of this section are 'De resurrectione Christi; 24 fructus penitentie; 24 catene qui ligant pectorem cum penitentia' and '24 tube qui vocant peccatorem ad penitentiam.'

135 'Vide hanc materiam in libro de timore Domini fratris Rub<ert>us carte 28. 42. Optime.'

136 A useful biographical profile of Robert of Lecce is Bastanzio, *Fra Roberto Caracciolo di Lecce*. On his preaching, see Gatto, 'I temi escatologici', and Visani Ravaioli, 'Testimonianze'; on the manuscript tradition of his works, see Gasparri, 'Sulla tradizione manoscritta', and Visani Ravaioli, 'Roberto Caracciolo e i sermonari del secondo Quattrocento'.

137 'Fraudulentissima, potentissima et crudelissima.'

138 'This is the dialogue between Death and a man: Man: "what is going to happen to my inheritance?" Death answers: "Should you worry about what suits you?" M: "what will my sons

power of reason and peacefully embraces death.[139] At this point, a marginal comment underlines the usefulness of this section by declaring that it is possible to make a complete sermon on death on St. Jerome's day.[140]

Another example of the employment of dramatic resources in the preparation for preaching can be found on fol. 46[r], where the rubric 'On the battle of demons against God almighty' introduces the narration of how a group of demons gathered and moved against God.[141] The demons chose four powerful weapons: vanity, avarice, luxury and gluttony.[142] However, they were defeated by the action of four great preachers: John the Baptist, Paul the Apostle, Francis of Assisi and Bernardino of Siena. The demons answer by choosing twelve captains to fight against the twelve apostles, but in the end, they are doomed to fail against the strength of the grace of God.

Additional resources assembled in MS 1789 can be found on fol. 52[r], where there is an anthology of topics written in the vernacular under a heading announcing the twelve privileges conceded to John the Baptist: 'Prerogative sancti Iohannis Baptiste que sunt 12.' Some of the headings describe how he was already a saint before being born, how he was the most virtuous of the children of God and how he was deemed to baptize the son of God.[143] Two features of this section should be underlined: first, it was written in the northern local vernacular, more precisely of the Paduan area as shown by the use of words such as '*mazor*' (higher) and '*fiolo*' (son); and second, some of the headings are not developed at all, which shows its character as a work in progress. Further, on fol. 67[v], there is an example of the interaction of different linguistic layers in the preparation for preaching. On the left-hand side of the written space, there is a heading presenting the

do?" D: "[The same as] you [did] after the death of [your] father." M: "And my beloved wife, whom I leave behind?" D: "It is not to say she is yours, because death makes her not yours any more. If she was not good, rejoice, because your binding to her will be dissolved; if she was good, then there are two possibilities: either she will be under the dominion of another, or she will go free." M: "And I die without any daughters!" D: "Then you will die even more pleasantly, because you will not have worries about them." The transcription of the text is as follows: on fol. 43[v]: 'Hic fac dyalogus inter mortem et hominem [...] On fol. 44[r]: 'H[omo]: quid de patrimonio meo erit? R[espondit]: quid curas de tibi accomodato? H: quid facient filii mei? R: Quid tu post obitum patris. H: En uxoram [sic] meam dilectam relinquo. R: Non dictis tuam, quod mors faciet non tuam. Si non bona fuit, gaude quod eius iugo solveris. Si bona, e duobus: aut altius subieriet [sic], aut libera vagabitur. H: En morior sine filiis. R: Moreris letior quod de eis non dolebis.'

139 On fol. 44[r]: 'Volo mori quod persuasisti veraciter.'

140 'Hic potes facere sermonem ad mortem die de Ieronymo, in transitu et post.'

141 'Proelium demoniorum contra deum omnipotentem.'

142 'vanitas, avaritia, luxuria et gula.'

143 'El foe sancto nel ventre de la madre; El foe attinente di Christo, El foe mazor e piu degno fiolo de lialtri, el batezoe el filiolo de Dio'

blessings of the holy religion, which are underlined by a list of oppositions between afflictions and joys.[144] On the right-hand side of the page there is a short poem praising the practice of confession, written in the vernacular.[145] Finally, there is a marginal note by the same hand that states that on fol. 78 there is the treatise on the joys of Paradise; the actual reference corresponds to the current fol. 80[r].[146]

On fol. 68[r] there starts a short section in which the scribe reminds Bonaventure's words concerning ten activities that endanger any religious order, but particularly the Minors: multiplicity of worldly affairs, the poisoned water of vices, straying of comforts, eagerness for and great expense in buildings, inappropriate request for honours, multiplication of acquaintances, reckless acceptance of commissioned services, usurpation of the rights to administrate last wills and burials, frequent changes of place, and excess in expenses.[147] This admonition is followed by a section that discusses forty of the most delightful joys of Paradise on fols. 80[r]-83[r].[148] At the end of this section, the scribe wrote a quick marginal note that refers to the book of Esther 1:5-8, where the magnificent banquet of king Ahasuerus

144 The heading is 'O sancta religio paradisus mundi'. Under the subheading 'Tu non', the following afflictions are listed: 'Mors, Dolor, Furor, Infamia, Afflictio'. In an opposite column, there is the subheading '[Paradisus] mundus es' under which the respective opposite joys are listed: 'Vita, Gaudem [sic], Tranquilitas, Sapientia, Letitia.'

145 The poem is presented under the title 'O stato mundano inferno temporale'. The text of the poem, composed of two stanzas in ottava rima, is as follows: 'O tu chi me resguardi, pensa bene/ E poni la mente chi devi tornare/ Che dove io sto venire te convene/ E non say lo ponto de lo traspassare// Io te conseglio che tu faci bene/ E delito y peccati te voglia confessare/ E far la penitentia in questa vita/ Se voy securo camino alla partita// Se lo mio conseglio tu non voray fare/ Zoe de mendare toa vita dolente/ Ne lo inferno te bisognera andare/ In quella gran pena e in quello foco ardente// Che cum li demoni staray ad habitare/ Insieme cum loro eternalmente/ Mendatine per Dio e non spetate la morte/ Che ley viene presto e gia e sule porte.'

146 'Require in hoc libro cartam 78 ubi reperies principium.'

147 'Nota qui dominus Bonaventura asserit X esse qui destruunt religiones. 1. Negociorum multiplicitas qua pecunia nostri ordinis paupertati fratribus omnia inimica avide petitur [...] 2. Ociositas sentina vitiorum [...] 3. Evagatio solatii [...] 4. Edificiorum curiositas et sumptuositas [...] 5. Importuna petitio [...] 6. Multiplicatio familiaritatum [...] 7. Improvida commissio officiorum [...] 8. Sepulturarum et testamentarum invasio [...] 9. Mutatio locorum frequens [...] 10. Sumptuositas expensarum.'

148 The introductory rubric to the treatise states: 'On the forty joys of Paradise. The joys in Paradise are so many that no arithmetic of this world can number them, no geometrics comprehend them, neither any grammar, dialectics or rhetoric explain them through words. Nevertheless, we will speak about the best forty among them.' The original text is as follows: 'De 40 gaudii paradisi. Tot et tanta sunt in paradiso gaudia quod omnis arismetica huius mundi non possent numerare, omnis geometria inserare, omnis gramatica dyalectici et rhetorica non possent sermonibus explicare. Tamen de 40 summum ad paradisis loquimur.' Nevertheless, the scribe adds three more items at the end.

is described.[149] Further, on fols. 88^v-94^v, the scribe transcribed a treatise on false prophets, wizards and witches, followed by another on the Last Judgement on fols. 95^r-100^r.

On fol. 100^r, there is the transcription of a poem in terza rima on the topic of death and attributed to Dante Alighieri's son, Iacopo, under the title 'Versus mortis domini Iacobi filii Dantis de Florentia'. In the poem, death personified claims that all the preoccupations and distractions of humanity are absurd and dangerous, especially because they lead the soul away from virtue. Death addresses the generic figures of the soldier, the nobleman, the young man and the sinner, explaining how all of their earthly efforts are useless and superfluous and that all of them will face judgement in the end.[150]

It is difficult to praise the literary virtues of the poem, but it is worth underlining three important features of this section. First, it is a piece of poetry that complements perfectly the poem on fol. 67^v, and it is reminiscent of the previous encounter between Man and Death. Second, although it is a literary piece composed originally in the Tuscan vernacular, it shows a strong influence of northern Venetian vernacular in the transcription. Third, it is clearly written with the *Commedia* as a model, not only in terms of the use of terza rima, but also in the discussion of the topic, in the description of the sinners, their sins and the afterlife, and in the perspective of the narration that proposes a constant ascent from sin towards a final admonition to experience the supreme good and virtue.[151] In this sense, the poem offers clues on the way in which the work of Dante was read in the context of the preaching of Observant friars, that is, as a moral treatise. A final observation on this section regards the writing. The hand remains the same, but the script becomes remarkably more formal in the transcription of the poem

---

149 'Hic potes competere convivium Assueri regis in figuram paradisi primo cape.'

150 Some verses of the poem: 'Io sum la morte principessa grande/ Che la superbia humana in basso pone/ Per tutto el mondo el mio nome se spande// Trona la terra tuta nel mio sono/ Li re e gran maestri in pericol hora/ per lo mio guardo cagion del suo trono// La forza iovenile non li demora/ che subito non vada in sepultura/ tra tanti vermi che cossi el divora// Soldato che te val tua armatura/ Che la mia falce non te sbata in terra/ E che non faci la partenza dura? [...] E tu che credi havere la zentileza/ per esser nato de gran parentato/ e per havere del corpo la belleza// Pegio che porco nato nel contato/ El gran macello cum desio te aspecta/ Se non ferai de virtu ornato// O zoveneto dalla çaçareta/ Che non cognosci li to gran pericli/ E in quanti modi porai morire in freta [...] Guardame in facia o latio iocatore/ Che te sconfunda el nostro gran spavento/ E piu a te che sey biastematore// O quanti son che se pascono di vento/ E per seguitare lo honor e le richezze/ Ne mai se trova alguno contento [...]'. The poem was published in Carducci, ed., *Rime da Cino da Pistoia e d'altri*, pp. 195-98.

151 The two final stanzas: 'E lalma toa semper sera dannata/ per uno poco de dolceza temporale/ perde la gloria e la vita beata// Ma quelo che in virtute semper sale/ desprecia el mondo e fuze suo veneno/ cercando Dio lassa l opere mala/ Stara nel celo perpetuo sereno.'

and abandons the swiftness of other parts of the volume. This suggests that the poem was considered an important section of the manuscript and that accordingly it was written carefully.

The poem is followed by another section. On fol. 109^r, there starts a treatise on the love of God; and particularly in the part where it discusses contrition, the scribe added marginal cross references.[152] The number of notes and comments with references to other places in the work increases from this point. A selection of excerpts on the topic of the disregard of the world or 'De contemptu mundi' starts on fol. 117^r, but very quickly ends on fol. 118^r and is followed by an excerpt in the vernacular with the initial exhortation of a sermon against superfluity and luxury that suddenly shifts into Latin.[153] This linguistic alternation reflects the nature of the excerpt as preparatory material for preaching. Another example can be found on fol. 134^v, where the scribe reproduces the Introduction to the elevation of the soul, or 'Prohemium de nobilitate anime', a short treatise in the vernacular on the proportions of the heavens and celestial bodies, and the place of the blessed souls within this arrangement. A characteristic feature of MS 1789 is the presence of unfinished topics that are listed as headings or rubrics but have no further development, as happens on fol. 119^r and especially on fol. 157^v, where a new section with unfinished paragraphs starts under the heading: 'Twelve paths of the ladder that leads to Paradise'.[154]

152 For example: 'look for chapter 148 where there is another introduction on the legend of [St.] Leo'; on fol. 109^v: 'Look in chapter 147 where there is more'; on fol. 110^r: 'Look this topic in master Leonard in St. Blas who clearly explains [on Augustine of Hippo].' The original comments are, on fol. 109^r: Aliud prohemium require cape 148 autem in legenda Leonis'; on fol. 109^v: 'Require cape 147 verbi est alia quod'; on fol. 110^r: 'Require hanc materiam in magistro Leonardo in sesto Sancti Blasii quod optime dicit Ipone.'

153 The sermon starts: 'O citadini mei! Reputaresti savio qolui el qual desiderasse tuti li piaceri de questo mundo come sono richeze, honor, bella dona, fioli, nobilità, reputatione et huius modi e che questa electione fosse libera, zoe senza alguno contrario et non seria bene stulto che in tanti beni luy se elegesse contrarietate alguna. O pazo mondo! O stulta gente! Ma qolui che se eleze richeza, honor et cetera quo se eleze se non pena, affani, tormenti, pro malo. Tria sunt in hoc modo, videlicet primo est appe[ti]tus est quedam passio quae numquam saturatur [...]'.

154 'First, examination of conscience; second, affliction of the heart; third, true confession; fourth, reconciliation with others or apologize; fifth hearing to the word of the Lord; sixth, endurance when in distress; seventh, overcoming of temptations; eight, opposing sins, that is, to be humble; ninth, looking carefully; tenth, communicating the good news; eleventh, the way of love; twelfth, persevering in all of the former.' The headings of each paragraph to be written are: '12 vie sive scala eundi paradisum. Prima: conscientie examinatio; Secunda via est cordis contritio; Tertia via est vera confessio; Quarta via, proximi reconciliatio sive satisfactio; Quinta via est verbi dominum auditio; Sexta via, tribulationum supportatio; Septima via, temptationum superatio; Octava via, peccatorum oppositio est esse humilem; Nona via previsio; Decima via

On fol. 175[r], there is a *tabula* with the contents of the manuscript; how-ever, some of the items listed are to be found on leaves located further in the volume. This suggests that the additional items belonged to another manuscript or that they were deliberately put in a different section, separated by the table of contents. In any case, the texts placed after the *tabula* are predominantly complete sermons or complete sections of sermons. There are significant variations in the codicological characteristics of this selection such as the use of rubrics, the variations in the hand of the scribe and from fol. 199[v], a change in the *mise en page* to a two-column layout. The main topics of these sermons are the danger of vices, the good effects of penitence, the mortal sins and admonitions addressed to women.[155]

From fol. 206[r] the manuscript again proposes a compilation of useful materials and hence the lists of virtues, vices and admonitions.[156] The main text finishes with a sermon on hope, from fol. 230[r] to fol. 237[v]. All the complete sermons are written in Latin, and the presence of different codicological features for this section suggests that most probably the sermons come from another volume. If that is the case, their inclusion here was not casual, since there is complete consistency in the topics of both sections of the manuscript. Summarizing, MS 1789 is a complex tool for the composition of sermons, offering a wide range of materials in different genres, languages and textual typologies.

The second tool for the composition of sermons that will be considered is the volume Padua, Biblioteca Universitaria, MS 1851, an anthology of different materials, mainly treatises on devotion. It is a manuscript in quarto of 215 × 154 mm, produced during the fifteenth century. The volume has a modern stiff binding and does not have traces of being chained. It has 282 leaves, written in a minuscule cursive script, heavily abbreviated, whose distribution varies from a full page to a two-column layout. The decoration of the manuscript is limited to the use of rubrics, initial letters decorated and some passages that are underlined in red.[157] The hand that transcribes

---

Bonorum communicatio; Undecima via per dilectionem; Duodecima, omnia predictarum perseveratio.'

155 On fol. 175[r]: 'De ambitione'; on fol. 182[r]: 'De superbia'; on fol. 183[r]: 'De nobilitate'; on fol. 186[r]: 'De contritione'; on fol. 187[v]: 'De eadem'; on fol. 194[r]: 'De adulteris'; on fol. 198[v]: 'De luxuria et incontinentia'; on fol. 199[r]: 'De incautu aspectu'; on fol. 199[v]: 'De aviditate mulierum', '12 mulierum magna fide', 'De sapientia mulierum', 'De pietate mulierum', 'De fortitude mulierum', 'De falaciis mulierum', 'De stiloquio mulierum', and 'De superfluo ornatu mulierum'.

156 On fol. 206[r]: 'De 8 impedimenti eundi ad vitam eternam'; on fol. 208[r]: 'De 8 remedii ad dissolvendum anteriora impedimenta'; on fol. 214[r]: 'De 27 vocationibus divinis' – and so on.

157 See Pantarotto, *La biblioteca manoscritta*, p. 192.

the text is the same that writes the comments and marginal references. On fol. 1ʳ, there is an incomplete table of contents and an inscription saying that the manuscript was given on long-term loan to friar Pellegrinus.[158]

From fol. 1ʳ to fol. 170ᵛ the manuscript contains the transcription of fragments of sermons and treatises by Iacopo della Marca, organized by topics and complemented by marginal comments.[159] On fols. 84ᵛ-86ᵛ, it has a table with a list of sins, a tool for quick reference under the title 'Tabula peccatorum', followed by a short sermon for the festival of St. Bernardino.[160] On fols. 171ʳ-176ʳ, there is a selection of sermons by Robert of Licio, very similar to those of Iacopo della Marca, followed by a sermon for the festival of Francis of Assisi, on fol. 186ʳ.[161]

From fol. 266ʳ to fol. 278ᵛ, a selection of texts appears under the heading 'Authorities, excerpts and examples', assembled as a quick reference resource.[162] Among the texts is a selection of fables by Aesop with specific indications as to their application, for example: 'Against the ungrateful, The Wolf; against envy, The Fox', and so on.[163] The final leaves of the manuscript, fols. 279ᵛ-282ᵛ, contain the transcription of some excerpts from the *Summa de essentia* by Bonaventure.

Despite gathering together numerous works of very different types, the selection of texts of MS 1851 is characterized by brief excerpts with essential information concerning the topic. This feature, and the absence of long single treatises on morality, pastoral care or consideration of cases such as the works of Antonino of Florence, suggests that this volume had the function of being a quick, efficient repository of primary materials for examples, admonitions and exhortations. The manuscript has traces of intensive use, especially in terms of cross references to other sections of the text, *maniculae* and marginal references indicated by the words 'Nota bene'.

Padua, Biblioteca Universitaria, MS 2103, an anthology of materials for the composition of sermons, is the third example to be considered. This is a paper manuscript in quarto of 218 × 152 mm, produced during the fifteenth

---

158 'Libri ad usum mei fratris Pellegrini'.

159 See Appendix 3, Plate 17. Some of the headings are: 'De fide', 'De iustitia', 'De predicatione', 'De penis inferni', 'De intemperantia', 'De blasfemia', 'De correctione fraterna', 'De virtutibus', 'De ligno vite', 'De caritatis ordine', 'De amore proximi', 'De mercanciis', 'De sacrilegio', 'De pace', 'De nomine Yesu', 'De vanagloria', 'De mendacio', 'De septem pecatis mortalibus', 'De lingua', 'De gracia et eius fructibus', 'De causis', 'De misericordia dei', 'De divite apulone', 'De mortuis', 'De morte' and 'De confessione'.

160 'In solempnitate sancti Bernardinis'.

161 'In solempnitate Patris nostri Francisci'.

162 'Auctoritates, excerpta and exempla'.

163 'Contra ingratos, dum lupum; contra invidiam, dum vulpem'.

century. The volume has a modern binding and does not have traces of being chained. It has seventy-four leaves, written in a minuscule cursive script, sometimes *al tratto*, carried out by several hands. The first writes from fol. 1ʳ to fol. 20ʳ: it is a very light hand, with traces of notarial training, heavily abbreviated. The second hand writes from fol. 21ʳ to fol. 25ʳ. This is a more organized and formal hand that uses a larger script, with traces of a book-hand style, less abbreviated.[164] A third hand writes from fol. 25ʳ to fol. 43ᵛ. This is a light, quick hand. A fourth hand writes from fol. 43ᵛ to fol. 70ᵛ. This hand shows a stronger gothic influence, very stylized, less abbreviated, being much more a book-hand script. It is probably German, as the scribe does not use the characteristic Italian abbreviations. The system of decoration in the volume consists of decorated initials and rubrics on fols. 72ᵛ-74ᵛ.[165] On fol. IIIʳ, an ownership inscription attributes the manuscript to master Augustine of Blaise.[166]

On fol. 1ʳ-20ᵛ, there is a selection of excerpts, notes and comments organized by topics or cases. The source for the selection is the *Coronula perusiva ad sermocinandum inventa*, written during the fourteenth century by John Calderinus. The work focuses on the practical application of scriptural excerpts. For example, under a heading that introduces ways to persuade the head of a house to come to a certain place, there is a selection of several biblical quotations.[167] A table of quick reference of the topics was prepared and included on fol. 69ᵛ. From fol. 71ᵛ to fol. 74ᵛ there are other texts and excerpts, mainly a selection from the Fathers of the Church. In this particular section, the texts are introduced by rubrics. The manuscript has a large

---

164 See Appendix 3, Plate 18.

165 See Pantarotto, *La biblioteca manoscritta*, pp. 208-9.

166 'Iste liber est mei Augustini magistri Blasii'.

167 Therefore, under the heading 'Ad invitandum aliquem dominum ut ad aliquem locum veniat', there are references such as 'Venite pone manum tuam super eam et vivet: Mathei VIIII' or 'Veniat dominus qui illuminabit abscondita: Ad Corinthi, 4' or 'Venite bene dicte patris miei percipite regnum: Marcus XXV'. Most probably this last reference is an error of the scribe, since the reference corresponds to Matthew 25, as confirmed by a quick comparison with Cologne, Historisches Archiv der Stadt, MS Best 7002, HS 146, fol. 301ʳ. Other examples are the following: Under the heading 'Ad acceptandum et promittendum ad aliquem locus', there are references such as 'Ego veniam et curabo eum: Mathei VIII' or 'Et surgens penitus est eum: Mathei VIIII'. Under the heading 'Ad excusandum se ab ambasiata [sic] vel alio officio', there is the reference 'Quis ego sum ut vadam ad pharaonem?: Exodus III'. Other headings are 'Ad impetrandam gratiam et ad recomendandum se vel alios'; 'Ad exortandum per habundantia virtutis'; 'Ad filios servos et quoslibet minores se ad aliquid agendum'; 'Ad suplicandum elemosinam fieri'; 'Ad pacem facendam et manutenendam'; 'Ad exortandum guerram contra iniquus opprimentes se vel amicos'; 'Ad confortandam gentem accedentem ad bellum; 'Ad corripiendum populum de aliquo enormi vicio; ad preveniendum aliquem turbantes comune bonum' – and so on.

number of marginal references, especially the marginal 'Nota' to identify passages of interest. There are some *maniculae*, such as on fol. 19ᵛ to highlight the passage on how to protect people from the peril of dangerous vice.[168]

The main characteristic of MS 2103 is that it is very fragmentary, and thus it does not offer a single complete work or a complete cycle of sermons. Instead, it presumably had a significant role as a swift and practical tool of reference for composing sermons and treatises, organized by cases and with strong support from biblical references.

The three examples of aids to preaching are all tools for quick reference for the composition of sermons. It is not possible to find in any of them a complete cycle of sermons or a complete anthology of the main works of a famous preacher. Instead, some of them are focused on devotional and moral questions, while others have a clear function of being a guide to the selection and first exploration of the topics for preaching. No one of them is constructed around a single concept, problem or situation. Another typical feature of this group of manuscripts is that they offer a perspective on the multilinguistic environment in which Observants undertook their preaching activity. The use of Latin and the vernacular in the sources for the preparation of sermons is an example not only of the adaptability of Observants as preachers but also of their flexibility concerning the practices of reading and study. The presence of literary works composed in the vernacular within the treatises on moral and devotional authority shows that Observants acknowledged the value of literary expressions as an important element of the cultural background of their audience. Nevertheless, the actual practice of Observant preaching to a wider audience remains uncertain and is still a matter of discussion. For some scholars, when preaching, Franciscan friars shifted from Latin to the vernacular according to the audience of their sermons; for others, they used a mixed language with traces of Latin and the vernacular in their preaching, as suggested by some manuscript evidence.[169] In any case, the group of manuscripts we have considered so far show that Observant friars employed multilingual resources for personal study and preparation.[170] It is unquestionable, then, that different linguistic layers were present in Observant sources for their preparation for preaching and that sometimes it was difficult to establish the linguistic boundaries between Latin and vernacular in the same single source. In their practice of

---

168 'Ad corripiendum populum de aliquo enormi vicio xxvi'.
169 David D'Avray discusses the relation between language, transmission of sermons and audience in D'Avray, *Preaching of the Friars*, pp. 90-131.
170 See Roest, *History of Franciscan Education*, pp. 311-12.

preaching to a wide and very mixed audience, there is no reason to believe the Observant preachers restricted themselves to one linguistic register, literary genre or rhetorical resource.

Conclusion

This chapter has explored the physical evidence of the Franciscan manuscripts in Padua and has shown how the manuscripts are a source of valuable information on the works they contained, as well as on the forms they took in the libraries. The analysis also offers evidence on the need for a typology of the Franciscan manuscript based on the practices of use, rather than subject matter. Even more interesting is the fact that this typology is substantially different for each library. The library of the convent of Sant'Antonio collected works to be studied, such as theological treatises, manuals and collections useful for the composition of sermons. The library of the Observant convent of San Francesco Grande had a different approach. Its books were mainly portable volumes written by their own readers and were, for the most part, compilations useful for internal or external pastoral care or compilations useful for preaching, containing topics, models of sermons, cases and 'exempla'. This substantial difference is underlined by some linguistic features. The Biblioteca Antoniana kept almost exclusively a collection of works written in Latin, while the manuscripts of San Francesco Grande show a wider variety, with works in the vernacular and in Latin and in different genres, such as poems, sermons, cases and treatises. The presence of two different approaches to production, study, use and collection of manuscripts in the same place, at the same time and within the Franciscan order could be summarized by saying that if reading was oriented towards learning in the convent of Sant'Antonio, it was oriented towards practical pastoral care in San Francesco Grande. In both cases, it is clear that there was a great distance between the ideal conception of the role and purpose of the Franciscan manuscript as conceived by the rule and the actual practices of scholarship and preparation for preaching in the convents, especially concerning ownership of manuscripts and practices of writing and reading.[171]

Sometimes the manuscripts reveal parts of their own history, for example through the presence of inscriptions 'ad usum', showing that long-term loans were common practice in both convents. The manuscripts from the

---

171 See Hernández Vera, 'Franciscan Observant Miscellanies'.

library of San Francesco Grande were, or had been, personal copies that satisfied the needs and expectations of an individual, a scribe who had produced a portable library 'per se ipsum'. In a sense, they were artefacts in which their creators left an imprint on their intellectual history. On the other hand, there were manuscripts which were less personalized but nonetheless intriguing, as shown by the sets of volumes from the Biblioteca Antoniana. Both are the result of an optimization of the bibliographical resources by 'releasing' manuscripts for loan as soon as other copies were available for consultation. This practice also constitutes a substantial difference between the libraries.[172] In effect, the library of Sant'Antonio was an old, well-established library with a double collection of books and a cycle of circulation according to which incoming manuscripts, after having been corrected, were chained, while the old copies became part of the collection for loan, as shown by the copies of Bonaventure's commentary on the *Sentences*.[173] There were no traces of such a practice in the library of San Francesco Grande, as suggested by the absence of traces of chains in its manuscripts. Most probably, the Observant library did not have a double collection, and all its books were available for loan.

The analysis of Franciscan regulations in Chapter 1 has shown that they were also a formulation of an ideal concerning the role of books in Franciscan convents. The study of Franciscan libraries in Chapter 2 revealed that they were not only repositories of the book collection but also spaces of study and production, and that they had a determining role in the development and intellectual success of the Franciscan order. This chapter has offered a more detailed picture of the actual manuscripts produced, read and studied by Franciscans from the thirteenth to fifteenth centuries in Padua. The evidence shows that these books had an enormous variety of formats, genres, scripts, topics and, most importantly, roles. This study has also shown that the manuscripts provide information on the interaction between readers and text and consequently are an excellent resource to gain a better understanding of their readership, which is the question to be considered in detail in the next chapter.

---

172 See Hernández Vera, 'From Chained Books to Portable Collections', pp. 102-4.
173 See Appendix 2.

4. The Readership

Reading Franciscan Manuscripts in Padua

Introduction

Piers Plowman is an allegorical poem written during the second half of the fourteenth century that narrates the quest of its eponymous hero for the true Christian life. It had a strong impact on popular culture, as shown by the large number of related compositions that appeared shortly after. One of *Piers Plowman*'s sequels was a poem known as *Jack Upland*, a polemical work arranged around a set of questions that aimed at condemning the hypocrisy of particularly the mendicant religious orders. At a certain point Jack, the main character, asks a sycophantic friar: 'Friar, what charity is it to gather up the books of God's word, many more than you need, and place them in your treasure room, and thus imprison them from secular clerks and curates, so that they are prevented from knowing God's word and from preaching the gospel freely?'[1] This excerpt provides an interesting depiction of the relationship between friars and books. In fact, according to the poem, friars were guilty of at least two sins, namely, avidly treasuring books and afterwards restricting access to them in a pronounced display of uncaring egoism.

Shortly after the poem's composition, between 1389 and 1396, the Franciscan friar William Woodford, a master at Oxford, prepared a threefold answer to these accusations.[2] William argued that friars restricted access to books, firstly, because that was the common practice within other orders, especially monastic ones. Secondly, friars needed to protect their books from mutilation and loss, and therefore they could not make them available to everybody. Thirdly, friars had the need and obligation to study, and so books should always be available to them.[3]

---

1   Heyworth, ed., *Jack Upland*, p. 70. A discussion of the passage and the sequel may be found in M. Rouse and Rouse, *Authentic Witnesses*, pp. 410-19.
2   M. Rouse and Rouse, *Authentic Witnesses*, p. 416.
3   'Respondeo et dico, primo, quod pars prima huius questionis queri potest ab abathiis et prioratibus monachorum et canonicorum, a communitatibus collegiorum et unitatibus, et a

Hernández Vera, R., *Franciscan Books and their Readers: Friars and Manuscripts in Late Medieval Italy*. Taylor & Francis Group, 2022
DOI 10.5117/9789463729512_CH04

As William's answer underlined, friars jealously protected their books because Franciscan convents had become centres of study, that is, places where books were written, collected and, most importantly, read. The essential role of reading for the purposes of learning in Franciscan life is well illustrated by the example of the Paduan convents, and this will be precisely the main topic to be discussed in this chapter. So far, this work has explored three dimensions of the manuscripts produced, studied and kept by the Franciscans in Padua from the thirteenth to the fifteenth century. The first chapter has explored the development of the relation between an ideal of what the Franciscan manuscript should be and the actual practices of learning and use of books through the regulations on the matter. The second chapter has explored the space where these manuscripts were produced and collected, namely the Franciscan libraries in general, and the Franciscan libraries in Padua in further detail. The third chapter has discussed the form of the manuscripts through the comparison and analysis of the characteristic features of the books held in the libraries. Regulations, libraries and manuscripts provide compelling evidence of the important role of books in the life of the communities, not only as tools for study and preaching, but as an element of Franciscan life. Nevertheless, in order to give a more complete idea of the role of the Franciscan manuscript, a further dimension needs to be explored, that is, the readership, and specifically the practices of reading in the convents. Therefore, if the previous chapter focused on the material evidence and on Franciscan manuscripts as physical objects, this chapter will consider the traces of interaction between the reader and the text.

To assess the use of the Paduan manuscripts it is necessary first to explore the meaning that terms such as 'reading', 'reader' and 'interpretive community' will have in the discussion. Afterwards, a brief overview of the

cathedralibus ecclesiis equale sicud secundum a fratribus. Nam quilibet predictorum habet librarias ad custodiendum libros in eisdem, tam de sacra scriptura quam de scientiis aliis, qui clauduntur, ita ut seculares ab eis excludantur pro maiori parte. [...] Quod fratres claudent libros tales ad cautelam ut impediant sacerdotes seculares a predicatione verbi Dei est manifeste falsum. Nam illa de causa, sic non faciunt fratres plus quam ecclesie cathedrales vel alii collegii, sed propter duas causas faciunt, quarum una est ut libri habeantur in sacra custodia ne furto exponantur; nam in quibusdam locis ubi libri in loco aperto iacebant et sacerdotes seculares accessum liberum ad eos habuerunt, libri frequenter fuerunt furtive sublati, non obstante quod ipsi fuerunt fortiter cathenati, et quaterni aliqui librorum fuerunt abscisi et catene cum asseribus relicte remanserunt [...] Alia causa est quod fratres servant libros suos sub custodia clausos ut magis essent in promptu pro fratrum usibus ad custodiendum ut fratres ipsi studeant in eis et illi libri non possunt simul servire fratribus et secularibus.' Oxford, Bodleian Library, MS Bodley 703, fols. 54^v-55^r; transcribed in M. Rouse and Rouse, *Authentic Witnesses*, p. 417.

development of medieval reading and the types of medieval reader will be introduced in order to provide the context for consideration of a set of questions proposed by the Robert Darnton as key concepts at the core of a history of the book. Darnton's set of methodological questions will be applied to the manuscripts of the Franciscan convents in Padua to discuss whether there were distinctive forms of reading in the convents, and whether there was a relation between practices of reading and the manuscripts used and produced in the convents. Finally, this section will discuss the typology of the medieval reader as proposed by Celine Van Hoorebeeck in terms of professional and amateur readers to outline a profile of the Franciscan friars as readers of manuscripts.[4]

Reading and Readers in the Middle Ages

One of the most effective definitions of reading describes it as 'lifting information from a page'.[5] In spite of being extremely simple, and perhaps reductive, this definition points to the usually overlooked fact that reading is essentially an action. It is possible to improve this definition by considering two key elements implicit in the action, namely the agent, the reader and the object, the text. Reading can also be seen therefore as a process of interaction between the reader and the text that results in a passage of information from one to another. Depending on which element the theory focuses on, different models may be developed for the process of reading.

The discussion of reading from the perspective of the reader is the central question of reception criticism or reception theory.[6] According to reception criticism, the text, which assumes the form of written words, is contained by a physical object, usually a book. The process of reading suspends the readers' links to material reality and creates an inner space for the abstract objects that constitute the universe of the text, allowing the text to become part of the world of the reader. During this process, the reader becomes the subject of the reality proposed by the text and assumes the identity, or at least the voice, of the author. This means that, through reading, the reader and the author each become someone different from

---

4   Van Hoorebeeck, 'Du livre au lire'.

5   Darnton, *Kiss of Lamourette*, p. 187. This process implies much more than the ability to decipher the units (letters, words) of the linguistic code employed to compose the text. See Certeau, 'La lecture absolue', p. 66.

6   Wolfgang Iser is perhaps the most influential scholar who considers reading from the point of view of the effect on the reader and the subsequent aesthetic response. See Iser, *Act of Reading*.

themselves. It is necessary, however, to keep in mind that the author is a textual entity, that is, the subject of the text, and should not be confused with the writer, namely the physical, historical person who arranged the words of the text. The writer is alien to the real meaning of the text before the experience of reading. Therefore, the effect of reading on the reader is the assumption of the identity of the author, not that of the writer, and this explains why any previous knowledge of the context of the writer fails to contribute to or essentially improve the experience of reading.[7] Naturally, the assumption of the identity of the author cancels out the distance between the text and the reader, allowing the latter to construct their own sense of the text, that is, to interpret it.[8] This reception approach has been of great importance for the understanding of reading as a complex process that implies more than decoding a fixed meaning contained in a book. However, as a methodology, it has also been controversial because it attributes a secondary role to the context; for example, one of the main criticisms addressed to reception theory argues that it 'erases the concrete modality of the act of reading and characterizes it by its effects, postulated as universals'.[9]

Actually, a better understanding of specific forms of reading can be achieved with the study of groups of readers in specific places and periods of time. From that point of view, which may be called 'historical', the reader is no longer an archetypical individual but a member of a community of fellow readers who share socio-historical circumstances and whose interaction determines the practices of reading of each one. Clear examples of such communities are groups that share a programme of education or intellectual training, as happens with medieval religious communities. Even though the criticism from the historical point of view reveals some significant limitations of reception theory, some of the notions proposed by reception criticism are relevant to medieval practices of reading, for example, the understanding of the reading experience as an individual, personal interaction, even though the subject can be member of a community with shared values and purposes, or the conception of the reader as an active player in the interaction with the text.[10] As a result, the methodological notion of reading as a process of personal interaction will be assumed in order to gain a better understanding of Franciscans' interface with their manuscripts. Accordingly,

7   Poulet, 'Phenomenology of Reading', pp. 54-58.
8   Chambers, 'Le texte "difficile" et son lecteur', p. 82.
9   Chartier, 'Labourers and Voyagers', p. 134.
10   Kimmelman, 'Trope of Reading', p. 28.

for the purpose of this analysis, it can be assumed that reading is a process in which a single member of the community of Franciscan friars interacted with a textual source, a manuscript, in the context of the conventual life, pastoral care or preaching.[11] In what follows, the topics of reading in the Middle Ages, medieval readers and the Franciscan community of readers will be outlined with further detail, in order to explore the process of reading undertaken by Franciscan friars in the Paduan convents.

Reading in the Middle Ages

One of the first questions discussed by scholarship on reading in the Middle Ages is whether reading aloud was preferred to silent reading. It has been argued that silent reading was practically unknown in late antiquity and that the situation remained unchanged during the high Middle Ages. Silent reading had then disseminated with the 'scholastic turn' during the eleventh and twelfth centuries. However, this assumption has been questioned, for example, by Armando Petrucci, who argues that excessive importance has been attributed to reading aloud during late antiquity and the early Middle Ages, that silent reading was already common practice during antiquity and that therefore it cannot be considered a medieval invention.[12] Nevertheless, it can be said that there was an effective transition in reading practices for purposes of study during the high Middle Ages, despite the fact that, as will be seen, not all readers had developed writing skills.[13]

Although not an innovation of scholastic culture, silent reading certainly was employed with an innovative purpose by medieval universities. Schematically, one can say that scholasticism took reading out of the monastic cell or library and found new spaces for silent reading with the purposes of study,

---

11   There were practices of reading that took place in locations different from the library such as, for example, the refectory, where friars shared common reading.

12   Petrucci, *Writers and Readers*, p. 133.

13   With the introduction of the practice of personal reflection on the scripture, there were at least three different types of reading: reading aloud, as happened in the refectories of religious houses; reading *sotto voce*, or 'meditari litteras', namely, reading in a whisper; and a different kind of private reading, in silence, as described in chapter 48 of the *Rule of St. Benedict* or in Isidore's *Libri sententiarum*, III, xiv, 8 and 9: 'Saepe prolixa lectio longitudinis causa memoriam legentis oblitterat. Quod si brevis sit, submotoque libro sententia retractetur in animo, tunc sine labore legitur, et ea quae lecta sunt recolendo memoria minime exciduntur. Acceptabilior est sensibus lectio tacita quam aperta; amplius enim intellectus instruitur quando vox legentis quiescit et sub silentio lingua movetur. Nam clare legendo et corpus lassatur et vocis acumen obtunditur.' Isidore of Seville, *Sententiae*, ed. Cazier, p. 240; see also Parkes, 'Reading, Copying and Interpreting', pp. 92-93, and Loutchitsky and Varol, eds., *Homo Legens*.

contributing significantly to the development of universities and schools. While reading in the monastic tradition was characterized by the rumination, or *ruminatio* of sacred scripture, scholastic reading aimed at the effective retrieval of information in the written text, and was circumscribed by specific and predetermined ways of interacting with the text, for example, by adding written marginal glosses and references.[14] More importantly, scholastic culture introduced a shift in the ultimate purpose of reading. While monastic reading was aimed at obtaining wisdom through reflective understanding, scholastic reading was aimed at achieving knowledge through the development of specific techniques retrieval and processing of information.[15]

Naturally, the development of scholastic culture and its practices of learning depended on the availability of copies of manuscripts for personal reading. As we have seen, medieval libraries organized their book collections around the needs of their users and provided places for personal reading in order to guarantee the availability of manuscripts for individual study.[16] These spaces were characterized by silence: books were studied individually in a common room, where the reader shared the space with fellow readers.[17]

The changes in the forms of reading also affected the development of writing. During the high Middle Ages, writing did not necessarily imply the ability to gain a full understanding of the text, which was presented in a continuous form without separation between the units of sense and without elements that provided guidance in reading. Writing was then an end in itself and was related to, but clearly separate from reading.[18] To a certain extent, the early medieval scribe's indifference to reading was the result of his lack of familiarity with its hard and laborious practice.[19]

14   Scholastic culture recognized the value of reading aloud, for example, during the *lectio*, that is, reading aloud in the class with the help of guided explanation and commentary. Nevertheless, personal reading with the purpose of study was carried out in silence. See Hamesse, 'Scholastic Model of Reading', pp. 105-10.

15   The university provided specific and demanding training to develop abilities in order to explain and comment on the text (*legere*), to discuss specific topics (*disputare*) and to discuss in public its spiritual dimension (*praedicare*). See Hamesse, 'Scholastic Model of Reading', pp. 110 and 112; see also Weijers, *Terminologie des universites au XIII[e] siecle*.

16   See the discussion of the development of university and mendicant libraries in Chapter 2. See also Saenger, 'Reading in the Later Middle Ages', p. 141.

17   Cavallo and Chartier, eds., *History of Reading in the West*, p. 19; Petrucci, *Writers and Readers*, p. 139.

18   Armando Petrucci discusses Paul Saenger's assessment of the contribution of the high Middle Ages to the history of literacy in terms of the introduction of the separation of words in the written text. See Saenger, 'Silent Reading', esp. pp. 377-79; see also Petrucci, *Writers and Readers*, p. 134.

19   The case of the monastery of St. Gall during the second half of the tenth century suggests that writing was secondary to reading, since the less talented young friars were assigned to the

With scholastic culture, reading and writing became the indispensable skills of a learned individual. Writing became more compatible with individual intellectual activity thanks to developments that guaranteed the personal, silent readability of the text. From the twelfth century, writing and reading became closely bound together, since both were necessary to study.[20] There was a diffusion of word-separated script, along with resources that helped to identify sections of the text such as rubrics, paraphs, chapter titles, commentaries, summaries, concordances, indexes and tables, all of which satisfied the need for individual, silent reading. In actual fact, the structure of the page and of the whole text from the fourteenth century on implied a reader who read only with their eyes.[21] In time, the demand for written material produced the figure of the professional scribe who, despite being a qualified reader, had a technical approach to writing. In this aspect, the professional scribe was no different from the early medieval one, apart from the fact that the professional scribe was able to read critically the contents of his writing although for professional reasons did not do so.[22] Nevertheless, students who copied their own books through the *pecia* system represented a very different kind of scribe, that is, a writer who wrote his own reading material, and who could freely leave signs of his interaction with the text in the margins of the work he had copied.[23] These works, usually written efficiently, that is, with a light, cursive script, were expected to be read in silence in an individual, personal fashion, instead of being read aloud within the community, and their authors, aware of their role, began to address their works to the reader, not to a community of listeners. During the last part of the Middle Ages many scribes assembled and copied their own reading materials, as shown for example by the miscellanies composed by Franciscan Observants.[24] All these developments of the forms of reading and writing responded to a simple need, that is, making reading as effective

copying of manuscripts. See Petrucci, *Writers and Readers*, pp. 135-36; see also Grotans, *Reading in Medieval St. Gall*, pp. 67-76.

20   Petrucci, *Writers and Readers*, pp. 138-39; Cavallo and Chartier, eds., *History of Reading in the West*, p. 18.

21   Saenger, 'Reading in the Later Middle Ages', p. 125; introd. to Cavallo and Chartier, eds., *History of Reading in the West*, p. 19; Kimmelman, 'Trope of Reading', p. 36.

22   Saenger, 'Reading in the Later Middle Ages', p. 129. In this sense, the admonition expressed by the regulations of Dominican friars against using valuable study time in the activity of copying texts is perfectly understandable.

23   Saenger, 'Reading in the Later Middle Ages', p. 132; Boyle, 'Peciae, apopeciae, epipeciae', pp. 39-40; Shooner, 'La Production du livre', pp. 17-37; Jean Destrez, *La Pecia dans les manuscrits universitaires*; Kimmelman, 'Trope of Reading', p. 35; and Saenger, *Space between Words*, p. 257.

24   Petrucci, *Writers and Readers*, p. 142.

as possible; and this certainly also contributed to the further diffusion of reading in non-scholastic environments at the end of the Middle Ages.[25]

The Medieval Reader

The reader as a key element of the process of reading can be seen in many different ways, for example, as a historical entity, as the agent and recipient of perception, as a selective cultural agent or even as a non-existent individual who is simply an effect of the act of reading.[26] From the point of view of the reader, the text guides the reading, and the reader is affected by the text. In this way, the act of reading implies a double role for the reader: they are an agent while reading but simultaneously transformed, not only by what they read but mainly by the act of reading itself. The criticism of reception theory is centred on that assumption.[27] For reception theory, the reader unfolds a network of connections from the text and selects some of them as significant. This selection is determined by the conformity of the text to the reader's experience; and precisely through reading, the text itself becomes part of the whole experience of the reader. As a result, what the reader believes are the thoughts of the author of the text, are their own.[28]

One of the main criticisms addressed to reception theory is that reading cannot be understood completely without a proper discussion of the context that affects the reader's performance. In this sense, an understanding of historical circumstances is essential to any discussion of the uniqueness of reception phenomena. However, reception criticism does not fully explore this dimension because it focuses on the atemporal aspects of reading.[29] As a response, historical criticism proposes a discussion of the reader as

25   Introduction to Cavallo and Chartier, eds., *History of Reading in the West*, p. 17; see also Nebbiai-Dalla Guarda, 'Lecteurs, bibliothèques et société'.

26   An effective synthesis of the main approaches to reading and the role of the reader can be found in the introduction to Bennett, ed., *Readers and Reading*. A summary of the approach to the reader as a historical figure can be found in Chartier, 'Labourers and Voyagers'. As mentioned above, the discussion of the central role of the reader in the process of reading can be found in Iser, *Act of Reading*. Some of the most important principles of criticism proposing that the reader does not exist as an individual, but rather as an effect of reading, may be found in Derrida, *Acts of Literature*, and in Felman, 'Turning the Screw of Interpretation'. Michel de Certeau explores the conception of the reader as a qualified decoder of cultural products in Certeau, 'Reading as Poaching', pp. 150-61.

27   Iser, *Act of Reading*, pp. 107, 134 and 163; see also Iser, 'Interaction between Text and Reader'.

28   Iser, *Act of Reading*, pp. 126 and 153; see also Iser, 'Interaction between Text and Reader', p. 21.

29   Chartier, 'Labourers and Voyagers', p. 134.

an individual who perceives the text in a specific context that determines the form of reading.

For historical criticism, the discussion of the reader as the subject of analysis derives primarily from the need to distinguish the history of reading from the history of what was read. The reader emerged in history as someone who perceived the contents of the book, and whose perception was conditioned by external factors. For example, in regard to reading during the *Ancien Régime*, Michel de Certeau has argued that reading was characterized by the independence of the text from its reader, a consequence of the control of the institution (the church) through clerks. This setting favoured a uniform interpretation, and this amounted to uniformity in reading. According to this interpretation, reciprocity in the interaction between the text and its readers developed only when the institution began to weaken.[30] The discussion of Certeau's approach has shown that this determinism is insufficient to explain complex phenomena such as variations in the practices of reading.[31] One of the most interesting principles of historical criticism proposes that a text is invested with new meaning and being when the physical form through which it is presented for interpretation changes.[32] In the context of the medieval manuscript, for example, the impact of the changes in the physical form is significant not only because of the changes in the techniques of writing but also because the changes are related to features such as portability, as shown in Chapter 3. Indeed, recent historical criticism has found analytical tools in disciplines such as textual criticism, bibliography and cultural history in order to define and describe the role and practices of the reader.[33]

For the purpose of this book, it is therefore necessary to establish the difference between the study and reconstruction of the processes of the perception of the text and the practices of reading. The former is the field of study of theories of reception and literary criticism, while the latter is discussed in further detail by historical criticism. Actually, for reception

---

30 Certeau, 'Reading as Poaching', p. 157.
31 Certeau aimed to challenge the assimilation of reading to passivity by underlining the autonomy of the reader as an achievement of modernity. The reader of the *Ancien Régime*, according to Certeau, would be the product of a controlled system of social relations. However, reception criticism has shown that the reader has enjoyed a great level of autonomy, even when the readable products were under control. See Certeau, 'Reading as Poaching', p. 155; Chartier, 'Labourers and Voyagers', p. 135; see also introd. to Cavallo and Chartier, eds., *A History of Reading in the West*, p. 3.
32 Chartier, 'Labourers and Voyagers', p. 134.
33 Chartier, 'Labourers and Voyagers', pp. 132-34.

criticism the text is at the centre of the discussion, almost regardless of its material support. However, a study of the medieval Franciscan practices of reading cannot exclude the physical support of the text, not only because the support may contain evidence of specific interactions between the reader and the text but also because the specific form of support, usually a manuscript, is the result of particular needs of the readers such as portability, flexibility, comprehensiveness or even the reader's personalization of the text. So a comprehensive, interdisciplinary historical approach that takes into account the literary perspective is the best option for an analysis based on manuscript evidence.

To describe the medieval reader and their practices of reading is a complex task that requires consideration of textual factors such as the contents and linguistic layers; material factors such as the physical characteristics of the text; and factors concerning the reader, such as their familiarity with the written word and their relation to writing. An example of a more complex approach that simultaneously takes into consideration socio-historical factors and the readers' actual practices of reading has been proposed by Céline Van Hoorebeek. Based on the study of the tradition and diffusion of works considered as fundamental to medieval culture, she aims to narrow the field delimited by the notions of communities and social groups of historical criticism by focusing on their relation to the book and the practices of reading. She proposes that, in general terms, any medieval reader can be described as one of two possible types: the 'professional' or the 'amateur' reader.[34]

The professional reader follows the models of scholastic and humanistic training. Their type of reading is personal, private and undertaken in silence and is to be found in a context where books are always available for consultation. Consequently, the library is a tool of work for the professional reader. More often than not, this reader handles copies of books written *manu propria*, which shows their specialist relationship to writing. This relation is also reflected in the traces this type of reader leaves on manuscripts, such as *notae bene*, corrections, comments and annotations. Usually, the material characteristics of the books used by this kind of reader reflect their relation to reading: volumes in regular or small formats, in paper, and full of notes and comments.[35] By contrast, the amateur reader would prefer reading out loud, or public readings; their reference books have a large format and are mainly objects, not tools of work. Finally, they would leave practically no textual

---

34 A more detailed description of the general traits of each one of these types of reader may be found in Van Hoorebeeck, 'Du livre au lire', p. 128.

35 Van Hoorebeeck, 'Du livre au lire', pp. 128-29.

traces in the manuscripts that would characterize their interaction with the text.[36] This proposal prudently foresees some instances where the types do not exclude each other and can even coexist.[37] But before contrasting this interesting proposal with manuscript examples from the Franciscan convents of Padua, it is necessary to explore an important methodological tool that will be employed in their description, that is, the notion of an interpretive community.

Franciscans and their Interpretive Community

When considering the importance of the context, it is necessary to take into account that the reader is not an isolated individual, but is, as a cultural agent, part of a community. The reader's community can be described from different points of view, such as the economic, sociological, historical and even the political angles. However, for the purposes of this study, the most relevant perspective is the historical, because it is the best suited to explain the complexities of the development of the community both in a synchronic and in a diachronic sense. Michel de Certeau had a strong intuition of its importance where he described the reading mechanisms of the *Ancien Régime*, although he focused on the power and extent of the influence of the institution rather than on the role of the community of readers as the determining factor in the interpretation carried out by the reader.

An attempt to develop a comprehensive theory of reading from the point of view of reception criticism was proposed by Stanley Fish through the notion of the interpretive community. This concept introduces into the theory the context of reading that intervenes in the interaction between the reader and the text. As the agent of interpretation or re-creation, the reader assumes an interpretive strategy in order to interact with the text, nevertheless their set of strategies of interpretation are prior to the act of reading and determine what is read.[38] However, it is important to keep in

---

36 Van Hoorebeeck, 'Du livre au lire', pp. 130-31. She argues that the amateur reader would leave some marginal glosses and *maniculae* to identify specific passages of the text. However, this argument can be disputed. For example, there are a significant number of instances in the manuscripts from the Franciscan convents in Padua where professional readers leave *maniculae* or glosses in the margins of the text. This would suggest that the use of *maniculae* is not a distinctive sign of non-professional reading. See Chapter 3 for a detailed description of some of these examples.

37 See Van Hoorebeeck, 'Du livre au lire', p. 131. Unfortunately, the analysis does not offer concrete examples of such coexistence.

38 Fish, *Is There a Text in This Class?*, pp. 14, 167-73 and 338-55.

mind that all the hermeneutic actions employed by the reader derive from the interpretive community to which they belong. From this perspective, at the centre of the meaning the reader finds in the text there is the interpretive community that could be described as a group of individuals who share a common cultural background, among which their interpretive strategies, not only for reading, but mainly for writing texts.

The notion of an interpretive community can be a very useful tool in exploring medieval practices of writing and reading. Roger Chartier proposed a study of modes of reading that identified and described communities of readers and their respective traditions of reading. In this regard, it would be necessary to explore, for example, the different levels of reading competence within the community, the significant contrasts and variations between the norms and conventions of reading, the actual uses of the book, the practices of reading, the instruments and procedures of interpretation, as well as the interests and expectations of the community concerning reading.[39] An example of that approach is the study of the 'mystical reader' carried out by Michel de Certeau, where he discussed the experiences of reading in the context of mystical spirituality during the sixteenth and seventeenth centuries. In the context of mysticism, reading, determined by norms and habits, invested the book with novel functions: to replace ecclesiastical institutions, to disseminate prayer and to indicate practices through which spiritual experience was constructed.[40] The mystical reading experience, as described by Certeau, reinforced the role of the individual as member of a community with a set of shared values such as the perception that words are a real extension of physical presence. In this sense, silent individual reading was a way of personally interacting with the superior, spiritual entity of the author.[41]

In the case of the Franciscan convents of the city of Padua, it is possible to explore their interpretive communities at different levels. The first and most general is the wider Franciscan community of friars, that is, a religious community that shared a set of institutional values and attitudes towards writing and reading, as established by their regulations and masters, and who also shared a distinctive ethos. In a very broad sense, within this community the main purpose of reading was to study in order to follow a programme of preparation for two activities: preaching and pastoral care.[42] A more specific

39   Chartier, 'Labourers and Voyagers', pp. 134-35.
40   Certeau, 'La lecture absolue'.
41   Kimmelman, 'Trope of Reading', pp. 28-30.
42   Roest, *History of Franciscan Education*, pp. 272-89; Şenocak, *Poor and the Perfect*, pp. 117-46.

interpretive community is constituted by the individual convents. Each convent constituted a community characterized by devotion to study, an activity supported by their libraries and by the practice of writing.[43] Specific differences concerning the practices of writing and study became clear with the examination of the manuscript evidence in the third chapter of this book. For example, the manuscripts from the convent of Sant'Antonio correspond to the format and configuration of the 'university manuscript', that is, parchment volumes of regular size – usually between 300 × 200 and 330 × 220 mm –, written in Latin with a gothic script and with a *mise en page* organized in two columns.[44] A much more modest, smaller version of these manuscripts, usually in paper, written in cursive script, with a *mise en page* more flexible and with excerpts in the vernacular and in Latin appeared later, and was typically used by the Observant friars of the convent of San Francesco Grande.

The following section will explore the manuscript evidence in search of forms of reading in the Franciscan convents of Padua. It will take into account the Franciscan convents as interpretive communities. The analysis aims to explore distinctive elements of the practices of reading in the convents and to verify and assess, if necessary, the typology of medieval reader as either amateur or professional. It will not attempt to reconstruct the history of the Franciscan reader in Padua or to establish a definitive phenomenology of Franciscan reading, but to describe practices of reading and their relation to the particular interpretive community of the convent as elements useful to the reconstruction of the Franciscan approach to books.

Some Important Questions

The first steps in the exploration of the practices of reading in the Franciscan convents in Padua can follow what Robert Darnton considers to be essential questions for the history of reading, namely, who reads, what do they read, where do they read and when? Two additional questions imply further analytical work, namely, why does the reader read, and how does the reader read?[45] These questions may be related to different theoretical approaches; for example, 'who reads?' is at the centre of reception theory, while 'when?' and 'where?' are questions that point to the context of reading, as well as

43   Humphreys, *Book Provisions*, pp. 108-9; Humphreys, *Library of the Franciscans of the Convent of St. Anthony*, p. 18; Pantarotto, *La biblioteca manoscritta*, pp. 11-12.

44   Giovè Marchioli, 'Il codice Francescano', pp. 392-93; see also Giovè Marchioli and Zamponi, 'Manoscritti in volgare', p. 312.

45   The study of the external history of reading as a social phenomenon helps to answer these questions satisfactorily and to constitute a solid base from which to explore the more difficult questions of why and how. See Darnton, *Kiss of Lamourette*, p. 157.

to reading as a process in terms of a developing action characterized by disruptions and movements forwards and backwards in the texts.[46] In the specific case of this study, the answer to the first question (who reads?) is that the reader is an individual member of the interpretive community of Franciscan readers and writers in the city of Padua from the thirteenth to the fifteenth centuries. The context of the friar as a reader is determined by the nature of the Franciscan order as a community devoted to study for purposes of preaching and pastoral care. At the same time, depending on whether the friar belongs to the unreformed Community or to the Observant movement, his perception of the written culture may change because the manuscripts that he read and eventually wrote would have distinct characteristics.[47] At this point, key methodological observations of Darnton, even though referring to printed books, are relevant to the particular case under discussion: the physical appearance of the volume is suggestive of the history of reading, since factors such as binding, typographical/script design, layout, paragraphing, punctuation and so on hold clues to historical developments in reading.[48] In manuscript culture, many significant developments in writing and reading were conditioned by specific needs such as the scarcity of the materials, the necessity of getting the best of the resources at one's disposal, or improving efficiency in writing.[49]

To describe more accurately who reads, the catalogue of the library is useful for outlining the profile of the reader, even if a single reader cannot read all the books available in the repositories of a library. Certainly, it is not the number of books read or held in the collection that becomes relevant for understanding the profile of a reader, but the type of books collected, because the typology of books usually reflects the expectations of the interpretive community the reader belongs to. This information is revealed by the catalogues of the libraries. In the case of the Paduan libraries, the catalogues of the libraries have been useful in establishing a common purpose for the collection of both communities, that is, the training of the preacher, although the composition of each collection shows significant differences in terms of the dynamics of the typology of books read.[50] Finally,

46 Introduction to Cavallo and Chartier, eds., *History of Reading in the West*, pp. 2-13.
47 See Chapter 3.
48 Introduction to Cavallo and Chartier, eds., *History of Reading in the West*, p. 8; Darnton, *Kiss of Lamourette*, pp. 182-86.
49 Derolez, *Palaeography of Gothic Manuscript Books*; Zamponi, 'Gothic Script in Italy'; Derolez, 'Nomenclature of Gothic Scripts'; Zamponi, 'Late Gothic', pp. 429-44.
50 For a description of the role and function of the libraries of the Paduan convents, see Chapter 2.

based on the characteristics of the interpretive community to which the friar belongs, one would expect the Franciscan friar to be a professional reader, a student who uses the library as a place for reading and writing, and a reader who takes an active role in his interaction with the text and who is willing to leave traces of his interaction with the text in the manuscript that becomes his object of study. It is also expected that this reader will be capable of writing his own material for study if required. We will see further on whether the manuscript evidence from the Paduan convents supports this description of the Franciscan friar as a reader.

The 'where' not only tells us the location where reading takes place but is helpful also for understanding whether or not reading was a communal activity. In the case of the Paduan convents, it is necessary to take into consideration the fact that the practices of reading were oriented towards spiritual edification and study. For the convent of Sant'Antonio, a common place for studying was the library, which offered a collection of books chained to the benches, and books available for loan, as shown by the earliest inventories available.[51] This suggests that the reader in the convent of Sant'Antonio could count on a space devoted exclusively to personal silent reading. The situation for the convent of San Francesco Grande is more difficult to establish. As Chapter 2 notes, it is certain that the convent had a library, as the earliest inventories available show, but unfortunately it has not been possible to establish whether it had a collection of chained books.[52] The absence of physical evidence of chaining on the examined surviving manuscripts does not allow one to confirm such a practice in the Observant convent. This addresses the question of whether the library was a space for silent, personal reading, to which it is possible only to offer an incomplete answer based on evidence present in the surviving manuscripts, that is, cross references and internal quotations, which suggest that intensive personal study could be carried out, preferably in a silent space.

Apart from the questions already discussed, another two about reading manuscripts in the Franciscan convents are of greater complexity: why did friars read, and how did they read? The answer to why has to do with the role of Franciscans as professional readers and with the nature of their interpretive community. Franciscans devoted themselves to study in order to acquire complete training as preachers and agents of pastoral care in accordance with the declared ideal purpose of their education. Nevertheless,

51   The current Padua, Biblioteca Antoniana, MS 572, a fourteenth-century inventory, and Padua, Biblioteca Antoniana, MS 573, a fifteenth-century inventory.
52   Pantarotto, *La biblioteca manoscritta*, pp. 10, 14-15 and 18-33.

it is worth remembering that, as shown in Chapters 1 and 2, the Franciscans' engagement with the highest levels of scholastic culture abundantly exceeded the levels of literacy required for preaching and pastoral care, and, as shown by Neslihan Şenocak, they reflected the characteristic medieval glorification of learning. Therefore, these complex conditions should also be considered when answering why Franciscans assumed the task of reading at a professional level. In order to determine how Franciscans read, it is necessary to take into account two dimensions of the friars as readers. On the one hand, there was the scholastic model of an ideal reader; on the other, the actual practice of reading in the convents, conditioned by the availability of the manuscripts and the particular circumstances of pastoral care. In any case, the manuscript evidence shows that Franciscan friars were highly skilled professionals and intellectuals familiar with writing and reading in a multilingual environment.

A detailed reconstruction of medieval practices of reading is difficult because sources do not describe learned readers at work. The pre-printing experience of reading has been described as 'intensive', that is, readers tended to read the same few books many times. An 'extensive' experience of reading would become characteristic of modern times when, thanks to social and cultural transformations, readers could enjoy a wider range of choices.[53] Unfortunately, this distinction is not helpful for understanding the context of the Franciscan convents, where friars used to read several manuscripts on diverse matters simultaneously, and where, if required, they could create personal anthologies of texts of different genres and languages, as shown by the evidence described in Chapter 3. Therefore, in order to balance the lack of accuracy in the description of the practices of reading in the sources, it is necessary to refer to the context of reading already studied through the convents, libraries and manuscripts.[54]

The Manuscript Evidence

To outline a profile of the Paduan friars as readers, this section will examine some textual evidence found in a set of manuscripts held in the libraries of the convents during the fourteenth and the fifteenth centuries.

---

53 Darnton, *Kiss of Lamourette*, pp. 165 and 157.
54 Jonathan Topham argues that the objective of book history is to reintroduce social actors engaged in social practices with respect to material objects into a history in which books have too often been understood as disembodied texts. Topham, 'BJHS Special Section: Book History and the Sciences; Introduction', p. 155.

It has been established that Franciscans, as readers, were professionals familiar with writing in the vernacular and in Latin, and read with the purpose of developing the required skills to preach or to provide pastoral care. Accordingly, the manuscripts to be considered in the analysis will include works for spiritual edification and devotion, works useful for pastoral care (such as compilations of cases, rules and treatises on confession and penance), works for study and works useful for preaching and writing sermons. Except for the books for study, examples of each type of book in both Franciscan libraries in Padua will be described. A comparative approach will be used, presenting the books of the Biblioteca Antoniana first, and then those held in the Observant library of San Francesco Grande.

Manuscripts from the Biblioteca Antoniana

The first manuscript to be discussed is a volume read as a source of spiritual edification and devotion: Padua, Biblioteca Antoniana, MS 267, a glossed volume containing the Gospels of Luke and John. This manuscript was part of a Bible in twenty-five volumes donated by Egidius, canon of the cathedral, to the Franciscan library in 1237.[55] It is a parchment volume of 355 × 240 mm, written during the thirteenth century. It has a stiff binding of wooden boards covered in leather, and traces of clasps in the binding suggest that the manuscript was chained. It has 145 leaves written in an elegant form of gothic book hand described as 'littera parisiensis'.[56] The script is distributed in three columns: the central one contains the main text and the two adjacent columns contain the gloss, plus an interlinear gloss to the main text. The initials of the manuscript are decorated in blue and red.[57]

The manuscript offers only a few but nevertheless significant instances of readers' interaction with the text. The main interventions by the readers take the form of notes, references to other biblical books, and complementary comments on the gloss. For example, on fol. 3^v, in the first chapter of the Gospel of Luke, a fourteenth-century reader added a cross reference to biblical sources in the passage where Gabriel announces to Zachary that he

---

55   There is a note on the pastedown: 'Iste liber est de conventus Padue et in eodem conventus debet permanere de voluntate eius cuius fuit. Si fuit autem ipsum alienaverit anathema sit et sunt Lucas et Iohannes in isto volumine.' See Cassandro et al., eds., *I manoscritti*, p. 53; see also Abate and Luisetto, *Codici e manoscritti*, I, xxvii.

56   Abate and Luisetto, *Codici e manoscritti*, I, p. 263.

57   See Appendix 3, Plate 19.

will conceive a son.[58] These references were intended to comment on the text of the gloss, which discusses the specific role of Zachary in the divine plan, the role of priests in ancient Israel, as well as their figurative role in the Christian community. In the same margin, another note on the gloss comments on the miraculous conception of Elizabeth as an example of how the laws of nature can be modified by the messengers of God to fulfil the divine plan of salvation. The comment states that in Elizabeth's case, it is to be understood that natural law was 'in hand', that is, it was subject to the purpose of the angelic mediator, who could alter the principles of nature, which means that the law is subject to the ministry of angels.[59]

On fol. 4[r], in the left margin, a reader wrote a number of comments, references and interpretations to complement the gloss on the visit of the angel Gabriel to Mary.[60] There is also a comment on the symbolic meaning of the conception: God wanted to be born and be nourished in a small city, giving a hint of his own crucifixion; similarly, small things allow the faithful to prefigure bigger sacrifices.[61] In the right margin the same hand comments on the gloss regarding the conception of Elizabeth, adding that the mystery of how she could conceive in her old age was not to be unveiled to her, but it was revealed in a clear form to the blessed Virgin.[62] These traces suggest an interaction that aims to establish references for personal, spiritual edification and devotion, and hence the marginal comments do not point to topics for preaching or theological debate.

---

58 'Ad Hebreos capitulus VII'; 'In Prima ad Timotheum, capitulus I', and further: 'Mala labia sacerdotem capitulus et ceterae'.

59 'Thus [it is to be understood that] the law was "in hand", that is, [subject to] the capability of the mediator, who could alter the law, that is add something or lessen the divine. Of the law itself, I say "ordained law", that is given in an ordered fashion, and given through angels, namely, by the ministry of angels.' According to the gloss to the main text, after divine law, ordained law was the second most important type of law in medieval jurisprudence, because it flowed from the operation of the divine law. The text of the marginal comment is: 'Ita <construe> lex erat in manu, id est potestate medi [sic.; most probably for 'mediatoris' as appears in the text of the gloss] qui poterat legem mutare vel addere aliquid vel minuere <divinem>. Ipsi legi. Lex dico ordinata, id est o<r>dinate data et data per angelos, id est ministerio angelorum.'

60 'In Genesis capitulum XVIII: postquam senui et dominus meus vetulus est voluptati operam dabo [Gen. 18:12]?'; 'In Exodo XXIII: ne coques edum in lacte matris [Exod. 23:19]. Idest, Christum ignorantie passionis est in die conceptionis'; and further: 'Ecclesiaste IIII [sic]: est temporis vacandi ab amplexibus [Eccles. 3:5]' and 'In Joel, capitulum II: Egrediatur sponsus de cubili suo [Joel 2.16]'. See Appendix 3, Plate 12.

61 'Per hoc que dominus voluit in parva civitate nasci et nutriri et immaginem crucifigi innuit velle nos in parvis <de lectari> ad magna pervenientes crucifigamus.'

62 'Quia non dum revelatum ei misterium conceptionis scilicet per quo misterio datum esset ei in senectute concipere quae post ea revelatum est ei <iam distinctu> beate virginis.'

Another example of manuscripts employed as materials for devotional purposes is Padua, Biblioteca Antoniana, MS 112, a copy of the *Life of Francis*, or *Legenda maior*, written by Bonaventure of Bagnoregio. This is a parchment manuscript of 390 × 280 mm, written during the thirteenth century. It has a stiff binding of wooden boards covered in leather with traces of clasps, which suggests that the manuscript had been chained. The volume has sixty-seven leaves written in an elegant gothic script organized in two columns. Apart from the rubrics, the text is decorated with some initials in red and turquoise.[63]

The text contains almost no evidence of written interaction of the readers. A set of comments provide orientation on the misplacement of some quires. On fol. 10^v, a sign indicates that the text is continued below, on fol. 58^r. In fact, after fol. 10^v, it follows fol. 18^v, where a note indicates that the reading continues further, where a matching sign can be found: 'Require in fine lectioni reperies hic signum'. On fol. 57^r, another annotation comments that there is one miracle missing and that it can be found at the end of the manuscript.[64] Apart from these annotations, the manuscript offers no further textual sign of interaction between the reader and the text, a feature explained by the fact that this was a text with a twofold value: as a source of devotional inspiration and as a cornerstone of the community's identity. Abate and Luisetto suggest, without further detail, that this manuscript was employed 'per uso di lettura pubblica', which means that it was used as a text to be read in the refectory and that the public character of this text was limited to the audience of friars and eventually to commemorative ceremonies.[65] In this case, it is not the presence, but the absence, of signs of interaction through intensive reading which constitutes a significant element of analysis in assessing medieval Franciscans as readers. If the absence of textual marks is the result of the interaction with amateur readers, one may argue, on the one hand, that devotional reading may not have left traces or, on the other hand, that the absence of marks does nothing to discount the possibility of a professional reader. It is necessary, then, to take into account the interpretive community to fully understand the dynamics of reading manuscripts of this kind.

One significant example of books used by the friars of Sant'Antonio for purposes of study is Padua, Biblioteca Antoniana, MS 125. It is a parchment manuscript that contains the commentary on the *Sentences* by Bonaventure

63 See Appendix 3, Plate 20.
64 'Hic deficit unum miraculum. Require illud in fine libri.'
65 Abate and Luisetto, *Codici e manoscritti*, I, p. 146.

of Bagnoreggio.[66] The manuscript has evidence of interaction between the reader and the text in the form of corrections, marginal annotations and *maniculae* to identify passages. Apart from these, there are additional forms of evidence in resources to identify parts of the text, cross references and ownership inscriptions referring to the concession of the manuscript 'ad usum'.

On fol. 10^v, along with some corrections to the text, marginal notes can be found to identify the main parts of Bonaventure's argument in the form of '1m' (*primum*), '2m' (*secundum*), '3m' (*tertium*) and so on. To identify the objections to these arguments, a fourteenth-century reader added in the margin 'Ad 1m', 'Ad 2m', 'Ad 3m' and so on. Similar corrections and resources to identify parts of the argument, as well as objections, can be found throughout the manuscript.

In addition, fol. 6^r provides evidence of the fact that this manuscript was still used as a tool for study during the fifteenth century. Where the author discusses the supreme and absolute goodness of God, a marginal note written by a fifteenth-century hand comments that goodness and virtue are said to be twofold and that integrity is a source of delight.[67] Further, on fol. 10^v, there is another example. There, in order to clarify the argument on whether is possible the knowledge of God through near similitudes or through the image, a fourteenth-century reader wrote in the margin that it was to be noted how image and impression differ.[68] The same reader commented further on the same topic that the ascension to God is twofold.[69] And once again this reader wrote marginal corrections and additions to the text on fol. 23^r, as well as on fol. 43^r, where the text reproduces the first question of the second article of the fourteenth distinction. Bonaventure discusses how the Holy Ghost gave himself in person, which constitutes divine grace, and then explains that what is given belongs to the recipient, following the principle that something is given to someone with a purpose.[70]

The ownership inscriptions on this manuscript are a source of additional information on the history and use of the volume. As already mentioned in Chapter 3, one of the inscriptions, written by a late thirteenth-century hand, appears on fol. 127^v and is followed by a second one, almost identical,

---

66   For a detailed description of this manuscript, see Chapter 3.
67   'Nota quod bonum honestum dicitur aliquid esse duplex et nota quod honesto sit fruendum.'
68   'Nota quomodo differunt ymago et vestigium.'
69   'Nota quod ascensus in deum duplex est.'
70   'Nota quod aliud datus alicui ad ita.' See Bonaventure of Bagnoregio, *Opera Omnia*, I, p. 250.

on fol. 143^r, written almost a century later.[71] Additionally, there is another ownership inscription from the late fifteenth century on fol. 141^v.[72] This set of ownership inscriptions suggests an intensive and continuous use of this manuscript for reasons of study during three centuries with at least two concessions 'ad usum', that is, as long-term loans.[73]

An example of books employed as source material in the preparation of sermons is the set of manuscripts of the sermons of Luke of Bitonto, namely MSS 417, 418, 419 and 527 of the Biblioteca Antoniana.[74] In this section, particular attention will be paid to manuscript 418, a parchment volume of 293 × 204 mm with a rigid binding that has traces of being chained. The text is written in gothic book-hand script by at least two hands from the thirteenth century, with no decoration added to the text.

A particular feature of this manuscript appears in the transition from fol. 16^v to fol. 17^r, where the distribution of the written text changes from across the page to a two-column layout.[75] Most probably, the alteration of the *mise en page* is due to a significant change in the format of the folio. In fact, the first quire measures 293 × 228 mm, while the format changes to 280 × 200 mm from the second quire on. The hand remains the same and the continuity of the text has no alteration, which suggests that the manuscript is not a composite volume, that is, a volume formed by piecing together different manuscripts, but a unitary one whose variations in format are the result of the availability of the parchment, a feature in complete accordance with the nature of the volume as a non-luxury book.[76]

The manuscript shows traces of interaction between the reader and the text in the form of corrections and comments written in a minuscule cursive script by a late fifteenth-century hand. Along with the examples of fols. 5^r, 6^v, 9^r and 10^r described in Chapter 3, there is an annotation that verifies the continuity of the text from fol. 16^v to fol. 17^r, where the text explains that faith allows insight into deep truths as if they were reflected in a mirror. The original text reads: 'per fidem quamvis per speculum [fol. 17^r] in enigmate'. A cursive fifteenth-century hand only corrects above,

---

71 On fol. 127^v: 'Iste liber datus est ad usum fratis [sic] Guidonis anno MCCCLXXXIIII'; and on fol. 143^r: 'Iste liber est concessus ad usum fratris Guidonis de Padua Ordinis Fratrum Minorum.' See Appendix 3, Plate 7 and 8.

72 'Liber fratris Francixi de Ordine Minorum'.

73 For a discussion of the long-term loans, or concessions *ad usum*, see Chapter 2.

74 The description of their physical characteristics can be found in Chapter 3.

75 See Appendix 3, Plate 9.

76 A swift synthesis of the material alterations and transformations of manuscripts can be found in Andrist et al., *La syntaxe du codex*, pp. 61-81.

'et imaginatione', which suggests that the change in the size of the folio did not change substantially the fluency of the text. There are a few other corrections and interventions of this kind; for example, on fol. 16^v, in the left margin, the same fifteenth-century hand corrects the first two words of the line, '[ad si]ni decli' for '[ad si]num declinat', and on fol. 17^r, in the left margin it corrects 'dispensatio eorum' for 'disputationem'. Similarly, the hand corrects words from the text, 'ipsios' for 'istis', and so on. This kind of correction might be the result of a revision of the text made to establish a reliable version of the sermons, most probably for long-term personal use once the manuscript, after being chained, became a volume destined for loan and eventually for loan *ad usum*.

Manuscripts from the Library of San Francesco Grande

The library of the convent of San Francesco Grande had a remarkable collection of works useful for the purposes of pastoral care and for the preparation and writing of sermons. In what follows some examples of the practices of reading these two types of manuscripts will be described.

The first example is Padua, Biblioteca Universitaria, MS 736, a miscellany of treatises useful for pastoral care. This is a paper volume in octavo from the mid-fifteenth century, written in a small minuscule cursive, whose decoration consists of modest ornaments on some capital letters. The text offers an anthology of excerpts, treatises and cases on confession, among which the treatise by Antonino of Florence. Most probably this was a personal selection of items and that is why it has been described as a volume of reference.[77]

The manuscript has only a few but nonetheless significant corrections and additions, all of them written by the same hand as the main text. For example, on fol. 1^r there is a marginal note that identifies the prologue to the treatise on confession and states that it was prepared by friar John of the order of Friars Minors in the penitentiary.[78] On the same folio there is another marginal note written with the purpose of identifying the first of the four preparative actions suggested by the author on confession and penance: to avoid propagation of sin, those who confess should first take action.[79]

77   For a detailed description, see Chapter 3. See also Pantarotto, *La biblioteca manoscritta*, p. 123.
78   'Incipit prologus formale confessionum <edite> a fratre Iohannes de Ordine Fratrum Minorum domini propter pennenciario.'
79   'Prima est qui de hiis qui confesit debent [sic] procedere.'

Another example may be found on fol. 71^r, where there is an addition in the form of a heading useful in identifying the section, namely the *Dubia*, that is questions on many topics addressed to master John of Capistrano, whose answers acquired an authoritative value.[80] Finally, on fol. 117^v, an ownership inscription allows one to establish that the manuscript was completed between 1454, the date of completion of the work of Antonino of Florence on confession, and 1462, when it was conceded in a long-term loan to friar Simon of Parma.[81]

The manuscript overall has a small number of notes, comments or further evidence of professional reading. The fact that the marginal notes and comments were written by the same hand that wrote the main text suggests that once the apparatus required to efficiently locate the information was completed, it was unnecessary to add anything further, except for the last folio, where there is an additional excerpt and the ownership inscription. This suggests that the manuscript was employed as a tool of reference and not as a manuscript for intensive study, or professional reading.

Another example of a manuscript used as a reference tool for pastoral care is Padua, Biblioteca Universitaria, MS 1159, a miscellany of treatises and cases on pastoral care. This is a paper manuscript in octavo, written during the fifteenth century in a special type of minuscule cursive *al tratto*, that is, employing a characteristic technique of the formal scripts. The decoration of the manuscript is limited to paraphs in red and some capital letters also highlighted in red.[82] On fol. 188^r, an ownership inscription in a late fifteenth- or early sixteenth-century script confirms that the volume was given on a long-term loan.[83] Despite being a volume given 'ad usum', and despite being a collection of excerpts of representative treatises and cases, the main characteristic of MS 1159 is the absence of traces of interaction with the reader. This feature is consistent with the nature of the volume as a tool, and thus it may be concluded that the work was used with the specific purpose of reference by the friars as professional readers, but not for doctrinal study.

---

80 'These are some questions as were proposed. Friar John of Capistrano answered them thoroughly, each and every one, as shown below.' The transcription of the heading is: 'Infrascripta sunt quidam dubia quae fuerunt proposita. Responsit <...> Johanni de capistrano qui respondit omnibus et singularis pro, ut infra patebit videlicet.'

81 'Hic liber pertinet ad locum sancti Francisci apud hospitale Padue. Concessus ad usum fratris Simonio de Parma Ordinis Minorum die X julii 1462.' See Appendix 3, Plate 21.

82 For a detailed description of the characteristics and contents of the volume, see Chapter 3. See also Pantarotto, *La biblioteca manoscritta*, p. 149.

83 'Ad usum fratris Antonii de Padua.' See Appendix 3, Plate 22.

Padua, Biblioteca Universitaria, MS 1511, offers a collection of treatises used for pastoral care by the Observant friars in Padua. The manuscript contains a miscellany of treatises and materials, among which are works by Antonino of Florence, Bernardino of Siena and Jacopone da Todi.[84] This is a paper manuscript in octavo of approximately 141 × 103 mm, written during the second half of the fifteenth century. The volume has a modern hard binding with no traces of being chained. The manuscript has 168 leaves written in minuscule cursive script by two different hands, the second of which started writing at fol. 155[r], where there is also a shift from a two-column *mise en page* to a full-page script. The overall decoration of the manuscript consists of a few paraphs, rubrics and initials in red.

This miscellany has the characteristics of a personal anthology of treatises on virtue, the nature of the Franciscan order, its spirituality and some elements of theological doctrine, as shown by the presence of dispositions concerning the order, its discipline and the proper way of living according to Franciscan principles. The excerpts from Jacopone da Todi's *Laudi* are a complement to the former texts as a source for spiritual edification. The presence of sections written in the vernacular and in Latin suggests flexibility on the part of the writer and eventual readers of the manuscript. Nevertheless, as with MS 1159, this manuscript is characterized by the absence of comments, notes or even corrections as signs of interaction between the reader and the text. On fol. 165[v], there is a set of recipes. The first one is written in the vernacular and is intended to cure diverse ailments such as abdominal pain and fever.[85] The second recipe is written in Latin, and its text transcribes an alternative formula to cure the same illnesses.[86] This section of the manuscript provides evidence

---

84   Pantarotto, *La biblioteca manoscritta*, p. 167. The works included in the miscellany are Antonino of Florence, *Confessionalis 'Defecerunt'*, plus excerpts from various works; Bernardino of Siena, *De restitutionibus*; Clement V, *Declaratio in regulam Fratrum Minorum*, transcribed in a version in the vernacular; and Jacopone da Todi, *Laudi*.

85   'Colico, mal di fianchi, stitico e quam lomo dubita de febre'.

86   The text of the recipes is as follows: 'Colico, mal di fianchi, stitico e quam lomo dubita de febre. [Below] Recipe: zedoaria/ meligrete/ peverlongo/ canella/ zenzevro/ garofoli/ aloepaturo/ zafrano/ eleboro negro. Mescola e pesta sutilmente e tamisa tante volte che de tute cavi la substantia e tolli mezo cuchiareto per volta a piu e meno secundo li corpi robusti e la etade cum un poco de vino a dezuno et ancho da altra hora qui non potesti indubiar.' Further down there is a second recipe: 'Recipe. Radices infra scriptas, videlicet, gencianam, trementillam, ditamum, bistortam, terram sigilatam ante uncia una. Terra sigillata est quedam terra alba que venduntur in apotecis. Item quilibet per se pistentur in mortario brazino et tamisentur suptiliter. Postea iugentur in simul ut supra dictum est.' And below: 'Item de isto pulvere accipitur tempore necessitatis dragma una statim quod sentit cum modico de vino albo optimo calido et quod sit bene copertus usque ad effusionem sudoris et sanabitur. Et caveat que non evomat.'

that the volume was used by a fifteenth-century reader who employed it as a portable device of reference meant to be consulted quickly rather than intensively studied.

Another miscellany useful for writing sermons is Padua, Biblioteca Universitaria, MS 1851. This is a paper manuscript in quarto, produced during the fifteenth century. The manuscript does not contain complete works but instead a selection of materials such as excerpts of sermons and treatises, especially by Jacopo della Marca. This set is complemented by a selection of 'auctoritates et exempla', that is authoritative excerpts. It has 282 leaves written in a swift minuscule cursive script. The decoration of the text consists of rubrics and coloured initials.[87]

The manuscript has evidence of the interaction between the reader and the text in the form of marginal comments and annotations, written by the same hand that wrote the main text. For example, on fol. 1[r] the text is organized in two columns, and it reproduces the beginning of the treatise on the nature of faith by Jacobus della Marca, as stated by the scribe with a very small script on the top of the page.[88] There is also a marginal rubric on the second column with the purpose of locating a specific passage of the text that discusses the role of Jews as those who, having previously abandoned God, are abandoned by him to their deities.[89] And further along on the same page, at the margin of the first column, the same hand wrote a similar synthesis of the topic, this time referring to the will of God of saving Jews from themselves.[90] Further, at the bottom of the folio, the scribe wrote an excerpt intended to complement the main topic. Most probably, this part was added later, as suggested both by the faintness of the ink employed and by the fact that the writing occupies the full extent of the page, instead of the original two-column *mise en page*. The added text refers to the contents of the exchange between two rabbis that was found in an unspecified volume containing works translated from Arabic, and has the purpose of supporting the main arguments of the treatise.[91]

---

87 A detailed description of the manuscript and its contents can be found in Chapter 3. See Pantarotto, *La biblioteca manoscritta*, p. 192.

88 'Fratris Jacobi de la Marcha in parte 3 post LXXam'.

89 '<Communicatio> dei contra Judeos qui derelinquunt di sunt a deo'.

90 'Vocat omnes Judeos.'

91 The incipit of the excerpt states: 'Unus judeus scribebat ad alium judeum. Reperitur in quadam translatione de Arabico in Latinum fratris Alfani cum datur cumdam [sic] libelli unus judei, ad <summi> summum pontificem. Et primo sciendum quod quae inter judeos multis gloriantur qui arabicam infimat latinam [...]'.

On fol. 8^r, there is another example of interaction with the text. The main argument of this passage is about the nature of preaching, and the text is enclosed by marginal notes added by the same hand that wrote the main text. Most of the notes are references to other texts and comments. There is, for example, a marginal annotation to clarify the argument of a treatise on the word of God, 'De verbo divino', where the writer transcribed notes and excerpts on the nature of preaching, as well as useful topics on which to write homilies according to the time of the year. In the right margin is a *manicula* and a cross reference: 'Libro 9'. Further, on fol. 84^v, an excerpt contains a set of rules and procedures to be considered in the preparation for confession and penance, complemented by a comment on the perils of the temptations of the flesh in the left margin.[92] The layout allows us to understand the original *mise en page* of the manuscript, with wide blank margins, which suggests an intention to complement the text with additional comments, annotations and references.

Finally, on fol. 187^v there is a recipe against the plague.[93] As with MS 1511, this feature reflects a practical purpose for the manuscript. The fact that there is only one hand commenting and complementing the text and that this hand is the same one that wrote the main text is consistent with its being a personal volume, and part of a set of personal manuscripts. Its personal character is suggested by the presence on fol. I^r of a heading allowing us to suppose that the scribe, friar Pellegrinus, intended to make a list of his books.[94]

Manuscript 1851 is an example of miscellanies used for the composition of sermons that show traces of active interaction with the text in the form of comments, aids to identifying significant parts of the text, additions, corrections and cross references. These marks constitute evidence of the use of the manuscript as material for study by professional readers. At the same time, the manuscript has strong similarities to volumes containing treatises on devotion or works for pastoral care such as portability, flexibility, being part of a personal set of works of reference, and eventual concession on long-term loan. However, even more significant are the differences between these manuscripts, as discussed in what follows.

---

92   The rules are to be found under the heading 'Here we will offer twelve exceedingly useful rules to confession'; the original heading states: 'Duodecim utlissimas regulas et necessarias <dabimus> ad confessionem'.

93   Under the heading: 'Recepta contra pestem cum in omni alia infermitatem possit infirmo dare spes salutis in sola pestilentia'.

94   'Libri ad usum mei fratris Pellegrini'.

Conclusion

Reading during the Middle Ages has been studied by disciplines such as the history of education, religious history, history of ideas and the history of literacy. Nevertheless, an approach from the perspective of the history of the book is still a relatively unexplored field. In this respect, there is a striking parallel with the history of the printed book. The medieval manuscript has been considered mainly from the perspective of the development of its physical form and the scripts employed by scribes. A very similar approach has been undertaken for the printed book, whose history has been until very recently the history of typography and forms of the physical composition of the volumes, isolated from the developments of societies, cultures and groups of readers.[95] The following few conclusive observations concerning the forms of reading manuscripts in the medieval Franciscan convents of Padua aim to identify significant elements of the interaction between the friars and their manuscripts in the context of their interpretive community and in the perspective of the history of the medieval manuscript.

A swift comparison between two manuscripts from the Observant library of San Francesco Grande will be helpful in exploring the relation between the purpose of the manuscripts and particular ways of reading them. This chapter has shown that MSS 1511 and 1851 were personal, portable, sophisticated and efficient devices used as tools of reference, that is, as sources of practical information. While the first volume was written in a very clear script and was used for pastoral care, the second was written in a very swift cursive script and was employed as a source for the writing of sermons. However, the most significant difference between them regards the forms of interaction with their readers. MS 1511 has no comments, annotations or references, while MS 1851 is extensively annotated and commented on. In actual fact, it shows striking similarities to the practices used to read the texts for study in the university, that is, the main text appears surrounded by an apparatus of comments, references, revisions and corrections.[96] In this particular case, the hand that added references and corrections was the same that wrote the main text.

If, at this point, one takes into consideration the traces of interaction and applies a typology of readers to describe the friars and their community,

---

95   Richardson, 'Inscribed Meanings', p. 85.
96   Some other examples are Padua, Biblioteca Universitaria, MSS 1098, 1789 and 2103; see also Giovè Marchioli, 'Il codice francescano', pp. 403-4, and Hamesse, 'Scholastic Model of Reading', pp. 114-16.

one has to conclude that although Franciscans were professional readers and active agents of scholarship, in some instances they left very few traces of interaction on their own manuscripts.[97] This suggests that, at least for the Observants of Padua, the text determines the reading and that therefore the types of reading were determined by features related to textual types produced within a given interpretive community. This allows us to understand Franciscans as flexible readers who could perfectly well undertake different forms of reading according to the nature of the text, their particular interests and the purpose of their reading, as shown by their different approaches towards texts of devotion, spirituality, pastoral care, theology and preparation for preaching.

The observations of friars as readers who were keen to write allows us to discuss the role of Franciscans as scribes of their own books, as suggested by the ownership inscriptions, particularly those from the Observant convent of San Francesco Grande. In this sense, the Franciscan friar as member of his interpretive community challenges the ontological disruption between writer and reader established by reception theory, and demands a more articulated approach to his agency in the context of the history of reading and the history of the book.[98]

Franciscan libraries played a fundamental role in the development of Franciscans' reading skills. Loans *ad usum* favoured active interaction with the text because they allowed the friars to build a long-term relationship with the book. The reader was able to verify the contents and reliability of the manuscript and to correct it to establish the best possible version of the text. The cases where active interaction has left traces reflect a scholastic approach to the text, but this does not necessarily imply that professional reading was carried out exclusively with manuscripts for study or for the preparation of sermons. Actually, manuscripts for spiritual edification or

---

97   To be highly skilled readers and writers was at the core of Franciscan identity, as shown by Bonaventure's description of his fellow friars as 'Fratres scribentes vel legentes'. See Bonaventure of Bagnoregio, *Opera Omnia*, VIII, p. 350.

98   When discussing the physical aspects of the contemporary printed book, Roger E. Stoddard proposed a clear distinction between the authoring and the writing of a text. Writing was possible only as a premodern form of book production: 'Whatever they may do, authors do not write books. Books are not written at all. They are manufactured by scribes and other artisans, by mechanics and other engineers, and by printing presses and other machines. Most manuscript books made before, say 1600 are copies. Each manuscript copy was transcribed from a particular manuscript exemplar, copied word for word, perhaps line for line.' This suggestive conception of writing, and therefore of reading, offers the possibility of further study of the phenomenology of reading. See Stoddard, 'Morphology and the Book', p. 4.

pastoral care were also conceded *ad usum*, as examples from the Paduan libraries show.

Perhaps because of the need to be as comprehensive as possible, theoretical approaches tend to propose sets of unique and separate forms of reading, and tend to conceive of the reader as capable of a unique type of reading, restricting dramatically the possibilities of their agency.[99] Nevertheless, as happens with any contemporary 'professional' reader who assumes different types of reading – for example, when reading a printed newspaper, a Wikipedia webpage, a printed novel or a fine piece of scholarship – it has been shown that Franciscans could also shift from an 'amateur' style of reading to a 'professional', or better, a scholastic style of reading, depending on the purposes and characteristics of the text, their expectations and the conditions set by their interpretive community. This allows us to understand that, just as there is need of a typology of the Franciscan manuscript in terms of its purpose as pointed out in Chapter 3, another typology based on the practices of reading would be a powerful tool in the study of the medieval manuscript.

99 Chartier, 'Labourers and Voyagers', p. 134.

Conclusions

This book has explored four aspects or dimensions of the manuscripts written and read by Franciscan friars in the convents of the city of Padua from the thirteenth to the fifteenth centuries. The first aspect is the ideal that these manuscripts should aim for, as expressed by the regulations on study and the use of books. To do so, the first chapter has explored the development of these regulations and has shown how the Franciscan rule constructed a specific ideal relationship with books and a specific image of the book allowed into the community. The ideal did not envisage dedication to study. After the death of Francis, in order to provide space for study and continuous learning within the order, Franciscans interpreted the rule in many different ways, although always with reference to what they perceived as Francis's original 'intentio'. As a consequence, there was a set of official explanations or interpretations of what the rule really meant to say, as well as more detailed regulations such as the general and provincial chapters which were meant to clarify these issues. The analysis has shown that even the interpretations of the most rigorous movements of reform found a place for study and the use of books within the order, and there was always a space of legitimacy for learning in the preparation for preaching and pastoral care. The extent of the Franciscans' intellectual achievement nevertheless surpassed their declared intentions, and this resulted in a gap between the ideal book, as proposed by the Franciscan rule, and the actual books used by the friars. The ideal book should be produced outside the community, be intended to support the performance of the divine offices and be available only to those friars who were already able to read at the moment of their arrival in the order. The most eloquent statements of the distance from such an ideal were the Franciscan libraries themselves, which were places where the original ideal developed, changed and adapted to the needs of a community who shared devotional, pastoral and intellectual expectations.

The second dimension explored is the space, represented by the Franciscan libraries. In fact, there is need of studies to compare the Franciscan book collections of the Community and the Observant reform at different levels. This book has shown that one of the common features of the libraries was

Hernández Vera, R., *Franciscan Books and their Readers: Friars and Manuscripts in Late Medieval Italy*. Taylor & Francis Group, 2022
DOI 10.5117/9789463729512_CONCL

the concession of long-term loans of books, or concessions *ad usum*. This was an extraordinary mechanism that allowed the user of a manuscript to establish a long-term relationship with the book, usually for life, and favoured the exercise of analytical study, since it was a process that permitted frequent rereading of some passages and interface with the text through written comments and references in the margins.

Concerning the differences between the libraries, the analysis of the fifteenth-century inventory of the Biblioteca Antoniana has shown that by the second half of the fifteenth century, this library was firmly established and had a complete set of tools for the study of theology, philosophy and natural sciences. The layout of the library, as revealed by the sources, showed that there was a double collection of books, one for consultation and one for loan. The palaeographical and codicological analysis of the copies of the commentary on the *Sentences* by Bonaventure revealed, for the first time, the mechanism of circulation within the two collections of manuscripts in the library: the availability of chained books and copies for loan was guaranteed thanks to a system of 'relay'. As soon as a new copy arrived in the library, it was corrected using the chained copy as a model. Once the text of the new copy was established, it was chained, and the older chained copy was released for concession on loan. Although further attempts to compare medieval libraries established in the same location could be limited in number, the principles of analysis employed in this study could be applied to describe single medieval libraries with the purpose of undertaking, for example, comparative studies between Franciscan and Dominican or even monastic libraries, both in male and female communities.

The organization of the volumes in the library of Sant'Antonio followed a principle of balance, reflected in the location of the books for loan on the opposite side of their respective chained volumes, most probably in order to guarantee a uniform distribution of the volumes in all the repositories, and therefore it was an additional, swift mechanism of controlling the stock of volumes.[1] Although the sources on the Observant library do not allow us to reconstruct the distribution of the volumes in the spaces of the convent, they reveal that there were significant differences from the library of the unreformed friars. While the Biblioteca Antoniana had a strong emphasis on collections of sermons and theological and philosophical literature, the main part of the collection of the library of San Francesco Grande was dedicated to treatises on pastoral care, confession and the preparation of sermons. Most importantly, the collection of this library was filled mainly

---

1   See Hernández Vera, 'From Chained Books to Portable Collections', pp. 96-97.

by paper manuscripts, smaller in size, and limited to miscellanies of texts. These manuscripts, as shown in Chapters 3 and 4, were examples of personal, portable libraries that reflected the expectations, needs and intellectual background of their owners who were usually also their scribes. In this regard, they challenge the notion of the humanist reader as the first figure to employ a personal library since late antiquity. Even though the humanist employed a collection of several volumes rather than one personal miscellany, a comparison between the agencies of the friar and the humanist would be very interesting to develop.

The third aspect of the Franciscan manuscript that has been explored is the form, as said above, in the Aristotelian sense of the term: the form refers not only to the physical configuration of the volumes but also to the relation between this layout and the purpose of the manuscripts themselves. The comparative analysis revealed the relationship between the convents and the types of books that were collected in their libraries. The books collected in the library of Sant'Antonio were parchment volumes of regular dimensions, between 300 × 200 and 330 × 220 mm, that frequently contained complete treatises or topical collections of texts. Those in the Observant library were small, portable paper manuscripts containing miscellanies of different genres and written both in Latin and the vernacular. This feature, very common in manuscripts used for the preparation of sermons, reveals that the Observant friars were well aware of the composition of their audiences, and they adapted to this circumstance by including a wide variety of textual genres in their materials, comprising dialogues, letters, treatises, poems, fables and narrative texts, among others.

The discussion of the profile of Franciscan friars as readers in Chapter 4 has revealed the dimension of the manuscripts' readership. It has shown that friars were flexible readers who adapted their performance of reading to the nature of the text and its purpose. Using the tools of reception theory, this chapter has also revealed the mechanisms of different practices of reading within the Paduan convents. Despite being highly trained readers, with a particularly intensive training as scholars, Franciscans adapted their form of reading, depending on whether the text was a devotional, a text for study, a manual for preaching, a literary piece written in the vernacular or a recipe against common ailments. This remarkable flexibility led us to apply the theoretical category of interpretive community to understand the Franciscan readers' choices. The Franciscan friar was an active member of an international community of scholars, was trained in intensive techniques of study with the purpose of undertaking pastoral care, producing new texts and engaging effectively with mixed audiences. The manuscript evidence studied in this chapter shows that friars were aware of the composition of their audience and used this knowledge to guarantee the maximum impact for their preaching. The study of Franciscans as readers also suggests that a similar approach could be followed to study other types of readers from different interpretive communities, such as the humanist or the female members of religious orders. This is one of the reasons why a study of this kind has important implications for scholarship beyond male mendicant communities.

A scholarly assumption that is challenged by Franciscans as readers keen to write is the ontological distinction between author, writer and reader. This is particularly true for Franciscan manuscript culture, where a friar could be the scribe of his own miscellany books, as suggested by the ownership inscriptions. The Franciscan friar as a member of his interpretive community was writer, reader and eventually the author of the selection of texts he intended to use. This form of agency demands a nuanced approach from the perspective of reception theory in the context of the history of reading and the history of the book.

The study of these elements of the Franciscan manuscript leads to two main conclusions. First, this book proposes the investigation of the concrete and rich complexity of the Franciscan manuscript as opposed to the abstract notion of a Franciscan book. The study of the manuscripts written, studied and collected by Franciscan friars shows that, outside of a theory, the Franciscan book does not exist in reality and that what exists, instead, is the wonderful arrangement of possibilities offered by the actual Franciscan manuscript. Second, this book has shown that a better understanding of the Franciscan manuscript as a cultural product can be achieved through consideration of four of its dimensions: idea, space, form and readership. This new form of understanding of these manuscripts could be applied not only to Franciscan written products but to medieval manuscripts in general. The four-dimensional model, as proposed here, has been shown to be flexible and to allow one to undertake the study of a set of manuscripts, of a particular type of manuscript or of manuscripts from the perspective of the interpretive community that produced and used them.

Appendix 1

Padua, Pontificia Biblioteca Antoniana, MS 573, fols. 64v-66v (1449)

[Fol. 64v]

[...]

Infrascripti sunt debitores librorum habentes infrascriptos libros apud se a quibus nunquam potui habere ad perfectionem inventarii, in quolibet descripserim libros simpliciter tamen non potui designare et scribere qualitates et signa librorum. Ideo hic pro debitoribus inscripti sunt

[Fol. 65r]

In primis, frater Baptista guardianus habet hos libros:

Et primo textum libri De anima.

Item Bibliam unam in magno volumine.

Item librum super Predicamentis.

Item aliam Bibliam unam parvulam.

Item librum in quo sunt opera Francisci et Maronis.

Item Primum Scoti.

Item Questiones plures super Sententias.

Item Quolibeta Scoti in magno volumine.

Item quinque volumina coperta coreo rubeo ad ligaturas.

Item Legendas sanctorum.

Item unum breviarium.

Item libretos III secundum diversas materias.

[*Cancelled:* Sanctissimus Domini noster papa Nicolaus habet:

Summa theologie Henrici de Gandavo. *In the margin, by a different hand:* Dedit. Restituit].

Magister Antonius de Rodigio habet:

Primum et secundum Scoti super Sententias.

Et Ugonem super secundum, tertium et quartum Sententiarum.

Item duos alios libros in theologia.

Hernández Vera, R., *Franciscan Books and their Readers: Friars and Manuscripts in Late Medieval Italy.* Taylor & Francis Group, 2022

DOI 10.5117/9789463729512_APP01

Magister Iohannes Lupatinus habet:
Textum Sententiarum de littera [*Cancelled:* antiqua] pulcra.
Item Summam Galensis.
Item Bonaventuram super Primo et Secundo et Quarto.
Item et super Omnes.
Item tabulam super Sententiis.
Item Augustinum De civitate Dei in pulcra littera.
Item Questiones varias in theologia.
Item Constitutiones regule.
Item Loycam Aristotilis.

Frater Nicolaus armarista habet:
Testus Sententiarum de littera antiqua.
Item unum breviarium.
Item parabolle Salomonis.

Frater Raynaldus habet:
Testum Sententiarum.

Frater Martinus de Cumis habet:
Testus Sententiarum [*In the margin:* dedit].

Frater Chatarinus habet:
Secundum Bonaventure abreviatum.
Item miracula et exempla sanctorum.

Frater Laurentius Venetus habet: [*In the margin:* dedit]
Secundum Francisci Maroni.
Et transitum sancti Ieronimi.

Magister Franciscus de Firmo habet:
Quartum Francisci Maroni.

Frater David Anglicus habet: [*In the margin by a different hand:* dedit]
Mamotretum in pulcra littera.

Frater Lambertus habet:
Mamotretum
et Legendas sanctorum.
Item unum breviarium.

[Fol. 65v]
Frater Matheus condam sacrista habet:
Librum de Vitis patrum.
Et Quadragesimale Iacobi Capre.

Frater Allexander de Padua habet:
Summam Brocardi.

Dominus Cosmas Contareno habet: [*In the margin by another hand:* dedit]
Duas decretales antiquas.

Frater Marsilius habet:
Sermones festivos.
Librum de VII donis.
Allexandrum De uxulis [sic].
et Sermonale quadragesimale.

Reverendus dominus generalis de Rusconibus habet:
Constitutiones regule.

Frater Galvanus habet:
Constitutiones regule.

Presbiter Iohannes Cavaza Petrus habet:
Psalterium glosatum.
Et Danielem glosatum.

Frater Bartholomeus de Veneciis habet:
Summam compendii theologie
et Danielem glossatum.
et unum librum in quo sunt multi tractatus.

Frater Iohannes Petrus de Galçegnano habet:
Summam Iohannis Theotonici.

Magister Franciscus de Civitate Beluni habet:
Constitutiones generales et provinciales.
Item librum De ordine officii.
Item Constitutiones domini Benedicti pape.
Item Privilegia ordinis.

Item Regulas sancte Clare.
Item tabulam per alfabetum.
Item Marmotretum.

Frater Iohannes Pacientia habet:
Unum Voraginem.
Item sermonale festivum.
Item apostilam [sic] super Apocalipsim.
Item Tertium Scoti.

Frater Iacobus de Padua habet:
Unum sermonale.
Item unum breviarium.
Item unum Psalterium glosatum.

Frater Antonius a Nigra habet:
Libros duos in papiro.

Frater Bartholomeus de Pulveraria:
Boclum [sic] De consolatione.

Frater Bartholomeus a Sancto habet:
Quartum Bonaventure.
Item librum Spere.
Item quoddam principium Sententiarum.
Item Compendium theologie.
Item librum unum parvum cum tabulis.
Item Sermones dominicales.

Magister Dyatalis habet:
Librum Aristotilis De anima et Physicorum.
Item unum breviarium.

[Fol. 66r]
Frater Iacobus de Placentia habet:
Unu [sic] librum Confessionum.

Magister Franciscus de Savona habet: [*In the margin:* dedit]
Quartum Francisci Maronis.
Item Quolibeta Scoti.

Magister Iohannes de Rodigio habet: [*In the margin:* dedit]
Sermones predicabiles Francisci de Maronis.

Frater Raymondus de Allexandria habet:
Unum testum Sententiarum.

Infrascripti sunt debitores librorum, quos reperi in libro antiquo alterius
armariste, non cançelatos usque ad tempus 1423.

In primis frater Antonius de Padue habuit de 1422:
Unum librum in quo sunt multi sermones.
Item habet Summam de penitentia.

Frater Benevenutus de Trivisio habet:
Duo breviaria.

Frater Bartholomeus de Plebe Sacii habet:
Postilas Monchalerii.

Frater Bernardus Memo vendidit:
Duo breviaria.

Frater Paulus de Padua habet:
Unum breviarium.

Frater Bartholomeus de Padua habet:
Unum librum sine nomine.

Frater Antonius vicarius conventus habet:
Postilam Blanchi.

Frater Franciscus de Plebe habet:
Librum Patrum.

Frater Franciscus bachalarius habet:
Quartum Maronis.

Magister Iohanes de Plebe habet:
Scriptum Averois.

Frater Guido de Montesilice habet:
Sermones dominicales et super Epistolas et Evangelia et festivos.
Item allium librum sermonum.
Item postilla super Evangelia.

Frater Iohannes a Ferro habet:
Sermones Luce.
Item Sermones quadragesimales.
Item Sermones festivum.
Item allium librum sermonum.
Item legendas sanctorum.

Frater Iacobus de Curtorodulo habet:
Unum breviarium.

Frater Iohannes habet:
Secundum Bonaventure.
Item librum Dyonisii con Ystoria scolastica et Ricardo.

Frater Iohannes de Montagnana habet:
Unum Voraginem
Et unum Sermonale festivum.

Frater Iacobus de Padua habet:
Unum sermonale.

Frater Madalenus de Veneciis habet:
Decretales.
Item Secundum Ricardi.

[Fol. 66v]
Frater Paulus de Padua habet:
Unum par legendarum.

Prosdocimus Cornaia habet:
Librum de Vitis patrum.

Frater Peregrinus de Plebe habet:
Librum in quo est ystoria Balaam et Iosafat.
Item Tract[at]um magistri Petri.

Frater Thomeus de Padua habet:
Unam Bibliam.
Item Compendium Sacre Scripture.
Item unam aliam Bibliam in parvo volumine.
Item unum breviarium.

Suprascripti nominati in dicto libro antiquo pro maiori parte sunt mortui et tamen non sunt depenati in ipso libro.
Unum *Decretum* pulcrum et *Decretales* pulcre fuerunt pignorati 1407 14 iullii pro pecunia quam debebat [*In the margin:* habere] ser Andreas, factor molendinorum Turiselarum, pro frumento dato conventui.

[Another hand writes:] die 7 iulii 1489. Memoria qualiter fuerunt consegnati nonnulli libri numero 52 [causa] illos ponendi in libraria et factum fuit inventarium [in quodam] folio manu mei Pasqualini de Mast[ellariis] a Sancto Thomeo, posito in scrinio usque quo fiet novum inventarium omnium librorum.

Appendix 2

The Set of Corrections of the Manuscripts of Bonaventure's Commentary on the First Book of the *Sentences*, Padua, Biblioteca Antoniana, MSS 120, 123, 124 and 125

The following table compares a set of corrections to the text of Bonaventure's commentary to the first book of the *Sentences* in four manuscripts of the Biblioteca Antoniana of Padua. Each row of the table reproduces an excerpt as it appears in the manuscripts. Textual interventions or corrections in MSS 120 and 125 appear IN SMALL CAPITALS. The groups of similar corrections in MSS 123 and 124 are identified with **bold** type.

Hernández Vera, R., *Franciscan Books and their Readers: Friars and Manuscripts in Late Medieval Italy*. Taylor & Francis Group, 2022
DOI 10.5117/9789463729512_APP02

Place in Bonaventure's commentary	MS 120	MS 123	MS 124	MS 125	Comments
Dist. 2 Commentarius: De unitate et Trinitate secundum quod creditur – Divisio textus	Fol. 8ᵛ: et in comparatione ad creaturas: [*In the margin*: IN SE, RATIONE TRINITATIS IN COMPARATIONE AD CREATURAS] ratione scientie, potentie et voluntatis.	et in comparatione ad creaturas: in se, ratione trinitatis **et unitatis;** in comparatione ad creaturas, ratione scientie, potentie et voluntatis.	et in comparatione ad creaturas: in se, ratione trinitatis **et unitatis;** in comparatione ad creaturas, ratione scientie, potentie et voluntatis.	et in comparatione ad creaturas: IN SE, RATIONE TRINITATIS IN COMPARATIONE AD CREATURAS ratione scientie, potentie et voluntatis.	Two groups of MSS: (a) MSS 120 and 125 (b) MSS 123 and 124
Dist. 3, pt. 1, art. 1, q. 2: 'Utrum Deus sit cognoscibilis per creaturas' *Whether God may be known through creatures*	Fol. 12ᵛ: Ad illud quod ultimo queritur de DIFFERENTIA vestigii et ymagis [sic] quidam assignant, quod vestigium est in sensibus, [sic] ymago in spiritualibus. [*In the margin:* SED HEC DIFFERENTIA NON VALET,] NAM unitas et veritas et bonitas in quibus consistit vestigium sunt conditione maxime universales et intelligibiles.	Ad illud quod ultimo queritur de DIFFERENTIA vestigii et ymaginis quidam assignant quod vestigium est in sensibilibus, ymago de spiritualibus. **Sed ista distinctio et positio non valet,** quia etiam vestigium est in spiritualibus. Nam unitas, veritas, bonitas in quibus consistit vestigium sunt conditiones maxime universales.	Fol. 12ᵛ: Ad id etiam quod ultimo queritur de **distinctio** vestigii et ymaginis quidam assignant quod vestigium est in sensibus, [sic] ymago in spiritualibus **sed ista distinctio et positio non valet** quia etiam vestigium est in spiritualibus. Nam unitas, veritas, bonitas, in quibus consistit vestigium, sunt conditiones maxime universales et intelligibiles.	Fol. 10ᵛ: Ad illud quod ultimo queritur de divina ymagine, [sic] quidam assignant quod vestigium est in sensibus, ymago in spiritualibus SED HEC DIFFERENTIA NON VALET, NAM unitas et veritas et bonitas in quibus consistit vestigium sunt conditiones maxime universales et intelligibiles.	MS 125 used to correct MS 120 MS 123: differentia – distinctio MS 124: distinctio – distinctio

Place in Bonaventure's commentary	MS 120	MS 123	MS 124	MS 125	Comments
	Fol. 13ʳ: Alia differentia est penes ea in quibus reperiuntur. Quoniam enim omnis creatura comparatur ad Deum et in ratione causae et in ratione triplicis causae IDEO EST UMBRA VEL vestigium sed quoniam sola rationalis creatura] comparatur ad Deum ut obiectum, quia sola est capax Dei per cognitionem et amorem et ideo sola est ymago.	Fol. 10ᵛ: Alia differentia est penes ea in quibus reperiuntur. Quoniam enim omnis creatura comparatur ad Deum et in ratione causae et in ratione triplicis causae ideo omnis creatura est umbra vel vestigium sed qoniam sola rationali comparatur ad Deum ut obiectum, quia sola est capax Dei per cognitionem et amorem et ideo sola est ymago.	Fol. 12ʳ: Alia distinctio est penes ea in quibus reperiuntur quoniam enim omnis creatura comparatur ad Deum et in ratione causae et in ratione triplicis causae ideo omnis creatura est umbra vel vestigium. Sed quoniam sola rationale creatura comparatur ad Deum ut obiectum, quia sola est capax Dei per cognitio-nem et amorem et ideo sola est ymago.	Fols. 10ᵛ-11ʳ: Alia differentia est penes ea quibus in reperiuntur quoniam enim omnis creatura comparatur ad Deum et in ratione causae et in ratione triplicis causae IDEO EST UMBRA VEL vestigium. Sed quoniam sola rationale creatura comparatur ad Deum ut obiectum quia sola est capax Dei per cognitionem et amorem ideo sola est ymago.	MS 125 used as model to correct MS 120 MSS 123 and 124 have the same variation

Place in Bonaventure's commentary	MS 120	MS 123	MS 124	MS 125	Comments
Dist. 7, art. 1, q. 2: 'Utrum potentia generandi sit in Filio' *Whether the power of generating is in the Son*	Fol. 26ʳ: Et tunc est sensus, non potuit, id est, impotens fuit; et tunc negatur potentia, et relinquitur aptitudo, sicud de truncato dicitur que non potest gradi [*Originally generandi, but the titulus was erased*] de Filio quia non habet ad hoc aptitudinem.	Fol. 21ʳ: Et tunc est sensus, non potuit, id est, impotens fuit. Et tunc negatur potentia et relinquitur aptitudo sicud de truncato dicitur, que non potest gradi **hec modo non potest dici** de Filio quia non habet ad hoc aptitudinem.	Fol. 24ᵛ: Et tunc est sensus, non potuit, id est, impotens fuit. Et tunc negatur potentia et relinquitur aptitudo, sicud de truncato dicitur quod non potest gradi **hoc modo non potest dici** de Filio quia non habet ad hoc aptitudinem.	Fol. 23ʳ: Et tunc est sensus, non potuit, id est, impotens fuit. Et tunc negatur potentia et relinquitur aptitudo sicud de truncato dicitur, quod non potest gradi [*Insertion mark, in the left margin, by a fifteenth-century hand in formal rotunda:* QUIA APTUS NATUS EST AD CONTRADICENDI ET GENERANDI NON POTEST HOC MODO NON POTEST DICI] de Filio, quia non habet ad hoc aptitudinem.	On MS 120, insertion mark, and in the margin, by a late hand, fifteenth century: 'et sic non intelligitur' The correction in MS 125 by late gothic hand, very close to the hand of the inventory of 1449; perhaps the hand of the fifteenth-century librarian Was MS 125 a 'safe copy'?

Place in Bonaventure's commentary	MS 120	MS 123	MS 124	MS 125	Comments
Dist. 14, art. 1, q. 2: 'Utrum processio Spiritus sancti aeterna et temporalis numerentur ut duae processiones' *Whether the eternal procession of the Holy Spirit and the temporal are to be numbered as two processions*	Fol. 46ʳ: Scilicet, aut quia duplex modus dicendi, non equivocus. Et per hoc patet sequens de homine picto et vero, quia illi non est analogia, sed EQUIVOCATIO pura.	Fol. 38ʳ: Scilicet aut quia duplex modus dicendi numquid equivocus *[Insertion mark, and in the margin, in a fifteenth-century hand:* non univocus sed analogicus] et per de *[Correction over the 'd' to form an 'h'; it should be* hoc] patet sequens de homine picto et vero, quia illi non est analogia sed **equivocacio** pura.	Fol. 44ᵛ: Scilicet aut quia duplex modus dicendi non equivocus. Et per hoc patet sequens de homine picto et vero, quia illi non est **analogica,** sed **equivoca** pura.	Fol. 43ʳ: Scilicet aut quia duplex modus dicendi, non equivocus. Et per hoc patet sequens de homine picto et vero, quia illi non est analogia sed EQUIVOCATIO pura.	MS 124 was not used to correct MS 123
Dist. 16, art. 1, q. 1: 'Quid sit missio visibilis' *What is a visible mission?*		Fol. 37ᵛ, col. a: Omne quod temporaliter procedit *[Insertion mark, and in the margin, in a late fourteenth-century hand:* : ab alio habet inicium essendi ex tempore; si ergo Spiritus sanctus temporaliter procedit] ergo eius essere incipit.	Omne quod temporaliter procedit ab alio habet inicium essendi ex tempore: si ergo Spiritus sanctus temporaliter procedit ergo eius essere incipit.		MS 125 used to correct MS 123 Paraphs absent in MS 123

Place in Bonaventure's commentary	MS 120	MS 123	MS 124	MS 125	Comments
Dist. 17, pt. 2, art. 1, q. 1: 'Tractatio questionum: Hic quaeritur, si caritas Spiritus sanctus est, cum ipsa augeatur et minuatur in homine' *Whether charity is the Holy Spirit, since it increases and diminishes in man*	Ad intelligentiam hoc partis est hic quaestio de augmento [sic] caritatiss et circa hoc quaeruntur iiiiuor. Primo queritur utrum caritas possit augeri. Secundo de modo augmenti ipsius caritatis. Tertio queritur de oppositio augmenti ipsius.	Fol. 48ᵛ: Ad intelligentiam hoc quaestio de augmento [sic] caritatis et circa hoc quaeruntur iiiiuor queritur utrum caritas possit augeri secundo substantiam. Secundo queritur de modo augmenti ipsius caritatis. Tertio queritur de op-positio augmenti ipsius **scilicet diminutione, utrum caritas possit diminui.**	Fol. 55ᵛ, col. b: Ad intelligentiam hoc partis est hic quaestio de augmento [sic] caritatis, et circa hoc queruntur iiiiuor. Primo queritur utrum caritas possit [*Cancelled:* diminuiri, *and above the word:* augeri; *insertion mark, and in the margin, by a late fourteenth-century early fifteenth-century hand:* secundo de modo augmenti ipsius caritatis. Tertio queritur de op-positio augmenti ipsius **scilicet diminutione utrum caritas possit diminui].**	Ad intelligentiam hoc partis es hic quaestio de augmento [sic] caritatis et circa hoc quaeruntur iiiiuor. Primo queritur utrum caritas possit augeri. Secundo de modo augmenti ipsius caritatis. Tertio queritur de oppositio augmenti ipsius.	MS 123 used as model to correct MS 124.

Appendix 3

Manuscript Images

Plate 1: Florence, Biblioteca Medicea Laurenziana, MS Amiat. 1, fol. 2ʳ.

Hernández Vera, R., *Franciscan Books and their Readers: Friars and Manuscripts in Late Medieval Italy.* Taylor & Francis Group, 2022
DOI 10.5117/9789463729512_APP03

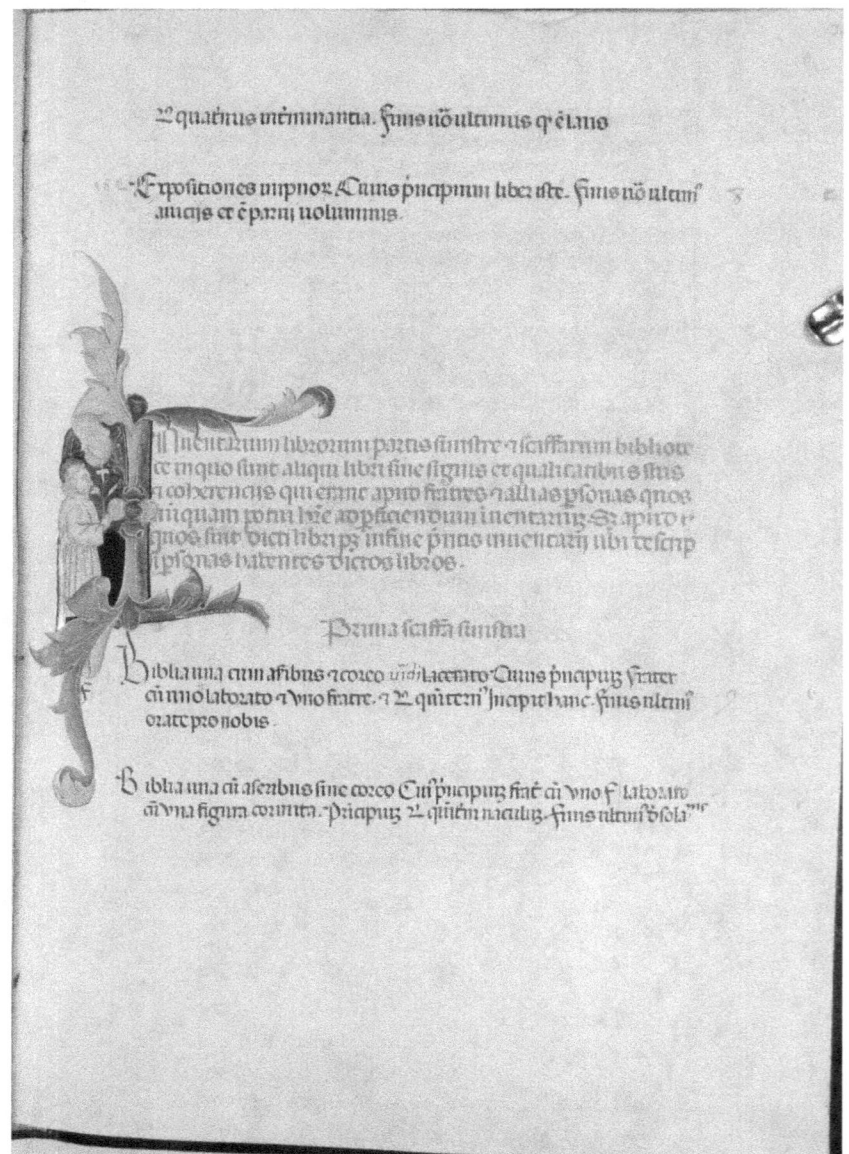

Plate 2: Padua, Biblioteca Antoniana, MS 573, fol. 30[r].

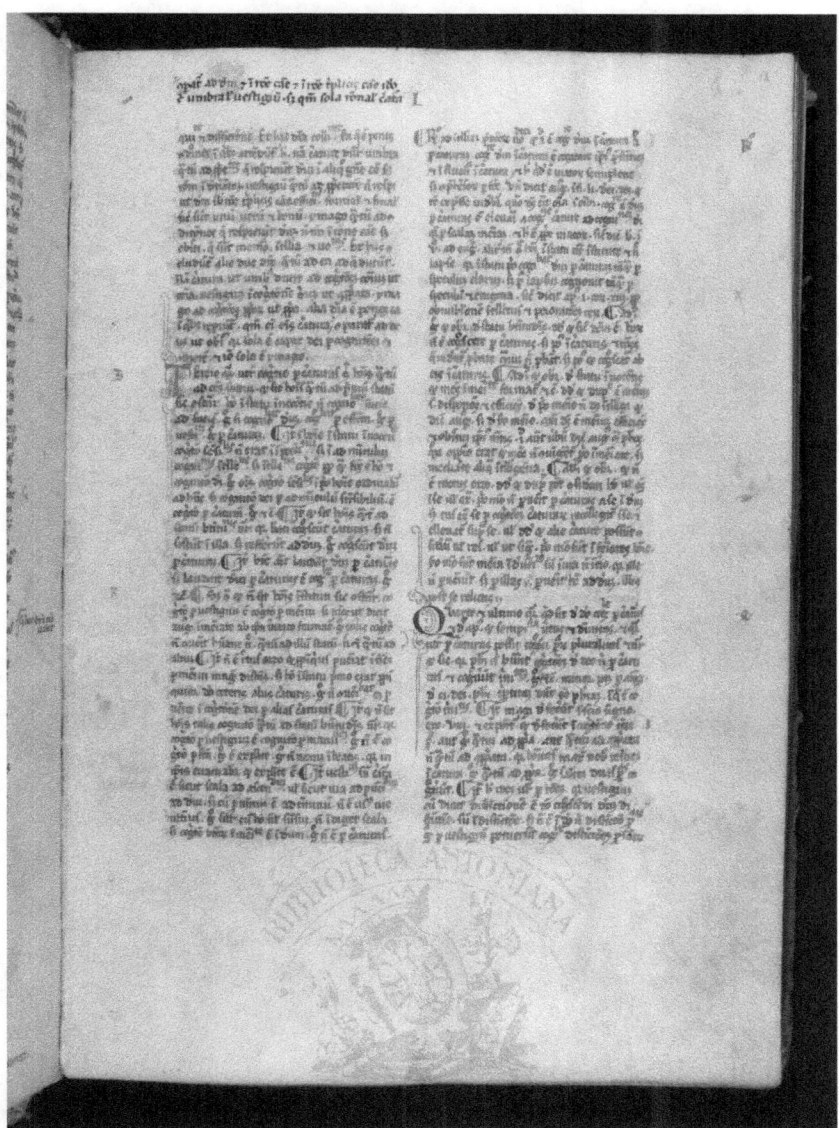

Plate 3: Padua, Biblioteca Antoniana, MS 120, fol. 13ʳ.

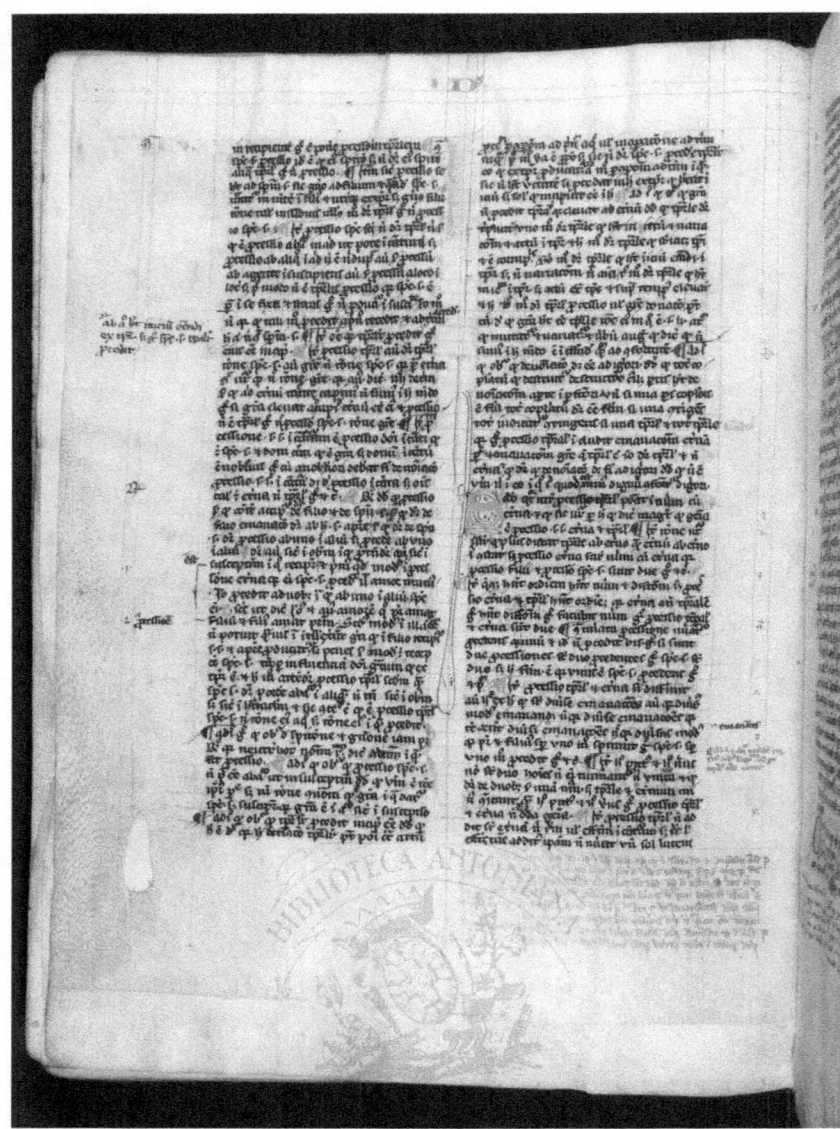

Plate 4: Padua, Biblioteca Antoniana, MS 123, fol. 37ᵛ.

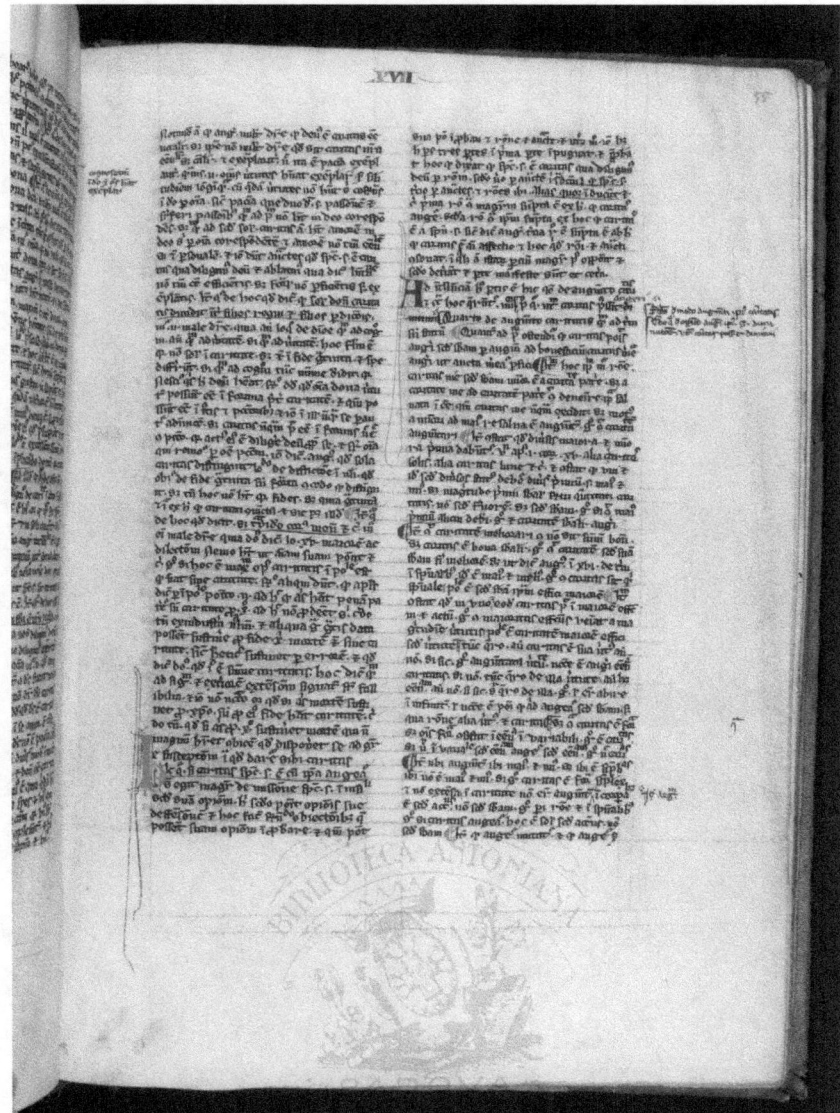

Plate 5: Padua, Biblioteca Antoniana, MS 124, fol. 55ʳ.

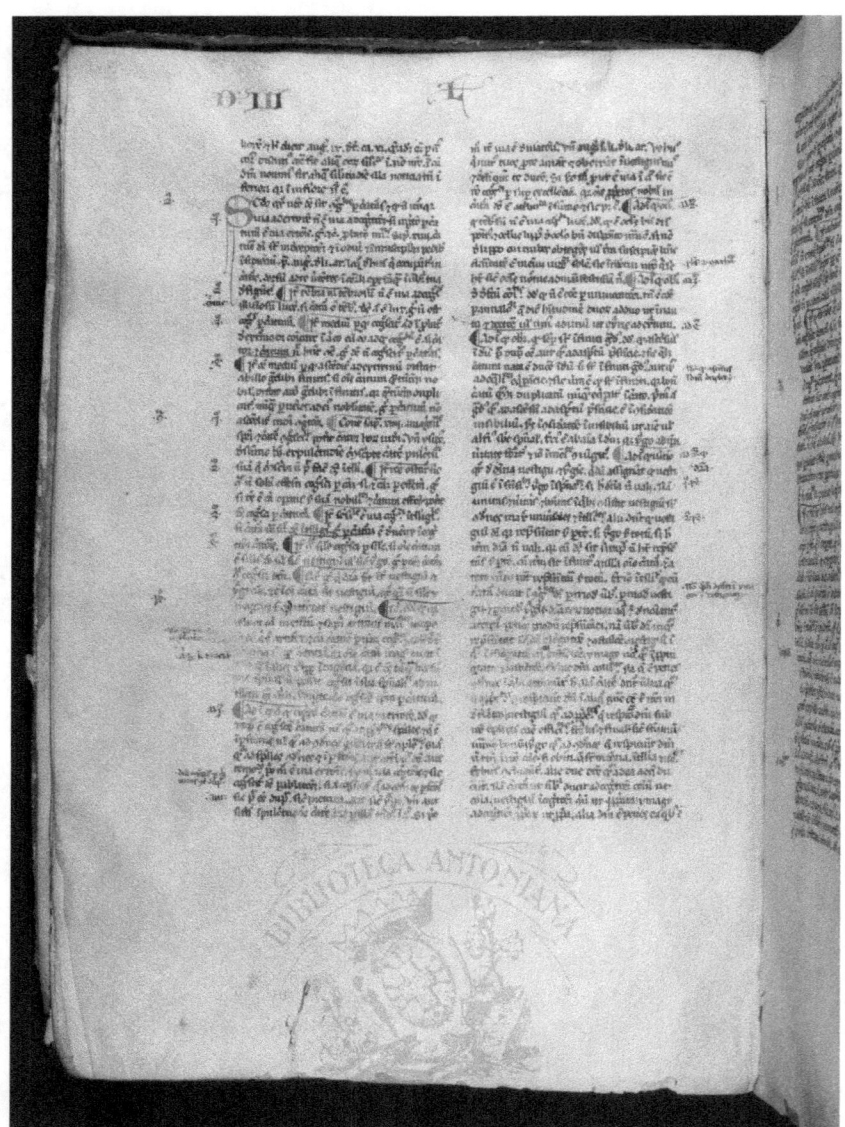

Plate 6: Padua, Biblioteca Antoniana, MS 125, fol. 10ᵛ.

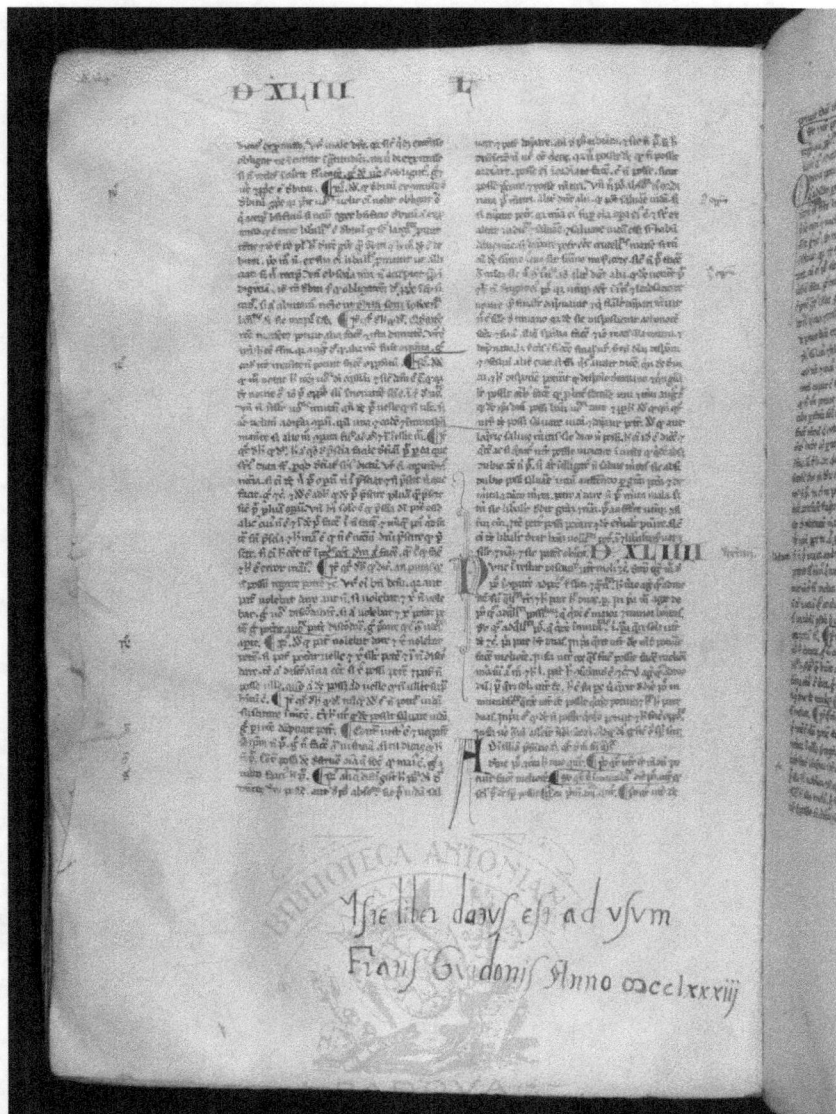

Plate 7: Padua, Biblioteca Antoniana, MS 125, fol. 127ᵛ.

Plate 8: Padua, Biblioteca Antoniana, MS 125, fol. 143ʳ.

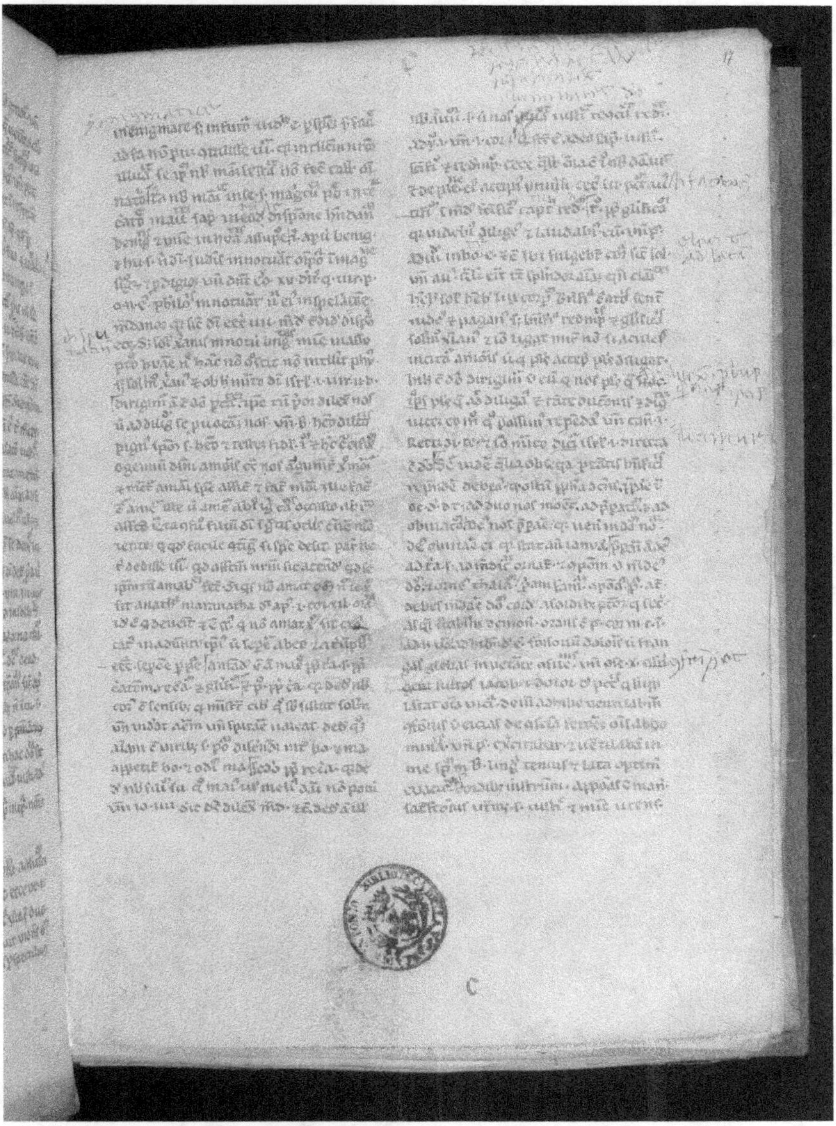

Plate 9: Padua, Biblioteca Antoniana, MS 418, fol. 17ʳ.

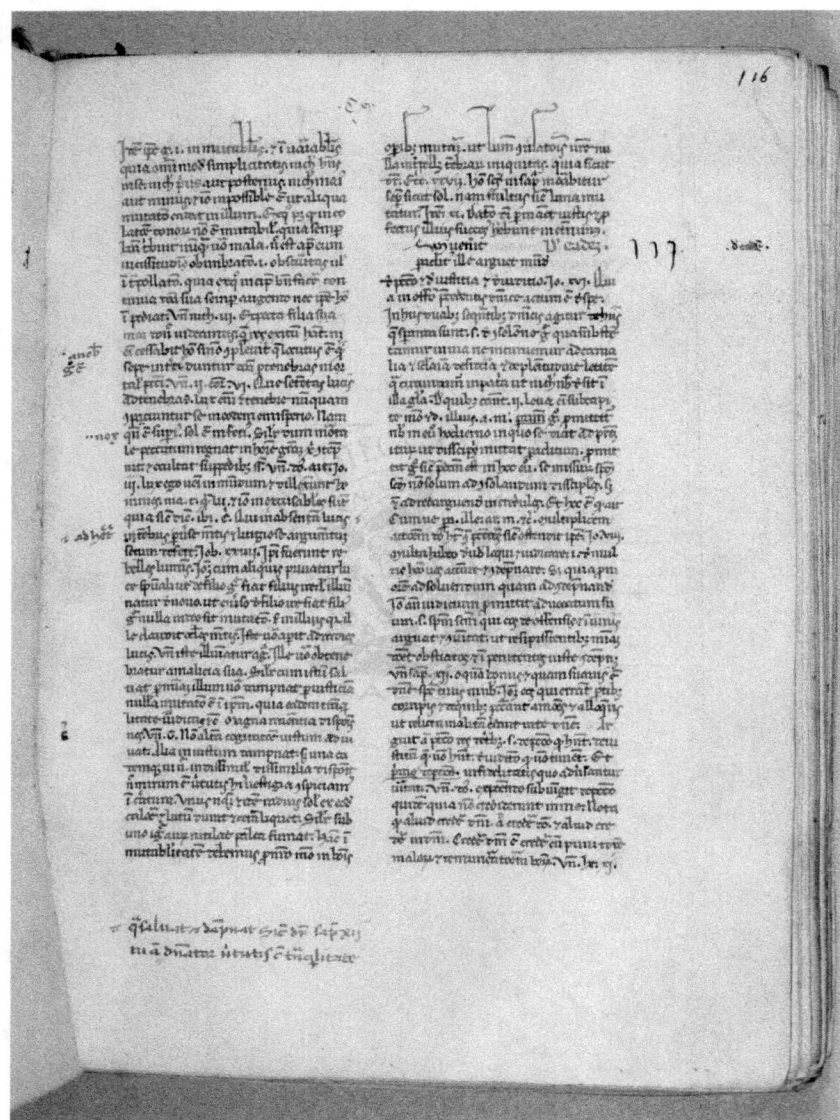

Plate 10: Padua, Biblioteca Antoniana, MS 419, fol. 116ʳ.

qb strenuue osstm sun tranc aut
tmedo · ptheodo · mglado · h resstrue
cichia vn pxra · Oqf magnos rolarit
latores · Suma dutul ut · so · xx · Instr
digitu mil huc · qt p̄ infacens man
· r · me · Septim e ostdaco pussionus · s
ouicor · spuror · ailaphor · flagellor
q clauor · ist̄ ois qn agn coxon se
obaqn · n a · o · s · h testtr un · q milla
sunt sustime uincia · ja · j · ta inti ni
d · n op · R · or mitaris · q it̄amaris ·
cdubi stara · q̄ u aune utsthea n i
qnar iure · Ao hos sene muti · cor
ruue unco Dn · Aug · Q fupbia sana
ti pot si similitate sibi cli · n sanat · q
audaia pot sanari si paupitat silu
cli · n sanat · q miracicha sanan pot · si
putia sibi · n sanari Omechena oib
silulctc · ora uniuq spmiec · oia xa
tesecia recitukec · oia sustlina tese
cant · oia uckia custether̄c · oia pli
ta rppmitc · oia depiraco corrigitie
s̄ · n q testrucus muris iericho so
sue speat · t dicit · oialedis q receuf
scamint ruinas iericho · ipmagenno
suo sindamna illi iaciat · q inouis
simo btor · ponat portal ts · supmo
genito sidumita iacit · q jp amore
ceatus timore cli q̄ e unu sapie pt
s nomsstio portal pon · q acetema
me uetris spe saturl amrapisd ·
xi · q mortuo hoie rmpio · nsla erit

uit spos · Sedm n e di irrene · nil usstn
hel h e resurrecto gre · de q ac · xr ·
Stb q sco q h · p mit · p · sic e cuplex
e mors · s mors aie psepareti · act · q
mors corpis psepareti abaia · mar
ctup e rt · t · ate a corpis · Resurrectev
aie optt e r ipmo couiectu · uicen ·
corpis psinier isto · Et sic corp̄ irice
sua mira q sensu recipiet · na cha
istia resuncecte recipiet ognintev
q chlectev cli · Cognitd e puta vn so
xvi · h e una et · d · et · st · sapia · xv ·
qosct te ossia · s · e · q scire msticia · a
iunne tua · mctx imoratmatis e
Valtecio au e sens · vn cap · j · scire
tdo itomtent · i · trmo coxtis affect
eu chligice jp tomeart siia · q bon
e set tc · Et sic qnq partie corpal est
sens na q spiual · indelicet · u nsudo
codt uncam tell · q cuicham q nob
sots · q cocem ton cdort · x a gutteni
qn stuaus e do · q pulpem e bto sosie te
uto mre iq socsu se nulla e aspinas
s oit mastieracus leuinas vunstcat
au nos ib maluc s uto vn jo · xro uit
hoea q nucd q m · a · u · s · q g · a · n · sse
sacimo · s corp suo vn jo · ur · Sigt na
du exh · pa · uicet · st spu sco vn jo vit
spe e q munficate · Ro · v · Catmi cli dit
qt teui n e de · q isignu e odi · qt mor
u r iub icup pgnam hicane malig
ste cht eu eranguie · q qosmi ton opt

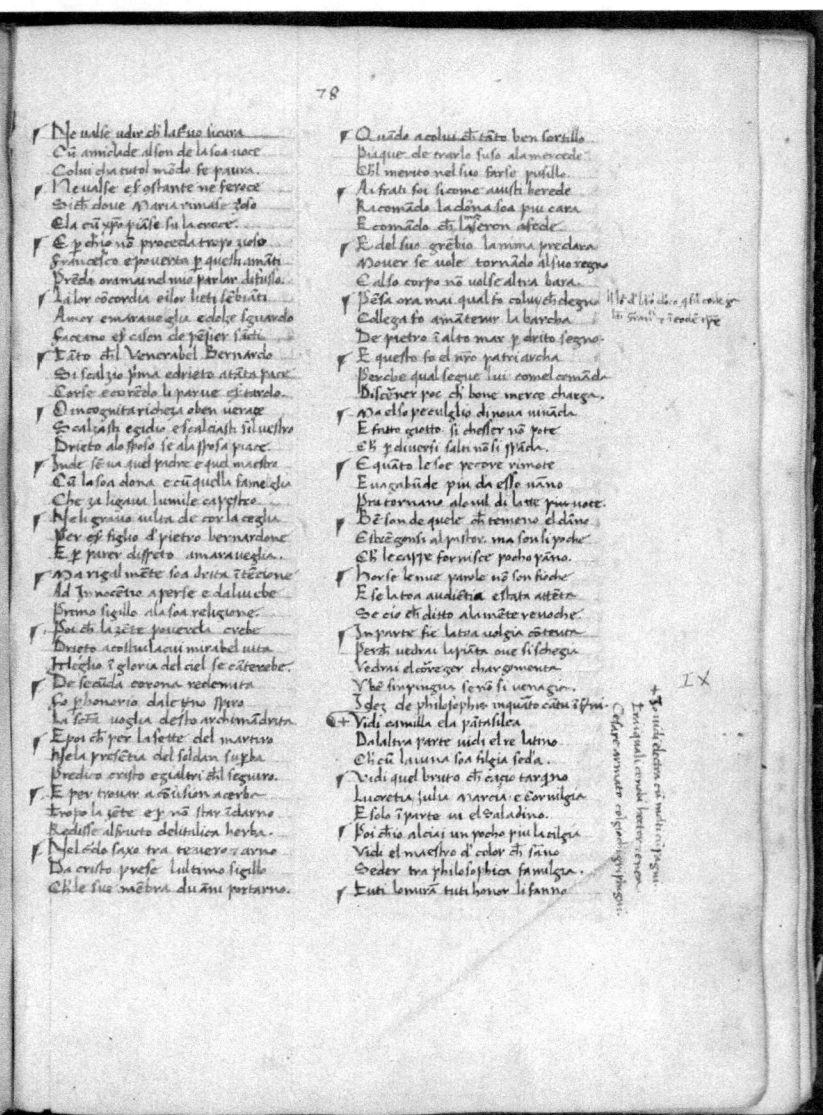

Plate 12: Padua, Biblioteca Universitaria, MS 1030, fol. 78ʳ.

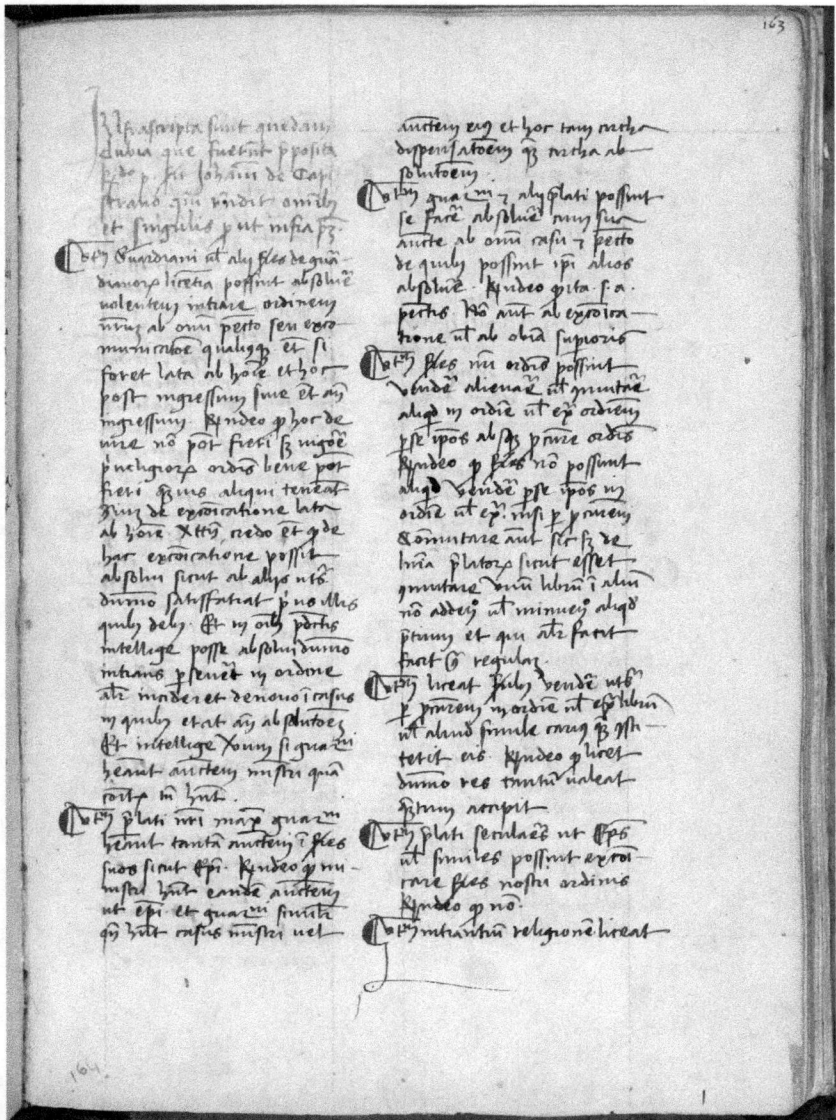

Plate 13: Padua, Biblioteca Universitaria, MS 586, fol. 164ʳ.

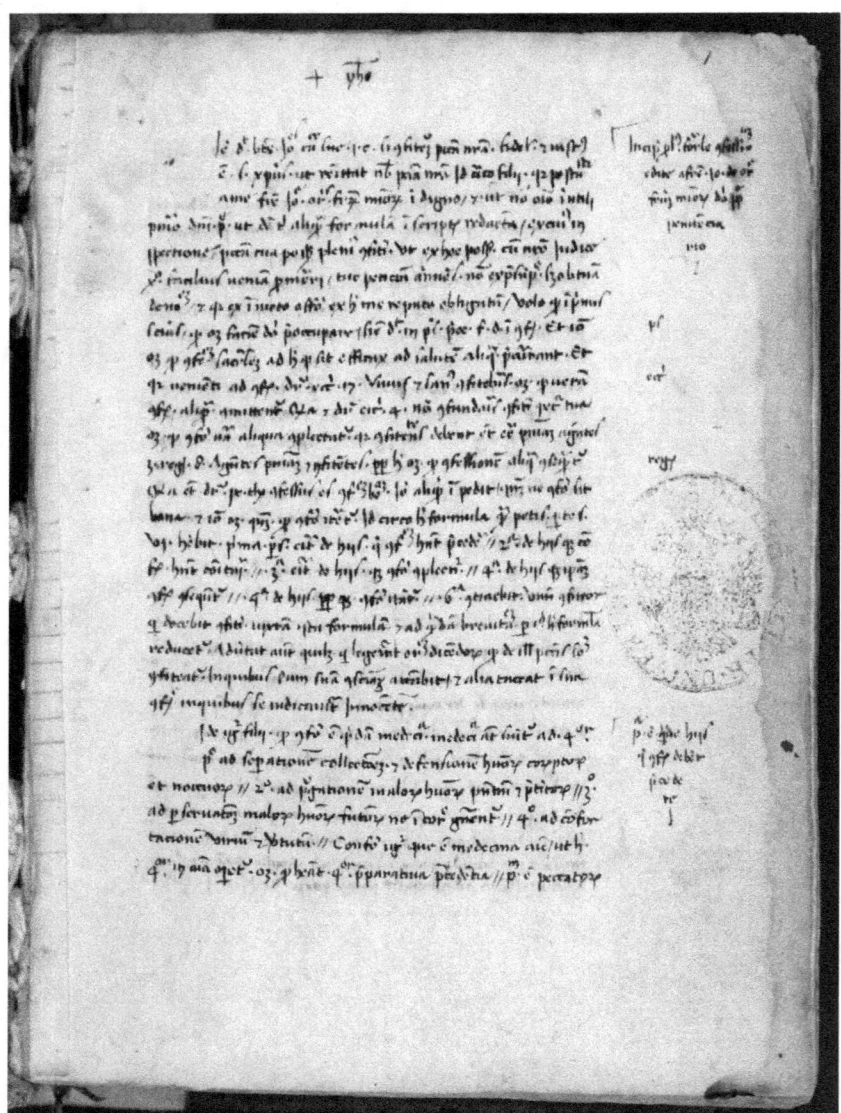

Plate 14: Padua, Biblioteca Universitaria, MS 736, fol. 1ʳ.

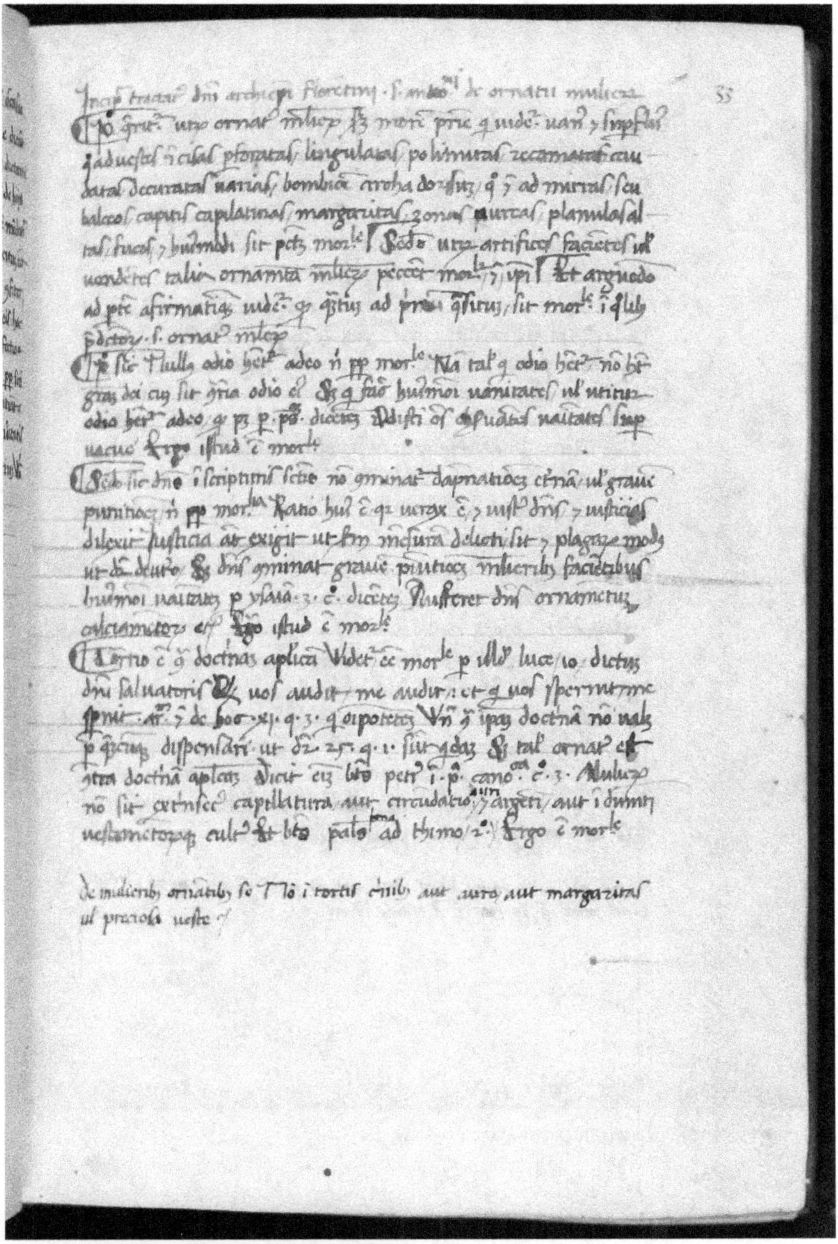

Plate 15: Padua, Biblioteca Universitaria, MS 1159, fol. 33ʳ.

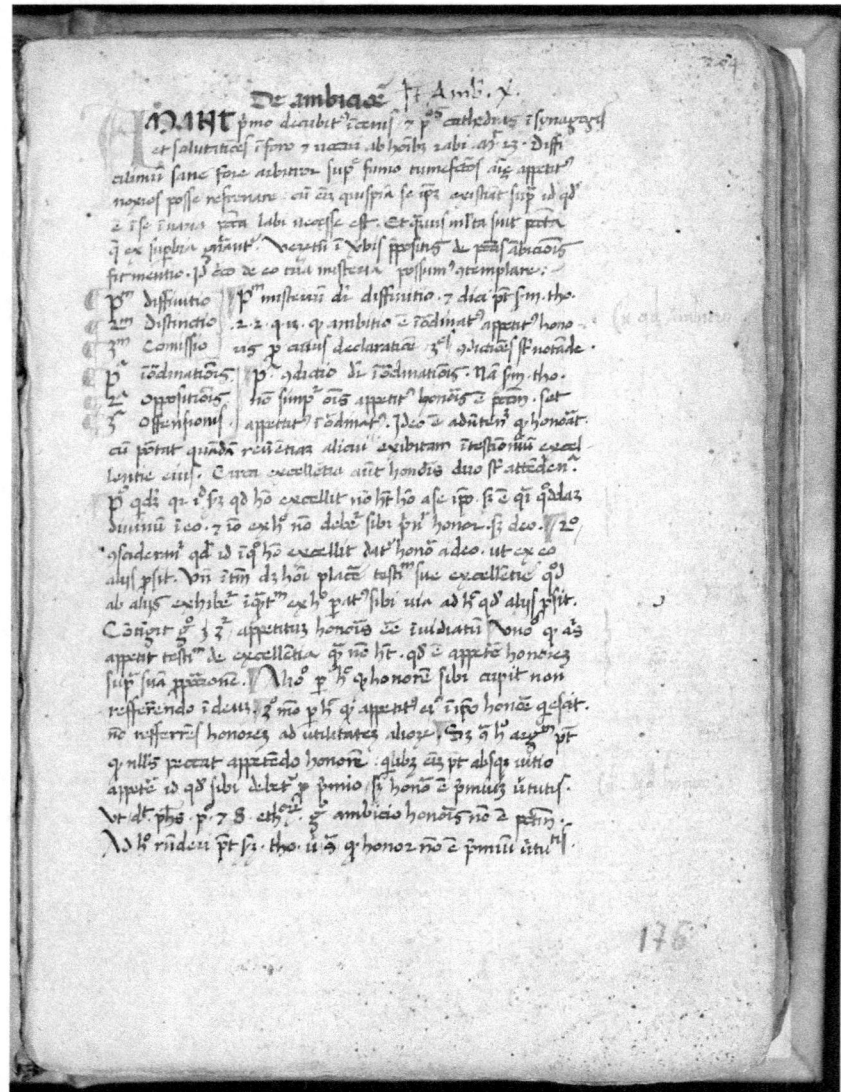

Plate 16: Padua, Biblioteca Universitaria, MS 1789, fol. 176ʳ.

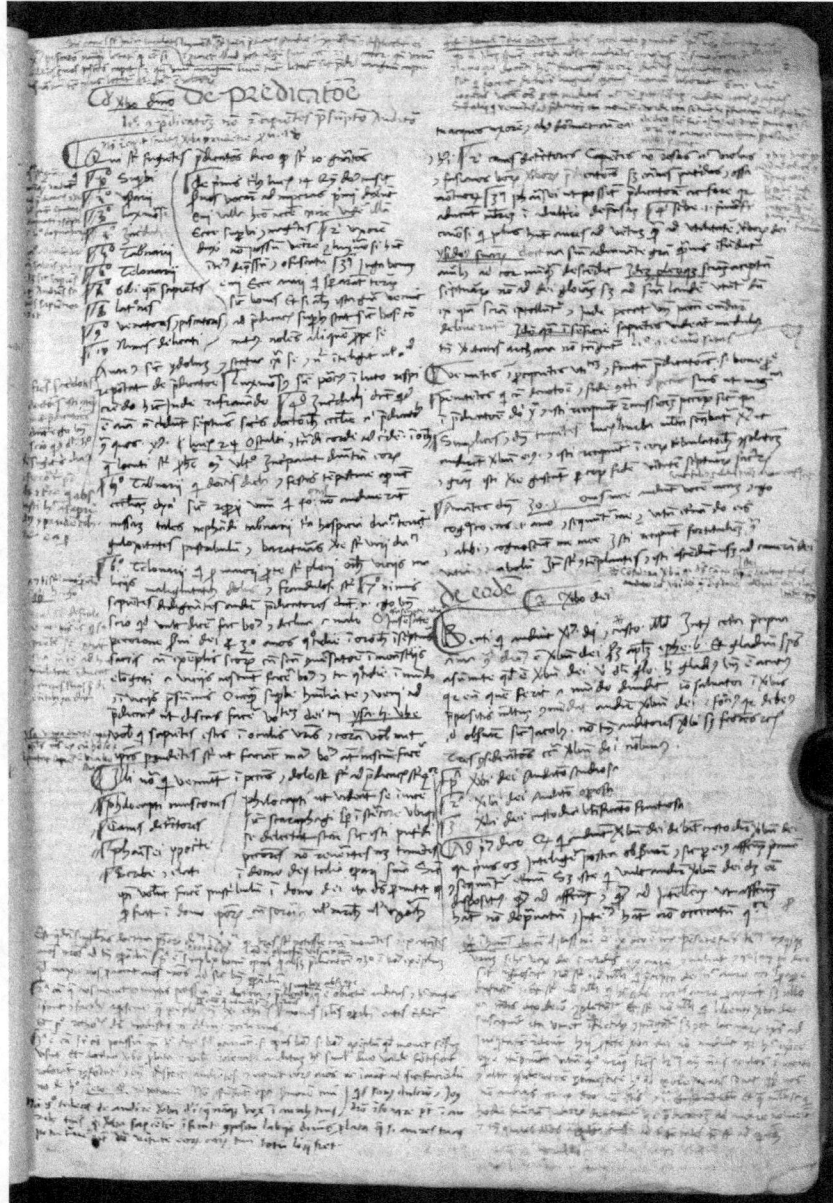

Plate 17: Padua, Biblioteca Universitaria, MS 1851, fol. 8ʳ.

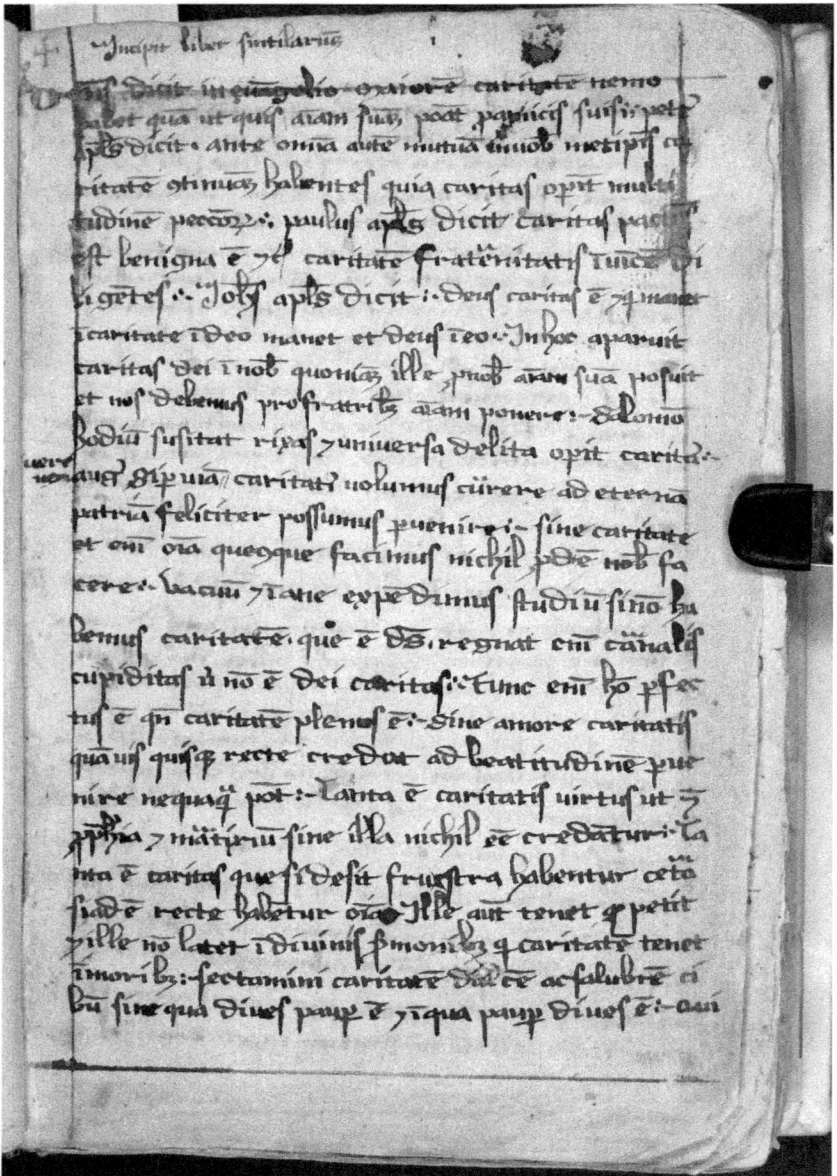

Plate 18: Padua, Biblioteca Universitaria, MS 2103, fol. 21ʳ.

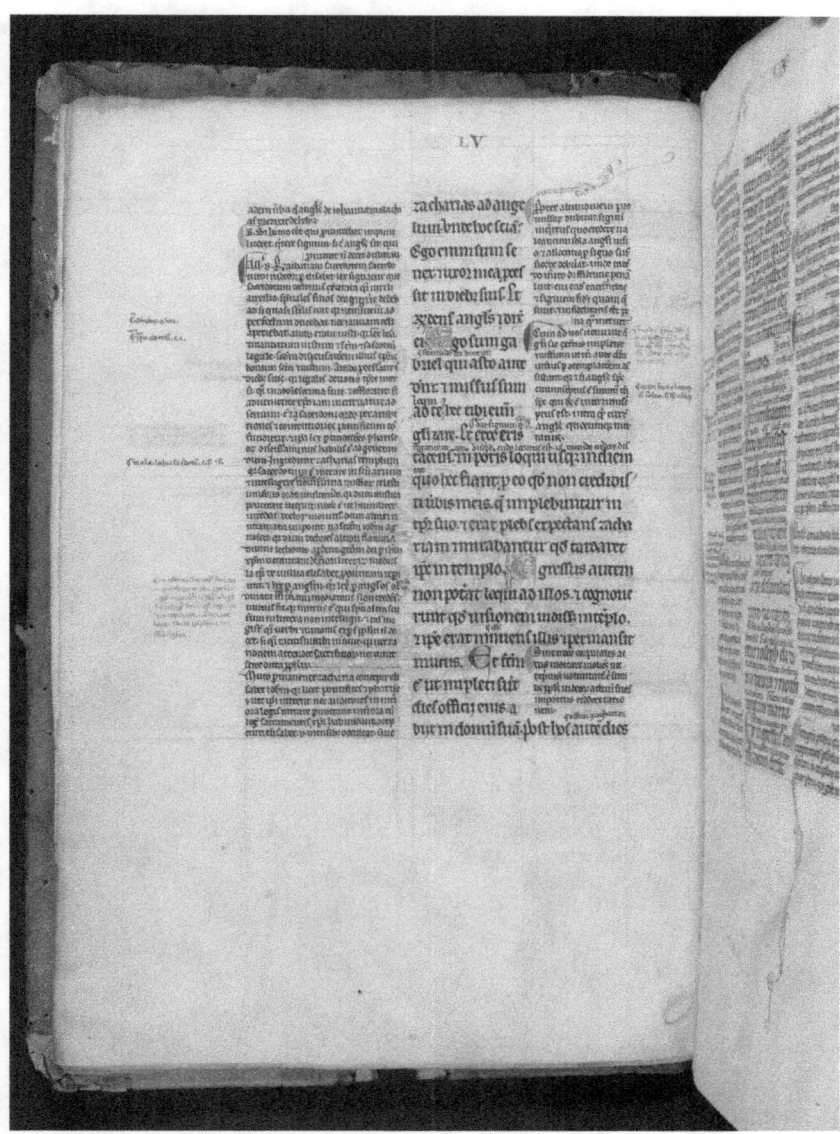

Plate 19: Padua, Biblioteca Antoniana, MS 267, fol. 3ᵛ.

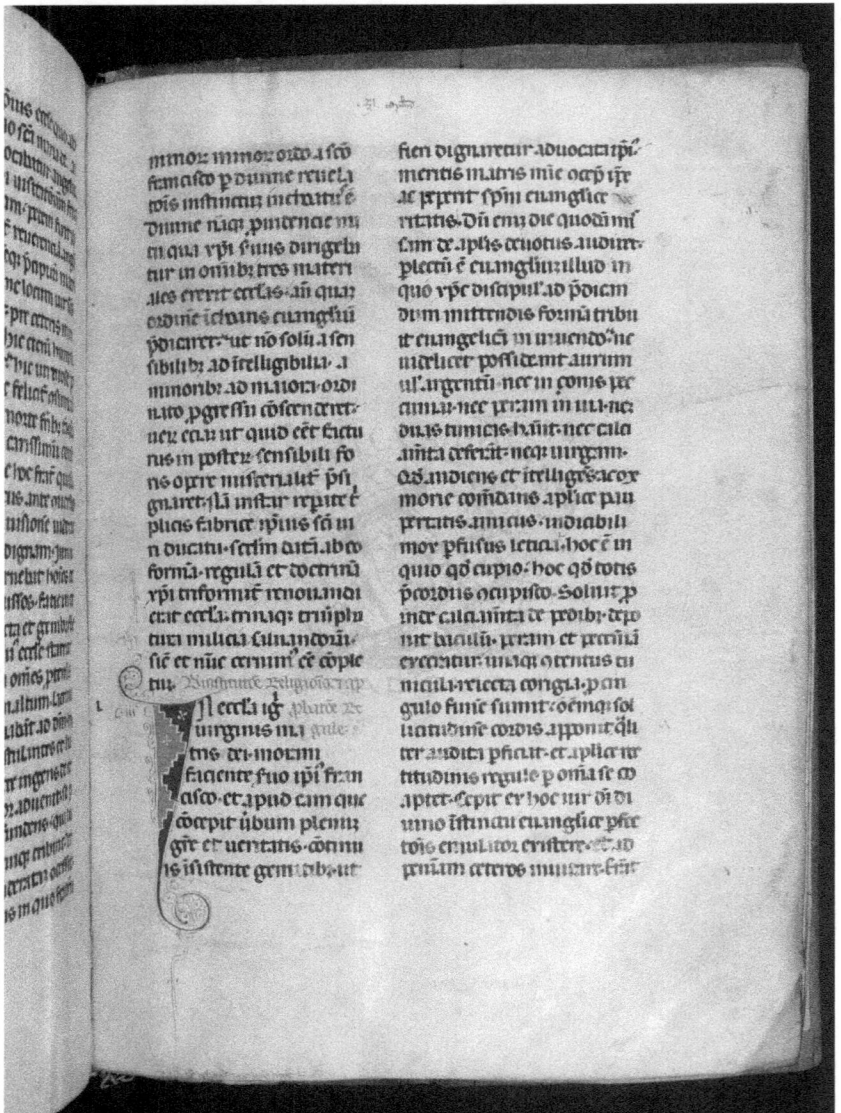

Plate 20: Padua, Biblioteca Antoniana, MS 112, fol. 7ʳ.

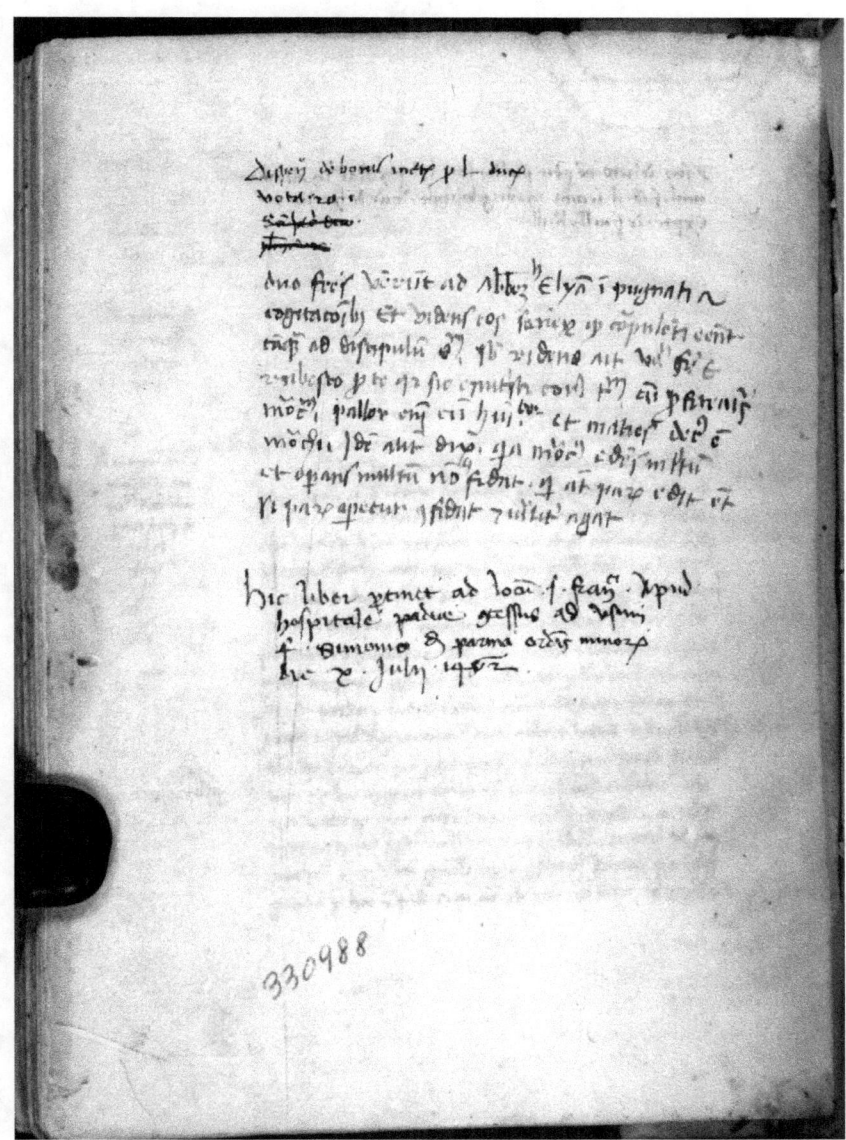

Plate 21: Padua, Biblioteca Universitaria, MS 736, 117ᵛ.

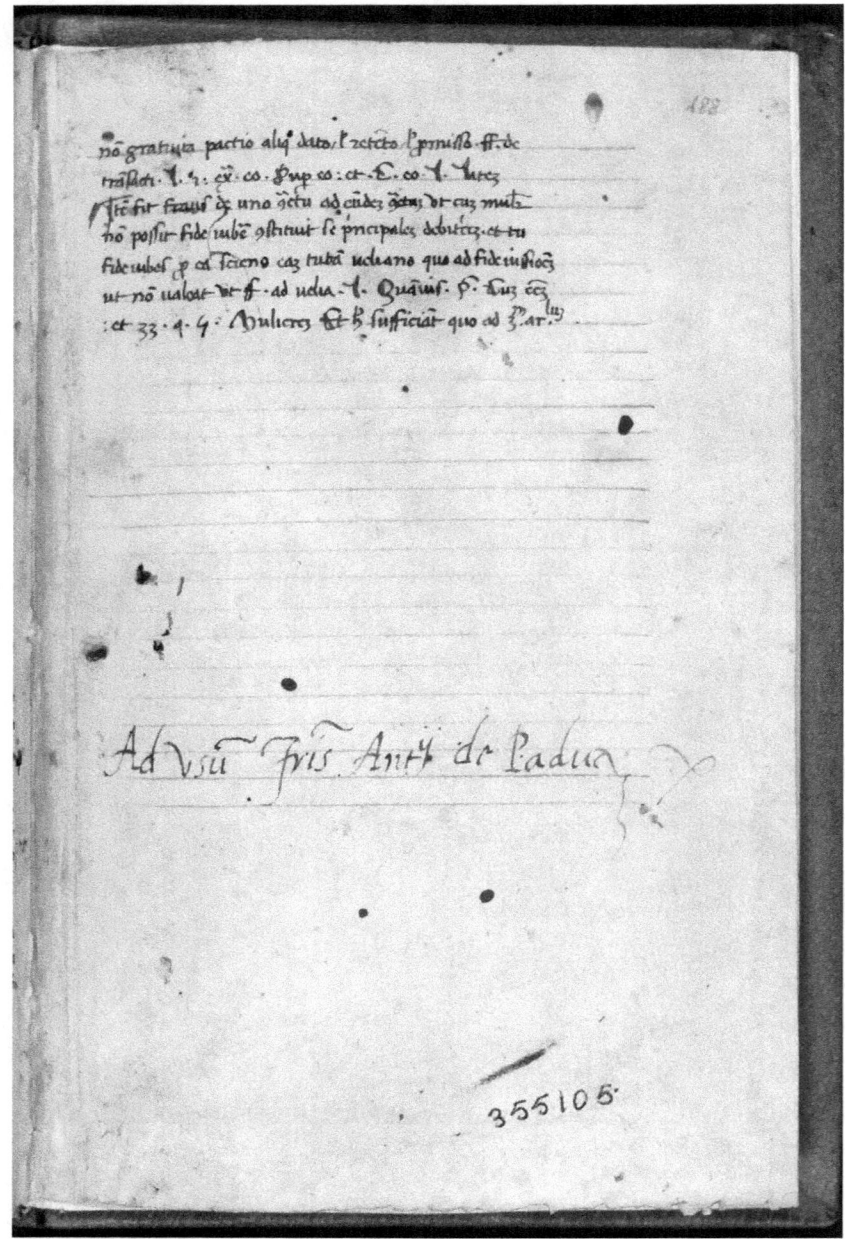

Plate 22: Padua, Biblioteca Universitaria, MS 1159, fol. 188ʳ.

Bibliography

Manuscripts

Assisi

Biblioteca Comunale
MS 505

Biblioteca del Sacro Convento
MS 1
MS 2
MS 3
MS 4
MS 5
MS 6
MS 7
MS 9
MS 10
MS 11
MS 12
MS 13
MS 15
MS 338

Cesena

Biblioteca Malatestiana
MS D.XXI.1
MS D.XXI.2
MS D.XXI.3
MS D.XXI.4

Cologne

Historisches Archiv der Stadt
MS Best 7002, HS 146

Florence

Biblioteca Medicea Laurenziana
MS Amiat. 1

Biblioteca Riccardiana
MS 1287

Padua

Pontificia Biblioteca Antoniana
MS 27
MS 112
MS 119
MS 120
MS 121
MS 122
MS 123
MS 124
MS 125
MS 126
MS 127
MS 128
MS 129
MS 130
MS 131
MS 213
MS 267
MS 274
MS 276
MS 277
MS 280
MS 283
MS 284
MS 285
MS 289
MS 309
MS 310

MS 313
MS 316
MS 322
MS 342
MS 417
MS 418
MS 419
MS 527
MS 572
MS 573
MS 590
MS 720

Biblioteca Civica
MS B.P. 929

Biblioteca Universitaria
MS 548
MS 586
MS 736
MS 1030
MS 1098
MS 1110
MS 1159
MS 1511
MS 1789
MS 1851
MS 2103

Rome

Biblioteca del Pontificio Ateneo Antonianum
MS 24

Trento

Castello del Buonconsiglio, Monumenti e collezioni provinciali
MS 1597

Vatican City

Biblioteca Apostolica Vaticana
MS Vat. Lat. 718
MS Vat. Lat. 11283

Vienna

Österreichische Nationalbibliothek
MS 1364
MS 1349

Primary Sources

Alanus de Insulis, *Summa de arte praedicatoria*, in *PL*, 210 (Paris: Typis L. Migne, 1855)

Abate, Giuseppe, ed., 'Memoriali, statuti ed atti di capitoli generali dei Frati Minori inediti dei secoli XIII e XIV', *Miscellanea Francescana*, 33 (1933), 15-45

Angelo Clareno, *Expositio regulae Fratrum Minorum*, ed. by Livarius Oliger (Quaracchi: Collegii S. Bonaventurae, 1912)

——, *Liber chronicarum sive Tribulationum Ordinis Minorum*, ed. by Giovanni Boccali, Pubblicazioni della Biblioteca Francescana Chiesa Nuova, Assisi, 8 (Assisi: Porziuncola, 1999)

Armstrong, Regis J. et al., eds., *Francis of Assisi: Early Documents*, 3 vols. (St. Bonaventure, NY: Franciscan Institute, 1999-2001)

Bernardino of Siena, *Opera Omnia, studio et cura PP. Collegii* S. *Bonaventurae*, 9 vols. (Quaracchi: Typographia Collegii S. Bonaventurae, 1950-65)

Bihl, Michael, ed., 'Statuta generalia Ordinis edita in Capitulis generalibus celebratis Narbonnae an. 1260, Assisii an. 1279 atque Parisiis an. 1292: editio critica et synoptica', *AFH*, 34 (1941), 13-94, 284-358

Bonaventure of Bagnoregio, *Opera Omnia*, ed. by the Fathers of the Collegii S. Bonaventura, 10 vols. (Quaracchi: Typographia Collegii S. Bonaventurae, 1882-1902)

Carducci, Giosuè, ed., *Rime da Cino da Pistoia e d'altri del secolo XIV* (Florence: Barbèra, 1862)

Cassiodorus, *An Introduction to Divine and Human Readings*, ed. and trans. by Leslie Webber Jones (New York: Octagon Books, 1966)

Cenci, Cesare, ed., *Bibliotheca manuscripta ad sacrum conventum Assisiensem*, 2 vols. (Assisi: Casa Editrice Francescana, 1981)

———, 'De fratrum minorum constitutionibus praenarbonensibus', *AFH*, 83 (1990), 50-95

Chiappini, Anicetus, ed., 'S. Iohannis de Capistrano Sermones duo ad studentes et Epistola circularis De studio promovendo inter observantes', *AFH*, 11 (1918), 97-131

Chronica XXIV generalium Ordinis Minorum, in *AF*, III (1897), pp 1-575

Chronica fratri Nicolai Glassberger, in *AF*, II (1887)

Chronologia historico-legalis seraphici Ordinis Fratrum Minorum Sancti Francisci, 4 vols. (Venice/Naples/Rome, 1650-1795)

Ehrle, Franz, ed., *Die ältesten Redaktionen der Generalconstitutionen des Franziskanerordens*, in *ALKG*, VI (1892), pp. 1-138

Esser, Kajetan, ed., *Die Opuscula des Hl. Franziskus von Assisi* (Grotaferrata: Il Collegio S. Bonaventura di Quaracchi, 1976)

Flood, David, ed., *Die Regula non Bullata der Minderbrüder* (Werl: Dietrich Coelde, 1967)

———, ed., *Hugh of Digne's Rule Commentary,* (Grottaferrata: Editiones Collegii S. Bonaventurae ad Claras Aquas, 1979)

Heyworth, Peter. L., ed., *Jack Upland, Friar Daw's Reply and Upland's Rejoinder* (London: Oxford University Press, 1968)

Humbert of Romans, *Opera de vita regulari*, ed. by Joachim J. Berthier, 2 vols. (Turin: Marietti, 1956)

Humphreys, Kenneth William, *The Library of the Franciscans of the Convent of St. Anthony, Padua at the Beginning of the Fifteenth Century* (Amsterdam: Erasmus, 1966)

———, *The Library of the Franciscans of Siena in the Late Fifteenth Century* (Amsterdam: Erasmus, 1978)

Isidore of Seville, *Etymologiarum sive originum libri XX*, ed. by W. M. Lindsay, 2 vols. (Oxford: Clarendon, 1911)

———, *Sententiae*, ed. by Pierre Cazier (Turnhout: Brepols, 1998)

John Climacus, *The Ladder of Divine Ascent,* trans. by Colm Luibheid and Norman Russell (New York: Paulist Press, 1982)

Kerval, Léon de, ed., *Sancti Antonii de Padua vitae duae quarum altera hucusque inedita* (Paris: Fischbacher, 1904)

Laurent, M. H., *Monumenta historica S. P. N. Dominici*, Monumenta Ordinis F. Praedicatorum Historica, 15 (Paris, J. Vrin, 1933)

Little, Andrew G., 'Definitiones capitulorum generalium Ordinis Fratrum Minorum 1260-1282', *AFH*, 7 (1914), 676-82

———, 'Statuta provincialia provinciae Franciae et Marchiae Trevisae (s. XIII)', *AFH*, 7 (1914), 447-65

Mansi, Johannes Dominicus, ed., *Sacrorum conciliorum nova et amplissima collectio*, 54 vols. (Venice: Antonio Zatta, 1759-98; repr. Paris: H. Welter, 1923-27), XXII (Venice: Antonio Zatta, 1778; repr. Paris: H. Welter, 1903)

Mattheus Parisiensis, *Historia Anglorum*, in *Monumenta Germania Historica, Scriptores*, 28 (Hannover, 1888)

Michaelis Savonarole, *Libellus de magnificis ornamentis regie civitatis Padue,* ed. by Arnaldo Segarizzi, in *RIS*, XXIV, 15 (Città di Castello: Lapi, 1902)

Peter Olivi's Rule Commentary, ed. by David Flood (Wiesbaden: Franz Steiner, 1972)

Petrus Cantorus, *Verbum abbreviatum*, in *PL*, 205 (Paris: Typis L. Migne, 1855)

Petrus Ioannis Olivi, *De usu paupere: The 'Quaestio' and the 'Tractatus'*, ed. by David Burr (Florence: Olschki, 1992)

Rolandinus Patavinus, *Cronica in factis et circa facta Marchie Trivixane aa. 1200-cc.1262*, ed. by Antonio Bonardi, in *RIS*, VIII, 1 (Città di Castello: Lapi, 1905)

Salimbene of Adam, *Cronica*, ed. by Giuseppe Scalia, 2 vols. (Bari: Laterza, 1966)

Sartori, Antonio, *Archivio Sartori: documenti di storia e arte francescana*, ed. by Giovanni Luisetto, 4 vols. (Padua: Biblioteca Antoniana/Basilica del Santo, 1983)

Statius, *Achilleid*, ed. by Oswald A. W. Dilke (Bristol: Phoenix, 2005)

Thomas of Celano, *Vita secunda S. Francisci Assisiensis* (Quaracchi: Typographia Collegii S. Bonaventurae, 1927)

Tomasini, Iacopo Filippo, *Bibliothecae Patavinae manuscriptae publicae et privatae* (Udine: Nicolai Schiratti, 1639)

Ubertino of Casale, *Sanctitas vestra*, in *ALKG*, III (Berlin, 1887), pp. 51-89

Wadding, Luke, *Annales Minorum seu trium ordinum a S. Francisco Institutorum*, ed. by Jose M. Fonseca, 32 vols. (Quaracchi: n. pub., 1931-64)

Secondary Literature

Abate, Giuseppe, 'Manoscritti e biblioteche francescane del medio evo', in *Il libro e le biblioteche: atti del primo congresso bibliologico francescano internazionale, 20-27 febbraio 1949*, 2 vols. (Rome: Pontificium Athenaeum Antonianum, 1950), II, pp. 77-126

Abate, Giuseppe and Giovanni Luisetto, *Codici e manoscritti della Biblioteca Antoniana col catalogo delle miniature*, 2 vols. (Vicenza: Neri Pozza, 1975)

Accrocca, Felice, *Un ribelle tranquillo: Angelo Clareno e gli spirituali francescani tra Due e Trecento* (Assisi: Porziuncola, 2009)

Andrews, Frances, *The Other Friars: The Carmelite, Augustinian, Sack and Pied Friars in the Middle Ages* (Woodbridge: Boydell Press, 2015)

Andrist, Patrick, Paul Canart and Marinela Maniaci, *La syntaxe du codex: essai de codigologie structurale* (Turnhout: Brepols, 2013)

Angelo Clareno francescano: atti del XXXIV convegno internazionale. Assisi, 5-7 ottobre 2006 (Spoleto: Fondazione Centro Italiano di Studi sull'Alto Medioevo, 2007)

Angotti, Claire, 'Les bibliothèques des couvents mendiants, un modèle pour les sèculiers? L'Exemple de deux premiers bienfaiteurs de la bibliothèque du collège de Sorbonne (Robert de Sorbon, Gèrard d'Abbeville)', in *Entre stabilitè et itinèrance: livres et culture des ordres mendiants XIIIe-XVe siècle*, ed. by Nicole Bèriou, Martin Morard and Donatella Nebbiai (Turnhout: Brepols, 2014), pp. 31-72

Asztalos, Monika, 'The Faculty of Theology', in *A History of the University in Europe*, ed. by Hilde de Ridder-Symoens and Walter Rüegg, 3 vols. (Cambridge: Cambridge University Press, 1992), I, pp. 409-41

Bailey, Michael, 'Religious Poverty, Mendicancy and Reform in the Late Middle Ages', *Church History*, 72 (2003), 457-83

Baldissin Molli, Giovanna, *La sacrestia del Santo e il suo tesoro nell'inventario del 1396: artigianati d'arte al tempo dei Carraresi* (Padua: Il Prato, 2002)

Barone, Giulia, 'La legislazione sugli "studia" dei Predicatori e dei Minori', in *Le scuole degli ordini mendicanti (secoli XIII-XIV), 11-14 ottobre 1976* (Todi: Accademia Tudertina, 1978), pp. 205-47

Bartoli, Marco, 'La biblioteca e lo *scriptorium* di Giovanni da Capestrano', *Franciscana*, 8 (2007), 239-59

Bartoli Langeli, Attilio, 'I libri dei frati: la cultura scritta dell'Ordine dei Minori', in *Francesco d'Assisi e il primo secolo di storia francescana* (Turin: Einaudi, 1997), pp. 283-305

Bassetti, Massimiliano, 'I libri "degli antichi"', in *Libri, biblioteche e letture dei frati mendicanti (secoli XIII-XIV): atti del XXXII convegno internazionale, Assisi, 7-9 ottobre 2004* (Spoleto: Fondazione Centro Italiano di Studi sull'Alto Medioevo, 2005), pp. 419-51

Bastanzio, Serafino, *Fra Roberto Caracciolo di Lecce, predicatore del secolo XV* (Isola del Liri: M. Pisani, 1947)

Bataillon, Louis J., 'Approaches to the Study of Medieval Sermons', *Leeds Studies in English*, 11 (1980), 19-35

————, 'Le letture dei maestri dei Frati Predicatori', in *Libri, biblioteche e letture dei frati mendicanti (secoli XIII-XIV): atti del XXXII convegno internazionale, Assisi, 7-9 ottobre 2004* (Spoleto: Fondazione Centro Italiano di Studi sull'Alto Medioevo, 2005), pp. 115-40

Bell, David, 'The Libraries of Religious Houses in the Late Middle Ages', in *CHLB*, I, pp. 126-51

Bennett, Andrew, ed., *Readers and Reading* (London: Longman, 1995)

Benoffi, Francesco A., 'Degli studi nell'Ordine dei Minori', *Miscellanea Francescana*, 31 (1931), 151-60, 257-59; 32 (1932), 23-27

Benvenuti, Anna, 'L'Osservanza e la costruzione dell'identità storica del francescane-
    simo', in *Il francescanesimo dalle origini alla metà del secolo XVI: esplorazioni e
    questioni aperte; atti del convegno della Fondazione Michele Pellegrino, Università
    di Torino, 11 novembre 2004*, ed. by Franco Bolgani and Grado Giovanni Merlo
    (Bologna: Il Mulino, 2005), pp. 189-97

Berardini, Valentina, 'Discovering Performance Indicators in Late Medieval
    Sermons', *Medieval Sermon Studies*, 54 (2010), 75-86

Bigaroni, Marino, 'Catalogo dei manoscritti della biblioteca storico-francescana
    di Chiesa Nuova di Assisi', *Atti dell'Accademia Properziana del Subasio di Assisi*,
    6th ser., 1 (1978), 9-43

Bordin, Bernardino, 'Profilo storico-spirituale della communità al Santo', in *Storia
    e cultura al Santo di Padova fra il XIII e il XX secolo*, ed. by Antonino Poppi
    (Vicenza: Neri Pozza, 1976), pp. 15-115

Bortolami, Sante, 'Studenti e città nel primo secolo dello studio padovano', in
    *Studenti, università, città nella storia padovana: atti del convegno, Padova 6-8
    febbraio 1998*, ed. by Francesco Piovan and Luciana Sitran Rea (Trieste: Lint,
    2001), pp. 3-28

Bougerol, J. Guy, *Introduction to the Works of Bonaventure*, trans. by Jose de Vink
    (Paterson, NJ: St. Anthony Guild Press, 1964)

Boyle, Leonard E., 'Peciae, apopeciae, epipeciae', in *La production du livre universi-
    taire au Moyen Âge: exemplar et pecia; actes du symposium tenu au Collegio san
    Bonaventura de Grottaferrata en mai 1983*, ed. by Louis J. Bataillon, Bertrand G.
    Guyot and Richard H. Rouse (Paris: Centre National de la Recherche Scientifique,
    1988), pp. 39-40

Briscoe, Marianne G., 'Artes Praedicandi', in *Artes Praedicandi and Artes Orandi*,
    ed. by Marianne G. Briscoe and Barbara H. Jaye (Turnhout: Brepols, 1992)

Brlek, Michael, *De evolutione iuridica studiorum in Ordine Minorum (ab initio ordinis
    usque ad an. 1517)* (Dubrovnik: Jadran, 1942)

Brooke, Rosalind B. *Early Franciscan Government: Elias to Bonaventure* (Cambridge:
    Cambridge University Press, 1959)

————, 'Hugh of Digne', in *New Catholic Encyclopedia*, 15 vols. (Washington, DC:
    Catholic University of America, 1976), VII, p. 190

Burr, David, *Olivi and Franciscan Poverty: The Origins of the Usus Pauper Controversy*
    (Philadelphia: University of Pennsylvania Press, 1989)

————, *The Spiritual Franciscans: From Protest to Persecution in the Century after
    Saint Francis* (University Park: University of Pennsylvania Press, 2001)

Cassandro, Cristiana, Nicoletta Giovè Marchioli, Paola Massalin and Stefano
    Zamponi, eds., *I manoscritti datati della provincia di Vicenza e della Biblioteca
    Antoniana di Padova* (Florence: SISMEL/Edizioni del Galluzzo, 2000)

Cavallo, Guglielmo and Roger Chartier, eds., *A History of Reading in the West*, trans. by Lydia G. Cochrane (Cambridge: Polity Press, 1999)

Cenci, Cesare, 'Manoscritti e frati studiosi nella Biblioteca Antoniana di Padova', *AFH*, 69 (1976), 496-520

Certeau, Michel de, 'La lecture absolue', in *Problémes actuels de la lecture*, ed. by Lucien Dällenbach and Jean Ricardou (Paris: Clancier-Guéhaud, 1982), pp. 65-80

——, 'Reading as Poaching', in *Readers and Reading*, ed. by Andrew Bennett (London: Longman, 1995), pp. 150-61

Chambers, Ross, 'Le texte "difficile" et son lecteur', in *Problémes actuels de la lecture*, ed. by Lucien Dällenbach and Jean Ricardou (Paris: Clancier-Guéhaud, 1982), pp. 81-93

Chartier, Roger, 'Labourers and Voyagers: From the Text to the Reader', in *Readers and Reading*, ed. by Andrew Bennett (London: Longman, 1995), pp. 132-49

Cicarello, Domenico, 'Tra grandi biblioteche e grandi lettori: i Conventuali', in *Libri e biblioteche: le letture dei frati mendicanti tra Rinascimento ed età moderna: atti del XLVI convegno internazionale, Assisi, 18-20 ottobre 2018* (Spoleto: Centro Italiano di Studi sull'Alto Medioevo/Società Internazionale di Studi Francescani, 2019), pp. 139-82

Clark, John Willis, *The Care of Books: An Essay on the Development of Libraries and their Fittings, from the Earliest Times to the End of the Eighteenth Century* (Cambridge: Cambridge University Press, 1909)

Colish, Marcia L., *Peter Lombard*, 2 vols. (Leiden: Brill, 1994)

Collodo, Silvana, 'Il convento di S. Francesco e l'Osservanza francescana a Padova nel '400', in *Riforma della chiesa, cultura e spiritualità nel quattrocento veneto: atti del convegno per il VI centenario della nascita di Ludovico Barbo (1382-1443), Padova-Venezia-Treviso, 19-24 settembre 1982*, ed. by G. B. F. Trolese (Cesena: Badia di Santa Maria del Monte, 1984), pp. 359-69

——, *Una società in trasformazione: Padova tra XI e XV secolo* (Padua: Antenore, 1990)

Courtenay, William J., 'Franciscan Learning: University Education and Biblical Exegesis', in *Defenders and Critics of Franciscan Life: Essays in Honor of John V. Fleming*, ed. by Michael Cusato and G. Geltner (Leiden: Brill, 2009), pp. 55-64

Cullen, Christopher M., *Bonaventure* (Oxford: Oxford University Press, 2006)

D'Avray, David L., *The Preaching of the Friars: Sermons Diffused from Paris Before 1300* (Oxford: Clarendon Press, 1985)

Da Campagnola, Stanislao, 'Introduzione', in *Fontes Franciscani*, ed by Enrico Menestò, Stefano Brufani, Giuseppe Cremascoli, Emore Paoli, Luigi Pellegrini, Stanislao da Campagnola and Giovanni Boccali (Assisi: Porziuncola, 1995), pp. 3-22

Dal Pino, Franco Andrea, *Rinnovamento monastico-clericale e movimenti religiosi nei secoli X-XIII* (Rome: Istituto Storico dell'Ordine dei Servi di Maria, 1973)

Dane, Joseph A., *What Is a Book? The Study of Early Printed Books* (Notre Dame, IN: University of Notre Dame Press, 2012)

Darnton, Robert, *The Kiss of Lamourette: Reflections in Cultural History* (London: Faber & Faber, 1990)

Davis, Charles T., 'The Early Collection of Books of S. Croce in Florence', *Proceedings of the American Philosophical Society*, 107 (1963), 399-414

Delcorno, Carlo, 'L'"Ars predicandi" di Bernardino da Siena', in *Atti del simposio internazionale cateriniano-bernardiniano: Siena, 17-20 aprile 1980*, ed. by Domenico Maffei and Paolo Nardi (Siena: Accademia Senese degli Intronati, 1982), pp. 419-49

——, 'La lingua dei predicatori: tra latino e volgare', in *La predicazione dei frati dalla metà del 200 alla fine del 300: atti del XXII convegno internazionale, Assisi, 13-15 ottobre 1994*, ed. by E. Menestò (Spoleto: Centro Italiano di Studi sull'Alto Medioevo, 1995), pp. 19-46

——, *'Quasi quidam cantus': studi sulla predicazione medievale*, ed. by Giovanni Baffetti, Giorgio Forni, Silvia Serventi and Oriana Visani (Florence: Olschki, 2009)

Derolez, Albert, 'The Nomenclature of Gothic Scripts', in *The Oxford Handbook of Latin Palaeography*, ed. by Frank T. Coulson and Robert C. Babcock (New York: Oxford University Press, 2020), pp. 301-20

——, *The Palaeography of Gothic Manuscript Books: From the Twelfth to the Early Sixteenth Century* (Cambridge: Cambridge University Press, 2006)

Derrida, Jacques, *Acts of Literature*, ed. by Dereck Attridge (New York: Routledge, 1992)

Desbonnets, Théophile, *Dalla intuizione alla istituzione: i francescani* (Milan: Biblioteca Francescana Provinciale, 1986)

Destrez, Jean, *La Pecia dans les manuscrits universitaires du XIIIe et du XIVe siècle* (Paris: Jacques Vautrain, 1935)

Deutscher, Thomas B., 'Angelo Carletti', in *Contemporaries of Erasmus: A Biographical Register of the Renaissance and Reformation*, ed. by Peter G. Bietenholz and Thomas B. Deutscher, 3 vols. (Toronto: University of Toronto Press, 1985)

Dickinson, Gary, 'Revivalism and Populism in the Franciscan Observance of the Late Quattrocento', in *Revival and Resurgence in Christian History: Papers Read at the 2006 Summer Meeting and the 2007 Winter Meeting of the Ecclesiastical History Society*, ed. by Kate Cooper and Jeremy Gregory (Rochester, NY: Boydell, 2008), pp. 62-76

Dolbeau, François, 'Noms de livres', in *Vocabulaire du livre et de l'écriture au Moyen Âge: actes de la table ronde Paris 24-26 septembre 1987*, ed. by Olga Weijers (Turnhout: Brepols, 1989), pp. 79-99

Doucet, Victorin, 'Maitres franciscains de Paris: supplément au "Répertoire des maitres en théologie de Paris au XIIIe siècle" de M. le Chan. P.Glorieux', *AFH*, 27 (1934), 531-64

Felder, Hilarin, *Geschichte der wissenschaftlichen Studien im Franziskanerorden bis um die Mitte des 13 Jahrhunderts* (Freiburg im Breisgau: Herder, 1904)

——, *Histoire des études dans l'Ordre de Saint François depuis sa fondation jusque vers la moitiè du XIIIe siècle*, trans. by Eusèbe de Bar-le-Due (Paris: Alphonse Picard, 1908)

Felman, Shoshana, 'Turning the Screw of Interpretation', *Yale French Studies*, 55-56 (1977), 94-207

Ferrari, Francesco, *Il francescanesimo nel Veneto dalle origini ai reperti di San Francesco nel Deserto: appunti per una storia della provincia veneta dei Frati Minori* (Bologna: Documentazione Scientifica, 1990)

Ferrari, Mirella, 'Gli scritti di san Francesco d'Assisi', in *Francesco d'Assisi nell'ottavo centenario della nascita* (Milan: Vita e Pensiero, 1982), pp. 34-59

Fink-Errera, Guy, 'La produzione dei libri di testo nelle università medievali', in *Libri e lettori nel medioevo*, ed. by Guglielmo Cavallo (Rome: Laterza, 2003), pp. 131-65

Fish, Stanley, *Is There a Text in this Class? The Authority of Interpretive Communities* (Cambridge, MA: Harvard University Press, 1980)

Fois, Mario, 'La questione degli studi nell'Osservanza e la soluzione di S. Bernardino da Siena', in *Atti del simposio internazionale cateriniano-bernardiniano: Siena, 17-20 aprile 1980*, ed. by Domenico Maffei and Paolo Nardi (Siena: Academia Senese degli Intronati, 1982), pp. 477-97

Fontana, Emanuele, *Frati, libri e insegnamento nella provincia minoritica di S. Antonio (secoli XIII-XIV)* (Padua: Centro Studi Antoniani, 2012)

——, 'La bibliothèque du convent des Frères Mineurs de Padoue (XIIIe-XIVe siècle)', in *Entre stabilitè et itinèrance: livres et culture des ordres mendiants XIIIe-XVe siècle*, ed. by Nicole Bèriou, Martin Morard and Donatella Nebbiai (Turnhout: Brepols, 2014), pp. 13-29

Francescanesimo e cultura universitaria: atti del XVI convegno internazionale (Assisi, 13-15 ottobre 1988) (Perugia: University of Perugia, 1990).

Frasson, Leonardo et al., eds., *In nome di Antonio: la "Miscellanea" del Codice del Tesoro (XIII in.) della Biblioteca Antoniana di Padova; studio ed edizione critica* (Padua: Centro Studi Antoniani, 1996)

Friedman, Russell L., 'The *Sentences* Commentary, 1250-1320: General Trends, the Impact of the Religious Orders, and the Test Case of Predestination', in *Mediaeval Commentaries on the Sentences of Peter Lombard*, ed. by Gillian R. Evans, 2 vols. (Leiden: Brill, 2002-10), I, pp. 41-128

Frioli, Donatella, 'Gli antichi inventari della Biblioteca Antoniana di Padova: lessicografia e concezioni codicologiche', *Le Venezie Francescane*, 4 (1987), 73-103

——, 'Gli inventari delle biblioteche degli ordini mendicanti', in *Libri, biblioteche e letture dei frati mendicanti (secoli XIII-XIV): atti del XXXII convegno internazionale, Assisi, 7-9 ottobre 2004* (Spoleto: Fondazione Centro Italiano di Studi sull'Alto Medioevo, 2005), pp. 301-73

Galbraith, Georgina R. *The Constitution of the Dominican Order: 1216 to 1360* (Manchester: Manchester University Press, 1925)

Gargan, Luciano, *Lo studio teologico e la biblioteca dei Domenicani a Padova nel tre e quattrocento* (Padua: Antenore, 1971)

Garzya, Antonio, 'Il modello della formazione culturale nella tarda antichità', in *Nuovo e antico nella cultura greco-latina di IV-VI secolo*, ed. by Isabella Gualandri, Fabrizio Conca and Raffaele Passarella (Milan: Cisalpino Istituto Editoriale Universitario, 2002)

Gasparri, Laura, 'Sulla tradizione manoscritta delle prediche di Roberto da Lecce (con due sermoni inediti)', *AFH*, 73 (1980), 173-225

Gatto, Ludovico, 'I temi escatologici nelle prediche di Roberto Caracciolo da Lecce', in *L'Attesa dell'età nuova nella spiritualità della fine del medioevo* (Todi: Accademia Tudertina, 1962)

Gavinelli, Simona, 'Per una biblioteconomia degli ordini mendicanti', in *Libri, biblioteche e letture dei frati mendicanti (secoli XIII-XIV): atti del XXXII convegno internazionale, Assisi, 7-9 ottobre 2004* (Spoleto: Fondazione Centro Italiano di Studi sull'Alto Medioevo, 2005), pp. 265-300

Genest, Jean-François, 'Le Mobilier des bibliothèques d'après les inventaires médiévaux', in *Vocabulaire du livre et de l'écriture au Moyen Âge: actes de la table ronde (Paris 24-26 septembre 1987)*, ed. by Olga Weijers (Turnhout: Brepols, 1989), pp. 136-54

Giannini, Massimo Carlo, 'Intellettuali militanti: i Frati Predicatori tra censura e Inquisizione nel cinquecento', in *Libri e biblioteche: le letture dei frati mendicanti tra Rinascimento ed età moderna; atti del XLVI convegno internazionale, Assisi, 18-20 ottobre 2018* (Spoleto: Centro Italiano di Studi sull'Alto Medioevo/Società Internazionale di Studi Francescani, 2019), pp. 327-54

Gibson, Margaret, ed., *Boethius: His Life, Thought and Influence* (Oxford: Blackwell, 1981)

Gilson, Etienne, *La philosophie de saint Bonaventure* (Paris: J. Vrin, 1924)

Giovè Marchioli, Nicoletta, 'Circolazione libraria e cultura francescana nella Padova del due e trecento', in *Predicazione e società nel medioevo: riflessione etica, valori e modelli di comportamento; atti del XII Medieval Sermon Studies Symposium*, ed. by Riccardo Quinto and Laura Gafurri (Padua: Centro Studi Antoniani, 2002), pp. 131-41

——, 'Codici francescani a Roma nel Duecento: le testimonianze, le assenze e i problemi', *Scripta*, 7 (2014), 127-138

———, 'I protagonisti del libro: gli ordini mendicanti', in *Calligrafia di Dio: la miniatura celebra la parola*, ed. by Giordana Mariani Canova and Paola Ferraro (Modena: Franco Cosimo Panini, 1999), pp. 51-57

———,'Il codice francescano, l'invenzione di un'identità', in *Libri, biblioteche e letture dei frati mendicanti (secoli XIII-XIV): atti del XXXII convegno internazionale, Assisi, 7-9 ottobre 2004* (Spoleto: Fondazione Centro Italiano di Studi sull'Alto Medioevo, 2005), pp. 375-418

———, 'La cultura scritta al Santo nel quattrocento: fra produzione, fruizione e conservazione', in *Cultura, arte, committenza al Santo nel quattrocento, Padova, Basilica del Santo, 25-26 Settembre 2009* (Padua: Centro di Studi Antoniani, 2010), pp. 361-88

———, 'Mitologia di un manoscritto, storia di un manoscritto, archeologia di un manoscritto: il cosiddetto "Codice del Tesoro" (ms 720) della Pontificia Biblioteca Antoniana di Padova', in *Antonio di Padova e le sue immagini: atti del XLIV convegno internazionale, Assisi, 13-15 ottobre 2016* (Spoleto: Fondazione Centro Italiano di Studi sull'Alto Medioevo, 2017), pp. 197-234

———, 'Note sulle caratteristiche dei codici francescani del quattrocento', in *Presenza ed opera di San Giacomo della Marca in Veneto: atti del convegno di studi (Monteprandone 18 ottobre 2008)*, ed. by Fulvia Serpico [= *Picenum Seraphicum*, 27 (2009)], pp. 19-53

———, 'Sante scritture: l'autografia dei santi francescani dell'Osservanza del quattrocento', in *Entre stabilité et itinérance: livres et culture des ordres mendiants XIIIe-XVe siècle*, ed. by Nicole Bériou, Martin Morard and Donatella Nebbiai (Turnhout: Brepols, 2014), pp. 162-87

———, 'Scriptus per me: copisti, sottoscrizioni e scritture nei manoscritti della Biblioteca Antoniana', *Il Santo*, 43 (2003), 671-90

———, 'Scritture (e letture) di donne. Il caso dei codici francescani', in *I manoscritti degli Ordini mendicanti e la letteratura medievale*, ed. by Agnese Macchiarelli (Bologna: Bononia University Press, 2021), pp. 143-56

———, 'Scrivere e leggere il libro francescano', in *Scriptoria e biblioteche nel basso medioevo (secoli XII-XV): atti del 51 convegno storico internazionale, Todi, 12-15 ottobre 2014* (Spoleto: Centro Italiano di Studi sul Basso Medioevo/Accademia Tudertina, 2015), pp. 179-212

Giovè Marchioli, Nicoletta and Stefano Zamponi, 'Manoscritti in volgare nei conventi dei Frati Minori: testi, tipologie librarie, scritture (secoli XIII-XIV)', in *Francescanesimo in volgare (secoli XIII-XIV): atti del XXIV convegno internazionale (Assisi, 17-19 ottobre 1996)* (Spoleto: Fondazione Centro Italiano di Studi sull'Alto Medioevo, 1997), pp. 301-36

Glorieux, Palemon, 'D'Alexandre de Halès à Pierre Auriol: la suite des maîtres franciscains de Paris au XIIIe siècle', *AFH*, 26 (1933), 257-81

Godet-Calogeras, Jean François, 'De la "Forma vitae" à la "Regula Bullata" et le Testament de Frère François', in *La regola dei Frati Minori: atti del XXXVII convegno internazionale, Assisi, 8-10 ottobre 2009* (Spoleto: Fondazione Centro Italiano di Studi sull'Alto Medioevo, 2010), pp. 31-59

Golubovich, Girolamo, *Biblioteca bio-bibliografica della Terra Santa e dell'oriente francescano*, 5 vols. (Quaracchi: Tipografia del Collegio di S. Bonaventura, 1906-27)

Govi, Eugenia, 'Il fondo manoscritto della biblioteca di S. Francesco di Padova conservato presso l'Universitaria Patavina', *Le Venezie Francescane*, 4 (1987), 137-57

Granata Giovanna, 'Dalle povere origini alle grandi biblioteche: gli Osservanti', in *Libri e biblioteche: le letture dei frati mendicanti tra Rinascimento ed età moderna; atti del 46 convegno internazionale, Assisi, 18-20 ottobre 2018* (Spoleto: Centro Italiano di Studi sull'Alto Medioevo/Società Internazionale di Studi Francescani, 2019), pp. 183-222.

Gratien, Badin, *Histoire de la fondation et de l'évolution de l'Ordre des Frères Mineurs au XIIIᵉ siècle* (Paris: Société et Librairie S. Francois d'Assise, 1928)

Grauso, Francesca, 'La biblioteca francescana medievale di Assisi, lo *scriptorium* e l'attività dello *studium*', PhD thesis, University of Lyon 2, 2014

Grotans, Anna A., *Reading in Medieval St. Gall* (Cambridge: Cambridge University Press, 2006)

Gutiérrez, David, 'De antiquis ordinis eremitarum Sancti Augustini bibliothecis', *Analecta Augustiniana*, 23 (1953-54), 240-51

——, *Gli Agostiniani nel medioevo (1256-1356)*, 2 vols. (Rome: Institutum Historicum Ordinis Fratrum S. Augustini, 1986)

Hamesse, Jacqueline, 'The Scholastic Model of Reading', in *A History of Reading in the West,* trans. by Lydia G. Cochrane (Cambridge: Polity Press, 1999), pp. 103-19

Hernández Vera, René, 'Franciscan Observant Miscellanies and Ownership of Books: The Paduan Case', *Il Santo*, 60 (2020) 177-93

——, 'From Chained Books to Portable Collections: Franciscan Libraries in Padua during the Fifteenth Century', in *Monastic Libraries in East Central and Eastern Europe between the Middle Ages and the Enlightenment: Proceedings of the International Conference, 7-9 December 2020 at the University of Hradec Králové*, ed. by Jakob Zouhar (Brno: Moravská zemská knihovna/St. Pölten: Diözesanarchiv, 2020), pp. 71-109

——, 'A Space in the Cupboard: The Organisation of the Book Collection in the Franciscan Convent of Sant'Antonio in Padua during the Fifteenth Century', *Bulletin of International Medieval Research*, 19 (2014), 101-21

Hinnebusch, William A., *The History of the Dominican Order*, 2 vols. (New York: Alba House, 1966-71)

Humphreys, Kenneth William, *The Book Provisions of the Medieval Friars: 1215-1400* (Amsterdam: Erasmus, 1964)

———, *The Friars Libraries* (London: British Library, 1990)

Iozzelli, Fortunato, 'Le edizioni scientifiche del Collegio S. Bonaventura di Quaracchi-Grottaferrata', in *Editori di Quaracchi 100 anni dopo: bilancio e prospettive; atti del colloquio internazionale (Roma, 29-30 maggio 1995)*, ed. by Alvaro Cacciotti and Barbara Faes de Mottoni (Rome: Pontificium Athenaeum Antonianum, 1997), pp. 21-39

Iser, Wolfgang, *The Act of Reading: A Theory of Aesthetic Response* (Baltimore: Johns Hopkins University Press, 1978)

———, 'Interaction between Text and Reader', in *Readers and Reading*, ed. by Andrew Bennett (London: Longman, 1995), pp. 20-31

Johnson, Timothy J., ed., *Franciscans and Preaching: Every Miracle from the Beginning of the World Came about through Words* (Leiden; Boston: Brill, 2012)

———, 'Introduction: The Franciscan Fascination with the Word', in *Franciscans and Preaching: Every Miracle from the Beginning of the World Came about through Words,* ed. by Timothy J. Johnson (Leiden; Boston: Brill, 2012), pp. 1-12

Kaeppeli, Thomas, *Scriptores Ordinis Praedicatorum medii aevii*, 3 vols. (Rome: S. Sabinae, 1970-80)

Kienzle, Beverly M., 'The Typology of the Medieval Sermon and its Development in the Middle Ages: Report on Work in Progress', in *De l'homélie au sermon: histoire de la prédication médiévale; actes du colloque international de Louvain-la-Neuve (9-11 juillet 1992)*, ed. by Jacqueline Hamesse and Xavier Hermand (Louvain-la-Neuve: Institut d'Etudes Médiévales de l'Université Catholique de Louvain, 1993), pp. 83-101

Kimmelman, Burt, 'The Trope of Reading in the Fourteenth Century', in *Reading and Literacy in the Middle Ages and Renaissance*, ed. by Ian Frederick Moulton (Turnhout: Brepols, 2004), pp. 25-44

Lambert, Malcolm D., *Franciscan Poverty: The Doctrine of the Absolute Poverty of Christ and the Apostles in the Franciscan Order 1210-1323* (St. Bonaventure, NY: Franciscan Institute, 1998)

Lambertini, Roberto and Tabaroni, Andrea, *Dopo Francesco: l'eredità difficile* (Turin: Abele, 1989)

Landini, Lawrence C., *The Causes of the Clericalization of the Order of Friars Minor, 1209-1260 in the Light of Early Franciscan Sources* (Chicago: Pontificia Universitas Gregoriana, 1968)

Langholm, Odd, *Economics in the Medieval Schools: Wealth, Exchange, Value, Money and Use, according to the Paris Theological Tradition, 1200-1350* (Leiden: Brill, 1992)

———, *The Merchant in the Confessional: Trade and Price in the Pre-Reformation Penitential Handbooks* (Leiden: Brill, 2003)

Lawrence, Clifford Hugh, *The Friars: The Impact of Early Mendicant Movement in Western Society* (London: Longman, 1994)

——, *Medieval Monasticism: Forms of Religious Life in Western Europe in the Middle Ages* (London: Longman, 1994)

Lebreton, Madeleine and Luigi Fioriani, eds., *Codices Vaticani latini: Codices 1126-11326* (Vatican City: Typis Polyglottis Vaticanis, 1985)

Leclercq, Jean, *The Love of Learning and the Desire for God: A Study of Monastic Culture*, trans. by Catharine Misrahi (New York: Fordham University Press, 1982)

Leff, Gordon, *Heresy in the Later Middle Ages: The Relation of Heterodoxy to Dissent c.1250-c.1450*, 2 vols. (Manchester: Manchester University Press, 1967)

Little, Andrew G., 'The Franciscan School at Oxford in the Thirteenth Century', *AFH*, 19 (1926), 803-74

——, *The Grey Friars in Oxford* (Oxford: Oxford Historical Society, 1892)

Little, Lester K., 'Les Techniques de la confession et la confession comme technique', in *Faire croire: modalités de la diffusion et de la réception des messages religieux du XIIe au XVe siècle; table ronde organisée par l'École Française de Rome, en collaboration avec l'Institut d'Histoire Médiévale de l'Université de Padoue, Rome, 22-23 juine 1979* (Rome: École Française de Rome/Turin: Bottega d'Erasmo, 1981), pp. 87-99

——, *Religious Poverty and the Profit Economy in Medieval Europe* (London: Elek, 1978)

Lombardi, Giuseppe and Donatella Nebbiai-Dalla Guarda, eds., *Libri, lettori e biblioteche dell'Italia medievale (secoli IX-XV): fonti, testi, utilizzazione del libro: atti della tavola rotonda italo-francese (Roma 7-8 marzo 1997)* (Rome: Istituto Centrale per il Catalogo Unico/Paris: CNRS Editions, 2001)

Lombardo, Eleonora, 'Ecclesia huius temporis: la chiesa militante nelle prime raccolte di Frati Minori (1225ca-1260)', PhD thesis, University of Padua, 2009

——, 'La production homilétique franciscaine: étude préliminaire de la structure des premiers recueils de sermons franciscains', *Études Franciscaines*, 5 (2012), 85-110

Lopez, Athanasius, 'Descriptio codicum franciscanorum Bibliothecae Riccardianae Florentinae', *AFH*, 1 (1908), 116-25, 433-42; 2 (1909), 123-30, 319-24, 480-84; 3 (1910), 333-40, 551-58, 739-48; 4 (1911), 360-65, 748-54; 5 (1912), 352-59; 6 (1913), 156-67, 328-37, 748-57

Loutchitsky, Svetlana and Marie-Christine Varol, eds., *Homo Legens: styles et pratiques de lecture; analyses comparées des traditions orales et écrites au Moyen Âge/Styles and Practices of Reading; Comparative Analyses of Oral and Written Traditions in the Middle Ages* (Turnhout: Brepols, 2010)

Lovatt, Roger, 'College and University Book Collections and Libraries', in *CHLB*, I, pp. 152-77

Maierù, Alfonso, 'Formazione culturale e tecniche d'insegnamento nelle scuole degli ordini mendicanti', in *Studio e studia: le scuole degli ordini mendicanti tra XIII e XIV secolo; atti del XXIX convegno internazionale (Assisi, 11-13 ottobre 2001)* (Spoleto: Centro Italiano di Studi sull'Alto Medioevo, 2002), pp. 3-31

Manselli, Raoul, 'Due biblioteche di "studia" minoritici: Santa Croce di Firenze e il Santo di Padova' in *Le scuole degli ordini mendicanti: secoli XIII-XIV* (Todi: Accademia Tudertina, 1978), pp. 353-71

——, 'L'Osservanza francescana: dinamica della sua formazione e fenomenologia', in *Reformbemühungen und Observanzbestrebungen im spätmittelalterlichen Ordenswesen*, ed. by Kaspar Elm (Berlin: Duncker & Humblot, 1989), pp. 173-87

——, 'Pietro di Giovanni Olivi spirituale', in *Chi erano gli spirituali: atti del III convegno internazionale, Assisi, 16-18 ottobre 1975* (Assisi: Società Internazionale di Studi Francescani, 1976), pp. 181-204

——, *San Francesco* (Roma: Bulzoni Editore, 1980)

——, *Studi sulle eresie del secolo XII* (Rome: Istituto Storico Italiano per il Medioevo, 1953)

Maranesi, Pietro, 'La normativa degli ordini mendicanti sui libri in convento', in *Libri, biblioteche e letture dei frati mendicanti (secoli XIII-XIV): atti del XXXII convegno internazionale, Assisi, 7-9 ottobre 2004* (Spoleto: Fondazione Centro Italiano di Studi sull'Alto Medioevo, 2005), pp. 171-264.

——, *Nescientes litteras: l'ammonizione della regola francescana e la questione degli studi nell'Ordine (sec XIII-XVI)* (Rome: Istituto Storico dei Cappuccini, 2000)

Marangon, Paolo, *Ad cognitionem scientiae festinare: gli studi nell'Università di Padova nei secoli XIII e XIV*, ed. by Tiziana Pesenti (Trieste: Lint, 1997)

Marenbon, John, *Boethius* (New York: Oxford University Press, 2003)

——, 'Imaginary Pagans: From the Middle Ages to Renaissance', in *Continuities and Disruptions between the Middle Ages and the Renaissance*, ed. by Charles Burnett, José F. Meirinhos and Jacqueline Hamese (Louvain-la-Neuve: Fédération Internationale des Instituts d'Études Médiévales, 2008), pp. 151-65

Mazzon, Antonella, 'Gli Eremitani tra normativa e prassi libraria', in *Libri e biblioteche: le letture dei frati mendicanti tra Rinascimento ed età moderna; atti del XLVI convegno internazionale, Assisi, 18-20 ottobre 2018* (Spoleto: Centro Italiano di Studi sull'Alto Medioevo/Società Internazionale di Studi Francescani, 2019), pp. 251-300

McGinn, Bernard, *The Calabrian Abbot: Joachim of Fiore in the History of Western Thought* (New York: Macmillan, 1985)

McKitterick, Rosamond, 'The Carolingian Renaissance of Culture and Learning', in *Charlemagne: Empire and Society*, ed. by Joanna Story (Manchester: Manchester University Press, 2005), pp. 151-66

——, *The Carolingians and the Written Word* (Cambridge: Cambridge University Press, 1989)

———, 'Charles the Bald (823-877) and his Library: The Patronage of Learning', *English Historical Review*, 95 (1980), 28-47

———, 'Le Rôle culturel des monastères dans les royaumes carolingiens du VIIIe au Xe siècle', *Revue Bénédictine*, 103 (1993), 117-30

———, 'The Scriptoria of the Merovingian Gaul: A Survey of the Evidence', in *Columbanus and Merovingian Monasticism*, ed. by H. B. Clarke and Mary Brennan (Oxford: British Archaeological Reports, 1981), pp. 173-207

Menestò, Enrico, 'Francesco, i Minori e i libri', in *Libri, biblioteche e letture dei frati mendicanti (secoli XIII-XIV): atti del XXXII convegno internazionale, Assisi, 7-9 ottobre 2004* (Spoleto: Fondazione Centro Italiano di Studi sull'Alto Medioevo, 2005), pp. 3-27

Merlo, Grado Giovanni, *Nel nome di San Francesco: storia dei Frati Minori e del francescanesimo sino agli inizi del XVI secolo* (Padua: Editrici Francescane, 2003)

——— 'Religiosità e cultura religiosa dei laici nel secolo XII', in *L'Europa dei secoli XI e XII fra novità e tradizione: sviluppi di una cultura; atti della decima settimana internazionale di studio, Mendola, 25-29 agosto 1986* (Milan: Vita e Pensiero, 1989), pp. 197-215

———, 'Storia di Frate Francesco e dell'Ordine dei Minori', in *Francesco d'Assisi e il primo secolo di storia francescana* (Turin: Einaudi, 1997), pp. 3-32

Meyvaert, Paul, 'The Date of Bede's *In Ezram* and his Image of Ezra in the Codex Amiatinus', *Speculum*, 80 (2005), 1087-1133

Monfrin, Jacques, 'Le catalogue et l'inventaire (résumé)', in *Vocabulaire du livre et de l'écriture au moyen age: actes de la table ronde (Paris 24-26 septembre 1987)*, ed. by Olga Weijers (Turnhout: Brepols, 1989), p. 135

Moorhead, John, 'Boethius' Life and the World of Late Antique Philosophy', in *The Cambridge Companion to Boethius*, ed. by John Marenbon (Cambridge: Cambridge University Press, 2009), pp. 13-33

Moorman, John R. H., *A History of the Franciscan Order: From its Origins to the Year 1517* (Oxford: Clarendon Press, 1968)

———, *The Sources for the Life of S. Francis of Assisi* (Manchester: Manchester University Press, 1940)

Moretti, Felice, *Luca Apulus: un maestro francescano del secolo XIII* (Bitonto: Arti Grafiche Nuovo Sud, 1985)

———, 'I sermoni di Luca da Bitonto fra cattedra e pulpito', *Il Santo*, 40 (2000), 49-69

Nebbiai-Dalla Guarda, Donatella, 'Le biblioteche degli ordini mendicanti (sec. XIII-XV)', in *Studio e studia: le scuole degli ordini mendicanti tra XIII e XIV secolo; atti del XXIX Convegno internazionale (Assisi, 11-13 ottobre 2001)* (Spoleto: Centro Italiano di Studi sull'Alto Medioevo, 2002), pp. 219-70

———, 'Lecteurs, bibliothèques et société. Observations pour un premier bilan', in *Lecteurs, lectures et groupes sociaux au Moyen Âge: actes de la journée d'étude organisée par le Centre de recherche 'Pratiques médiévales de l'écrit' (PraME) de l'Université de Namur et le Département des Manuscrits de la Bibliothèque Royale de Belgique, Bruxelles, 18 mars 2010*, ed. by Xavier Hermand, Étienne Renard and Céline Van Hoorebeeck (Turnhout: Brepols, 2014), pp. 195-98

——, 'Les inventaires des bibliothèques mèdiévales', in *Le livre au Moyen Âge*, ed. by Jean Glenisson (Paris: Centre National de la Recherche Scientifique, 1988), pp. 88-91

——, 'Modelli bibliotecari pre-mendicanti', in *Libri, biblioteche e letture dei frati mendicanti (secoli XIII-XIV): atti del XXXII convegno internazionale, Assisi, 7-9 ottobre 2004* (Spoleto: Fondazione Centro Italiano di Studi sull'Alto Medioevo, 2005), pp. 141-70

Nimmo, Duncan, 'The Franciscan Regular Observance: The Culmination of Medieval Franciscan Reform', in *Reformbemühungen und Observanzbestrebungen im spätmittelalterlichen Ordenswesen*, ed. by Kaspar Elm (Berlin: Duncker & Humblot, 1989), pp. 189-205

——, *Reform and Division in the Medieval Franciscan Order: From Saint Francis to the Foundation of the Capuchins*, ed. by Theo Jansen (Rome: Capuchin Historical Institute, 1987)

Noonan, John T., *The Scholastic Analysis of Usure* (Cambridge, MA: Harvard University Press, 1957)

Noone, Timothy B., 'The Franciscans and Epistemology: Reflections on the Roles of Bonaventure and Scotus', in *Medieval Masters: Essays in Memory of Msgr. E. A. Synan*, ed. by R. E. Houser (Houston: Center for Thomistic Studies, 1999), pp. 63-90

O'Donnell, James J., *Cassiodorus* (Berkeley: University of California Press, 1979)

O'Gorman, James F., *The Architecture of the Monastic Library in Italy: 1300-1600* (New York: New York University Press, 1972)

O'Malley, John W., 'Introduction: Medieval Preaching', in *De Ore Domini: Preacher and the Word in the Middle Ages*, ed. by Thomas L. Amos, Eugene A. Green and Beverly Mayne Kienzle (Kalamazoo: Medieval Institute Publications, 1989), pp. 1-11

Origo, Iris, *The World of San Bernardino* (London: Jonathan Cape, 1963)

Pacheco, Maria Candida, ed., *Le vocabulaire des écoles des mendiants au Moyen Âge: actes du colloque (Porto, 11-12 octobre 1996)* (Turnhout: Brepols, 1999)

Pantarotto, Martina, *La biblioteca manoscritta del convento di San Francesco Grande di Padova* (Padua: Centro Studi Antoniani, 2003)

Paolazzi, Carlo, 'I Frati Minori e i libri: per l'esegesi di "ad implendum eorum officium" (Rnbu III, 7) e "nescientes litteras" (Rnbu III, 9; Rebu X, 7)', *AFH*, 97 (2004), 3-59

Parkes, Malcolm B., 'Reading, Copying and Interpreting a Text in the Early Middle Ages', in *A History of Reading in the West*, ed. by Guglielmo Cavallo and Roger Chartier, trans. by Lydia G. Cochrane (Cambridge: Polity Press, 1999), pp. 90-102

Pasquini, Emilio, 'San Francesco e i frati Minori in Dante', in *Francescanesimo in volgare (secoli XIII-XIV); atti del XXIV convegno internazionale, Assisi, 17-19 ottobre 1996* (Spoleto: Centro Italiano di Studi sull'Alto Medioevo, 1997), pp. 143-58

Pásztor, Edith, *Intentio Beati Francisci: il percorso difficile dell'Ordine francescano (secoli XIII-XV)*, ed. by Felice Accrocca (Rome: Istituto Storico dei Cappuccini, 2008)

Paul, Jacques, 'Le commentaire de Hughes de Digne sur la règle franciscaine', *Revue d'Histoire de l'Église de France*, 61 (1975), 231-41

Pellegrini, Letizia, 'Cultura del libro e pratiche dei libri nell'Osservanza italiana (XV secolo)', in *Entre stabilitè et itinèrance: livres et culture des ordres mendiants XIIIe-XVe siècle*, ed. by Nicole Bèriou, Martin Morard and Donatella Nebbiai (Turnhout: Brepols, 2014), pp. 189-201

——, *I manoscritti dei Predicatori* (Rome: Istituto Storico Domenicano, 1999)

Pellegrini, Luigi, *L'Incontro tra due invenzioni medievali: università e ordini mendicanti* (Naples: Liguori, 2003)

Petrucci, Armando, 'La concezione cristiana del libro fra VI e VII secolo', in *Libri e lettori nel medioevo: guida storica e critica*, ed. by Guglielmo Cavallo (Rome: Laterza, 1989), pp. 3-26

——, *Writers and Readers in Medieval Italy: Studies in the History of Written Culture*, ed. and trans. by Charles M. Rading (New Haven, CT: Yale University Press, 1995)

Pini, Giorgio, 'Le letture dei frati agostiniani: Egidio Romano e Giacomo da Viterbo', in *Libri, biblioteche e letture dei frati mendicanti (secoli XIII-XIV): atti del XXXII convegno internazionale, Assisi, 7-9 ottobre 2004* (Spoleto: Fondazione Centro Italiano di Studi sull'Alto Medioevo, 2005), pp. 79-114

Ponesse, Matthew, 'The Augustinian Rules and Constitutions', in *A Companion to Medieval Rules and Customaries*, ed. by Krijn Pansters (Leiden: Brill, 2020), pp. 393-428

Poppi, Antonino, 'La teologia nell'università e nelle scuole', in *Storia della cultura veneta*, 6 vols. (Vicenza: Neri Pozza, 1976-[86]), III, 3: *Dal primo quattrocento al Concilio di Trento*, ed. by Girolamo Arnaldi and Manlio Pastore Stocchi (1981), pp. 1-33

Potestà, Gian Luca, 'Maestri e dottrine nel XIII secolo', in *Francesco d'Assisi e il primo secolo di storia francescana* (Turin: Einaudi, 1997), pp. 307-36

Poulenc, Jerome, 'Hughes de Digne' in *Dictionnaire de spiritualité ascétique et mystique, doctrine et histoire*, 17 vols. (Paris: Beauchesne, 1969), VIII, cols. 875-79

Poulet, Georges, 'Phenomenology of Reading', *New Literary History*, 1 (1969), 53-68

Prinzivalli, Emanuela, 'Un santo da leggere: Francesco d'Assisi nel percorso delle fonti agiografiche', in *Francesco d'Assisi e il primo secolo di storia francescana* (Turin: Einaudi, 1997), pp. 71-116

Ragazzini, Severino, 'Presenza di Dante al Santo', in *Storia e cultura al Santo di Padova fra il XIII e il XX secolo*, ed. by Antonino Poppi (Vicenza: Neri Pozza, 1976), pp. 641-47

Rasolofoarimanana, Jean Désiré, 'La tradition manuscrite des sermons de Fr. Luca de Bitonto, OMin', *AFH*, 97 (2004), 229-74; 99 (2006), 33-131

——, 'Luc de Bitonto, OMin, et ses sermons', in *Predicazione e società nel medioevo: riflessione etica, valori e modelli di comportamento: atti del XII Medieval Sermon Studies Symposium*, ed. by Riccardo Quinto and Laura Gaffuri (Padua: Centro Studi Antoniani, 2002), pp. 239-47

——, 'Sermons anonymes *De Sanctis* attribués a Luca de Bitonto, OMin', *AFH*, 96 (2003), 301-72

——, 'Un sermon anonyme et inédit attributé à Luca da Bitonto, OMin', *AFH*, 102 (2009), 391-418

Reeves, Marjorie, *The Influence of Prophecy in the Later Middle Ages: A Study in Joachimism* (Oxford: Clarendon, 1969)

Richardson, Brian, 'Inscribed Meanings: Authorial Self-fashioning and Readers' Annotations in Sixteenth-Century Italian Printed Books', in *Reading and Literacy in the Middle Ages and Renaissance*, ed. by Ian Frederick Moulton (Turnhout: Brepols, 2004), pp. 85-104

Riché, Pierre, *Éducation et culture dans l'Occident barbare : VIe-VIIIe siècles* (Paris: Éditions du Seuil, 1962)

Rigon, Antonio, 'San Antonio e la cultura universitaria nell'Ordine francescano delle origini', in *Francescanesimo e cultura universitaria: atti del XVI convegno internazionale, Assisi, 13-15 ottobre 1988* (Perugia: Università degli Studi di Perugia/Centro di Studi Francescani, 1990), pp. 69-72

Roberts, Phyllis B., 'Medieval University Preaching: The Evidence in the Statutes', in *Medieval Sermons and Society: Cloister, City, University, Proceedings of the International Symposia at Kalamazoo and New York*, ed. by Jacqueline Hammesse, Beverly Mayne Kienzle, Debra L. Stoudt and Anne T. Thayer (Louvain-la-Neuve: Fédération Internationale des Instituts d'Études Médiévales, 1998), pp. 317-28

——, 'Sermon Studies Scholarship: The Last Thirty-Five Years', *Medieval Sermon Studies*, 43 (1999), 9-18

Robson, Michael J. P., *The Franciscans in the Middle Ages* (Woodbridge: Boydell Press, 2006)

——, *The Greyfriars of England (1224-1539): Collected Papers* (Padua: Centro Studi Antoniani, 2012)

——, 'Sermons Preached to the Friars Minor in the Thirteenth Century', in *Franciscans and Preaching: Every Miracle from the Beginning of the World Came about through Words,* ed. by Timothy J. Johnson (Leiden; Boston: Brill, 2012), pp. 273-96

Roest, Bert, *A History of Franciscan Education (c. 1210-1517)* (Leiden: Brill, 2000)

———, *Franciscan Learning, Preaching and Mission c. 1220-1650: Cum scientia sit donum Dei, armatura ad defendendam sanctam fidem catholicam...* (Leiden; Boston: Brill, 2015)

———, '"Ne Effluat in Multiloquium et Habeatur Honerosus": The Art of Preaching in the Franciscan Tradition', in *Franciscans and Preaching: Every Miracle from the Beginning of the World Came about through Words* (Leiden; Boston: Brill, 2012), pp. 381-412

———, 'The Role of Lectors in the Religious Formation of Franciscan Friars, Nuns, and Tertiaries', in *Studio e studia: le scuole degli ordini mendicanti tra XIII e XIV secolo; atti del XXIX convegno internazionale, Assisi, 11-13 ottobre 2001* (Spoleto: Centro Italiano di Studi sull'Alto Medioevo, 2002), pp. 83-115

———, 'Sub humilitatis titulo sacram scientiam abhorrentes. Franciscan Observants and the Quest for Education', in *Rules and Observance. Devising Forms of Communal Life*, ed. by Mirko Breitenstein, and others (Berlin; Münster; Vienna: LIT, 2014)

Rosemann, Philip W., *Peter Lombard* (New York: Oxford University Press, 2004)

Rouse, Mary A. and Richard H. Rouse, *Authentic Witnesses: Approaches to Medieval Texts and Manuscripts* (Notre Dame, IN: University of Notre Dame Press, 1991)

Rouse, Richard H., 'The Early Library of the Sorbonne', *Scriptorium*, 21 (1967), 42-71

Ruiz, Damien, *La vie et l'ouvre de Hugues de Digne* (Spoleto: Fondazione Centro Italiano di Studi sull'Alto Medioevo, 2018)

Saak, Eric L., 'Augustine in the Later Middle Ages', in *The Reception of the Church Fathers in the West: From the Carolingians to the Maurists*, ed. by Irena Backus, 2 vols. (Boston: Brill, 2001), II, pp. 367-404

———, *Creating Augustine: Interpreting Augustine and Augustinianism in the Late Middle Ages* (Oxford: Oxford University Press, 2012)

Saenger, Paul, 'Reading in the Later Middle Ages', in *A History of Reading in the West,* trans. by Lydia G. Cochrane (Cambridge: Polity Press, 1999), pp. 120-48

———, 'Silent Reading: Its Impact on Late Medieval Script and Society', *Viator*, 13 (1982), 367-414

———, *Space between Words: The Origins of Silent Reading* (Stanford: Stanford University Press, 1997)

Sambin, Paolo, 'Tre notizie per la storia culturale ed ecclesiastica di Padova (secoli XII e XIII)', *Archivio Veneto*, 56 (1955), 1-11

Sartori, Antonio, 'Gli studi al Santo di Padova', in *Problemi e figure della scuola scotista del Santo* (Padua: Messagero, 1966), pp. 67-180

———, 'La "Ratio Studiorum" nella Provincia del Santo', in *Storia e cultura al Santo di Padova fra il XIII e il XX secolo*, ed. by Antonino Poppi (Vicenza: Neri Pozzi, 1976), pp. 119-52

Şenocak, Neslihan, 'Book Acquisition in the Medieval Franciscan Order', *Journal of Religious History*, 27 (2003), 14-28

———, 'Circulation of Books in the Medieval Franciscan Order: Attitude, Methods, and Critics', *Journal of Religious History*, 28 (2004), 146-61

———, 'The Earliest Library Catalogue of the Franciscan Convent of St. Fortunato of Todi (c. 1300)', *AFH*, 99 (2006), 467-505

———, *The Poor and the Perfect: The Rise of Learning in the Franciscan Order, 1209-1310* (Ithaca: Cornell University Press, 2012)

Severino Polica, Gabriella, 'Libro, lettura, "lezione" negli studia degli ordini mendicanti (sec XIII)', in *Le scuole degli ordini mendicanti, secoli XIII-XIV (11-14 ottobre 1976)* (Todi: Accademia Tudertina, 1978), pp. 373-413

Sharpe, Richard, *Titulus: Identifying Medieval Latin Texts: An Evidence-Based Approach* (Turnhout: Brepols, 2003)

Shooner, Hugues V, 'La Production du livre par la pecia', in *La Production du livre universitaire au Moyen Âge: exemplar et pecia: actes du symposium tenu au collegio san Bonaventura de Grottaferrata en mai 1983*, ed. by Louis J. Bataillon, Bertrand G. Guyot and Richard H. Rouse (Paris: Centre National de la Recherche Scientifique, 1988), pp. 17-37

Somigli, Elena, *'Hoc est registrum omnium librorum*: le biblioteche e la circolazione libraria in ambito francescano nella Provincia di Toscana dei secoli XIV-XV; fonti edite e inedite', PhD thesis, Istituto di Studi Umanistici, Florence, 2009

Stam, David H., ed., *International Dictionary of Library Histories*, 2 vols. (London: Fitzroy Dearbom, 2001)

Stoddard, Roger E. 'Morphology and the Book from an American Perspective', *Printing History*, 9 (1987), 2-14

Teeuwen, Mariken, *The Vocabulary of Intellectual Life in the Middle Ages* (Turnhout: Brepols, 2003)

Thorndike, Lynn and Pearl Kibre, *A Catalogue of Incipits of Mediaeval Scientific Writings in Latin* (London: Mediaeval Academy of America, 1963)

Thompson, James Westfall, *The Medieval Library* (New York: Hafner, 1957)

Todeschini, Giacomo, 'Credito ed economia della civitas: Angelo da Chivasso e la dottrina della pubblica utilità fra quattro e cinquecento', in *Ideologia del credito fra tre e quattrocento: dall'Astesano ad Angelo da Chivasso; atti del convegno internazionale, Asti, 9-10 giugno 2000*, ed. by Barbara Molina and Giulia Scarcia (Asti: Centro Studi sui Lombardi e sul Credito nel Medioevo, 2001), pp. 59-83

Topham, Jonathan, 'BJHS Special Section: Book History and the Sciences; Introduction', *British Journal for the History of Science*, 33 (2000), 155-58

Tosti, Salvatore, 'Descriptio codicum franciscanorum Bibliothecae Riccardianae Florentinae', *AFH*, 8 (1915), 226-73, 618-57; 9 (1916), 395-442; 13 (1920), 587-603; 14 (1921), 243-58; 15 (1922), 155-70, 508-24; 16 (1923), 545-56

Turrini, Miriam, *La coscienza e le leggi: morale e diritto nei testi per la confessione della prima età moderna* (Bologna: Il Mulino, 1991)

Van Hoorebeeck, Céline, 'Du livre au lire: lectures et lecteurs à l'épreuve des catégorisations sociales', in *Lecteurs, lectures et groupes sociaux au Moyen Âge: actes de la journée d'étude organisée par le Centre de recherche "Pratiques médiévales de l'écrit" (PraME) de l'Université di Namur et le Département des Manuscrits de la Bibliothèque Royale de Belgique, Bruxelles, 18 mars 2010*, ed. by Xavier Hermand, Étienne Renard and Céline Van Hoorebeeck (Turnhout: Brepols, 2014), pp. 123-31

Vauchez, Andrè, *Ordini mendicanti e società italiana (XIII-XV secolo)* (Milan: Il Saggiatore, 1990)

Visani Ravaioli, Oriana, 'Roberto Caracciolo e i sermonari del secondo quattrocento', *Franciscana* 1 (1999), 275-317

——, 'Testimonianze della predicazione di Roberto da Lecce a Padova', in *Predicazione francescana e società veneta nel quattrocento: committenza, ascolto, ricezione; atti del II convegno internazionale di studi francescani, Padova 26-28 marzo 1987* (Padua: Centro Studi Antoniani, 1995), pp. 185-220

Weijers, Olga, *Terminologie des universités au XIIIe siècle* (Rome: Ateneo, 1987)

Weitzmann, Kurt, *Late Antique and Early Christian Book Illumination* (London: Chatto & Windus, 1977)

Zamponi, Stefano, 'Gothic Script in Italy', in *The Oxford Handbook of Latin Palaeography*, ed. by Frank T. Coulson and Robert C. Babcock (New York: Oxford University Press, 2020), pp. 411-28

——, 'Late Gothic: Italy (XIVth-XVIth Centuries)', in *The Oxford Handbook of Latin Palaeography*, ed. by Frank T. Coulson and Robert C. Babcock (New York: Oxford University Press, 2020), pp. 429-44

Zarri, Gabriella, 'Le monache e i libri nel secolo XVI: produzione, letture, uso', in *Libri e biblioteche: le letture dei frati mendicanti tra Rinascimento ed età moderna: atti del XLVI convegno internazionale, Assisi, 18-20 ottobre 2018* (Spoleto: Centro Italiano di Studi sull'Alto Medioevo/Società Internazionale di Studi Francescani, 2019), pp. 355-76

Index

For Product Safety Concerns and Information please contact our EU
representative GPSR@taylorandfrancis.com
Taylor & Francis Verlag GmbH, Kaufingerstraße 24, 80331 München, Germany

www.ingramcontent.com/pod-product-compliance
Lightning Source LLC
Chambersburg PA
CBHW071521110726
47908CB00003B/915